THE MORAL RESPONSIBILI

Eric W. Orts is the Guardsmark Professor at the Wharton School of the University of Pennsylvania. He is a professor in the Legal Studies and Business Ethics Department with a secondary appointment in the Management Department. He directs the Initiative for Global Environmental Leadership. He is the author, co-author, and co-editor of many other books and articles, including *Business Persons: A Legal Theory of the Firm* (Oxford University Press).

N. Craig Smith is the INSEAD Chaired Professor of Ethics and Social Responsibility at INSEAD, France. He is also Director of the INSEAD Ethics and Social Responsibility Initiative (ESRI), a part of the INSEAD Hoffmann Global Institute for Business and Society, and a specialist professor at the INSEAD Corporate Governance Centre. His current research projects examine the "price-tag society", corporate political activism, the purpose of the firm, social contract theory, stakeholder theory, strategic drivers of CSR/sustainability, marketing ethics, and sustainable consumption. He is the author, co-author, or co-editor of eight books and over forty academic journal articles.

The Moral Responsibility of Firms

Edited by
ERIC W. ORTS
and
N. CRAIG SMITH

OXFORD
UNIVERSITY PRESS

Great Clarendon Street, Oxford, OX2 6DP,
United Kingdom

Oxford University Press is a department of the University of Oxford.
It furthers the University's objective of excellence in research, scholarship,
and education by publishing worldwide. Oxford is a registered trade mark of
Oxford University Press in the UK and in certain other countries

© Oxford University Press 2017

The moral rights of the authors have been asserted

First published 2017
First published in paperback 2020

Published in the United States of America by Oxford University Press
198 Madison Avenue, New York, NY 10016, United States of America

British Library Cataloguing in Publication Data
Data available

Library of Congress Cataloging in Publication Data
Data available

ISBN 978–0–19–873853–4 (Hbk.)
ISBN 978–0–19–885705–1 (Pbk.)

Preface

Thomas Donaldson

It has been said that the most important philosophical question is "So what?" For purposes of this volume, if it should be determined that organizations qualify as "moral agents" and are able to sustain predicates such as "is responsible," "is to blame," and "has rights," then we must ask, "So what?"

And the answer is, "A lot."

Corporations, sometimes known as "persona ficta" or fictional persons, are taller and richer than most of us yet have disturbingly narrow personalities. They neither cry at funerals nor experience pain and pleasure. Most are chartered for financial purposes and lead sheltered lives. They enjoy unlimited lifespans and can protect their shareowners from financial liability; which is to say, governments grant them unlimited longevity and limited liability. As an English jurist once quipped, a corporation has no soul to damn, nor pants to kick. Perhaps it should have both.

Yet these queer beings have huge power. It is well known that multi-national corporations boast revenues and influence that rival that of the largest nation-states. But it is less well known that corporate power filters its way throughout multiple corners of our political and social life. For example, by virtue of the *Citizens United* ruling by the US Supreme Court in 2010, corporations are able in the United States to make independent contributions on behalf of political candidates, and along with labor unions can spend unlimited sums of money on advertisements and other means to support or defeat the or election of particular political candidates. Moreover, corporations are often immune from criminal prosecution despite flagrant behavior. Germany disallows criminal charges against corporations, and yet in 2015, Volkswagen, Germany's largest corporation, announced that it had intentionally planted software in 11 million diesel cars that cheated on emissions tests, allowing the cars to disgorge far more deadly pollutants than regulations permitted.

Hence, the arcane, abstract issue of moral agency has weighty practical consequences that underscore the relevance of the current volume. Good fortune combined with a superb organizational effort permitted some of the best scholars in the world to gather in December of 2013 in Fontainebleau, France, for a special conference sponsored by the Wharton School of the University of Pennsylvania and INSEAD. The list of attendees reads like a Who's Who of contributors in the areas of corporations and moral agency. Attending were not only early, heralded writers on the topic, such as Peter

French from Arizona State University, but leading emerging scholars such as Amy Sepinwall from the Wharton School. Philosophers such as Michael Bratman at Stanford and Philip Pettit at Princeton joined business academics such as Joakim Sandberg of the Stockholm School of Economics and Nien-hê Hsieh of Harvard Business School to weave moral concepts into our understanding of concrete corporate behavior.

The chapters collected in this volume are a joy to read. Readers will delight when they discover the innovative analyses that the authors have used to cut the long-resistant Gordian knot of moral agency. The result is a mosaic that reveals a compelling picture of both the clear and hazy aspects of corporate moral agency; a mosaic that shows strong lines of agreement as well as options for disagreement. It is no exaggeration to say that this volume marks the best overall contribution to the question of corporate moral agency in the past fifty years.

Contents

Notes on the Contributors

Michael E. Bratman is the U.G. and Abbie Birch Durfee Professor in the School of Humanities and Sciences and Professor of Philosophy at Stanford University.

Thomas Donaldson is the Mark O. Winkelman Professor of Legal Studies and Business Ethics at the Wharton School of the University of Pennsylvania.

Peter A. French is the Lincoln Professor of Ethics and Professor of Philosophy at Arizona State University.

John Hasnas is Professor of Business in the McDonough School of Business at Georgetown University.

Kendy Hess is the Brake-Smith Associate Professor in Social Philosophy and Ethics at the College of the Holy Cross.

Nien-hê Hsieh is Professor of Business Administration at Harvard Business School.

Waheed Hussain is Assistant Professor of Philosophy at the University of Toronto.

Ian Maitland is Professor of Management at the Carlson School of Management of the University of Minnesota.

Eric W. Orts is the Guardsmark Professor of Legal Studies and Business Ethics at the Wharton School of the University of Pennsylvania.

Philip Pettit is the L.S. Rockefeller University Professor of Politics and Human Values at Princeton University and also Distinguished University Professor of Philosophy at the Australian National University.

David Rönnegard is a visiting scholar at INSEAD.

Joakim Sandberg is Professor of Practical Philosophy at the University of Gothenburg.

Amy J. Sepinwall is Associate Professor of Legal Studies and Business Ethics at the Wharton School of the University of Pennsylvania.

N. Craig Smith is the INSEAD Chaired Professor of Ethics and Social Responsibility at INSEAD.

Manuel Velasquez is the Charles J. Dirksen Professor of Business Ethics at the Leavey School of Business at Santa Clara University.

Introduction

The Moral Responsibility of Firms: Renewed Interest in a Perennial Question of Business Ethics

N. Craig Smith

> "Sure, cried the tenant men, but it's our land...We were born on it, and we got killed on it, died on it. Even if it's no good, it's still ours.... That's what makes ownership, not a paper with numbers on it."
>
> "We're sorry. It's not us. It's the monster. The bank isn't like a man."
>
> "Yes, but the bank is only made of men."
>
> "No, you're wrong there—quite wrong there. The bank is something else than men. It happens that every man in a bank hates what the bank does, and yet the bank does it. The bank is something more than men, I tell you. It's the monster. Men made it, but they can't control it."
>
> John Steinbeck, *The Grapes of Wrath*

Are firms morally responsible for their actions? Individuals are generally considered morally responsible for their actions. Who or what is responsible when those individuals become part of business organizations? Can we correctly ascribe moral responsibility to the organization itself? If so, what are the grounds for this claim and to what extent do the individuals also remain morally responsible? If not, does moral responsibility fall entirely to specific individuals within the organization and can they be readily identified? What are the practical implications of these positions? These are the questions at the heart of this book.

In many ways, these are old questions, going back at least as far as the debate around corporate moral agency of the 1970s and 1980s (French 1979; Velasquez 1983). While they have remained of interest to philosophers since (for example, Arnold 2006; French 2006; Tuomela 2007; Velasquez 2003), they have more recently assumed greater theoretical significance given new work on the topic, not least by some of the authors featured in this book (for example, Bratman 2014; Hess 2013; List and Pettit 2011; Rönnegard 2013).

Their implications are also of increased practical significance in light of seemingly rampant corporate misconduct in some sectors of business (for example, the banking, pharmaceutical, and automotive sectors) and questions about who is to blame, who should be punished, and how such misconduct can be prevented. Recent court cases in the USA, that seem to give corporations rights of religious expression and freedom of speech normally reserved for individual human beings, also heighten the importance of these questions. As Hussain and Sandberg observe in this book (Chapter 4), we seem to care a great deal about whether we can treat corporations as moral agents.

The banking sector provides the most flagrant examples of business misconduct of late, relating especially to sales of US mortgage-backed securities, money laundering, and the manipulation of LIBOR and of foreign exchange markets. It has cost the sector dearly—or, at least, its shareholders. Morgan Stanley research estimates that since the 2007–08 financial crisis, fines and lawsuits for misconduct have cost the big banks $260 bn—more than the GDP of medium-sized countries such as Greece or Chile (Noonan 2015). Bank of America, Morgan Stanley, JPMorgan, Citi, and Goldman Sachs alone have paid out a massive $137 bn. In these cases, regulators and prosecutors have attributed responsibility (legal, if not moral) to the organization. However, despite these large fines, few individuals have been held criminally responsible, not even as yet the Barclays' trader involved in the rigging of foreign exchange markets who said to his co-conspirators, "if you ain't cheating, you ain't trying" (Odell 2015). This has prompted widespread criticism of the government agencies tasked with regulating the sector and prosecuting its miscreants as well as the agencies' political taskmasters.

It is often argued that only individual human beings can be morally responsible. Corporate moral agency raises the possibility that a corporation can be morally responsible for an action but no individual person or that both individuals and the organization can have moral responsibility. In the event of corporate misconduct, do we blame the company or the individuals within? A widespread, if not prevalent view is that we should blame the organization, so we speak of BP being responsible for the Gulf of Mexico oil spill and actions are taken against the company. Does this let individuals off the hook? The absence of prosecutions on Wall Street and in the City of London in the wake of the fraud that gave rise to the financial crisis suggests the answer is a clear "yes."

A CONFERENCE ON MORAL RESPONSIBILITY OF FIRMS

Renewed interest in these questions of corporate moral agency prompted the editors of this book to organize a conference on the theme of "The Moral

Responsibility of Firms: For or Against?"[1] We were fortunate to be able to involve some of the leading thinkers on the topic, including philosophers, business ethicists, legal scholars, and governance specialists. The conference was not intended to provide a definitive answer to the question of firm moral responsibility. Nonetheless, it confirmed that the debate continues, introduced new thinking on the topic, and explored its practical implications. Given the stimulating presentations and debates at the conference, we then solicited chapters for this book from those speakers who had offered particularly interesting and original theoretical developments and insights.

PART I OF THE BOOK

The four chapters of Part I are from contributors who are generally proponents of the idea of corporate moral agency (Pettit, Bratman, and French) or, at least, believe that corporations as collective agents can be held morally responsible for their actions under certain conditions (Hussain and Sandberg).

In the first chapter, Philip Pettit writes about "The Conversable, Responsible Corporation." He asserts that corporations are conversable agents and that conversable agents are fit to be held responsible for their actions. The agency of corporations, akin to that of animals and human beings because of their purposes and representations, is grounded in their central decision-making structure (consistent with French 1979). Unlike animals, but similar to human beings, corporations make commitments via their words and generally live up to them. We hold corporations responsible if they don't keep to their word. In this view, the corporation has a voice of its own—evident, for example, in the words of a corporate spokesperson—and distinct if not different from those of its members. It is a person not in a moral sense but "in the functional sense of agents who can speak for themselves in a commissive manner" (p. 23), and it has a mind to the extent that it is sensitive to the requirements of consistency.

Pettit goes on to claim that corporations are fit to be held responsible; particularly in regard to actions that breach common shared expectations. Accordingly, a firm cannot claim not to be able to make normative judgments (this in itself would presume that it knows what is moral) or that it is incapable

[1] The conference was held on the INSEAD Fontainebleau campus, December 12–13, 2013. It was organized under the auspices of the INSEAD–Wharton Alliance and was jointly co-chaired by myself (INSEAD) and Eric Orts (Wharton). The conference was sponsored by: Dreyfus Sons & Co. Ltd., Banquiers, the INSEAD–Wharton Alliance, the INSEAD Social Innovation Centre, the Wharton School's Legal Studies and Business Ethics Department, Wharton's Initiative for Global Environmental Leadership, and Wharton's Carol and Lawrence Zicklin Center for Business Ethics Research.

of living up to them. Thus Volkswagen could not claim that it did not know that designing its vehicles to cheat on emissions tests was wrong or that it was incapable of preventing this from happening. However, this claim for corporate moral responsibility does not mean that individual human beings are not also potentially morally responsible, neither does it mean that if individuals are held responsible that there isn't good reason to hold the corporation they are part of also responsible.

In Chapter 2, "The Intentions of a Group," Michael Bratman extends his prior work on *Shared Agency* (2014), where he developed a "plan-theoretic model" of the shared intentions of a group. He proposes that groups (and thus, potentially, firms) may be morally responsible if the group has intentions that are not shared and, by extension, this also becomes a plausible claim when there is a corresponding shared intention.

Bratman starts by establishing that his plan-theoretic approach to shared intentions of groups has application to group intentions that are not shared. Human planning capacity is evident in groups as well as in individual planning, but shared intentionality goes beyond individual planning agency. Groups have a plan-theoretic architecture that can include weights attached to certain decision considerations and policies guiding decision-making procedures, consistent with the Corporate Internal Decision Structures (CIDS) of French (1979) and such that the group can in effect govern itself. This can give rise to group intentions that are not shared intentions. Thus, through ignorance of the outcome of a group decision-making procedure (for example, in a large organization) or through awareness of the outcome and believing it to be a mistake, there can be procedure-based group intentions that are not shared intentions. By showing how in small groups common intentions do not need to satisfy some further condition of a shared state of mind (for example, two people choosing to go for a walk), Bratman also asserts, in contrast to List and Pettit (2011), that this is the case even if the group intentions are not embedded in a web of group attitudes.

Peter French, in "The Diachronic Moral Responsibility of Firms" (Chapter 3), revisits his earlier work on corporate moral agency, noting how his initial ideas have been modified (including his incorporation of Bratman's planning model), before turning to the issue of corporate moral agency over time. He observes that there are cases involving both human and corporate actors in which assessments of responsibility for the same event at later times may differ from the assessment at the time of the event. These diachronic responsibility ascriptions (at a later time) are "revisitations of moral assessments of an agent's previous actions, but they are not revisions of justified synchronic responsibility assessments" (p. 55), that is, the original assessment. More simply put, without questioning the original assessment of (synchronic) responsibility, he asks: Is BP still morally responsible today for the Gulf of Mexico oil spill of 2010?

French explores and endorses two approaches for examining the question of agent sameness that could be applied in ascribing (diachronic) responsibility to BP today. Psychological connectedness is applied to individual human beings in asserting diachronic moral responsibility. With corporations, French suggests, the diachronic responsibility depends on the degree to which the firm's CIDS remain the same as those that causally connected them to the past action. Thus, if a firm addresses failings in its CIDS that gave rise to misconduct, corporate moral responsibility may diminish over time—but it could potentially increase. The narrative coherence approach examines the stories that people or, conceivably, corporations tell about themselves. An agent is morally responsible for a past action to the extent that the action coheres with the agent's self-told (non-delusional and non-fictional) narrative. French suggests that corporations have various highly accessible self-narratives that are internally coherent and consistent with reality (for example, in annual reports but not in corporate image projections).

In "Pluralistic Functionalism about Corporate Agency" (Chapter 4), Hussain and Sandberg eschew the "pre-institutional" approach of the other contributors to Part I. While not denying the possibility of group agency, they offer instead a normative functionalism account. Under this approach, "questions about the collective agency of business corporations must be answered by asking what forms of treatment for business corporations would serve the justifying aims of the competitive market" (p. 67). Hussain and Sandberg thus argue that corporations are collective agents because of the corresponding social practices with which they are engaged and the relevant structural activity of involvement in a competitive market economy. This leads to a claim of collective agency for corporations because it serves an important purpose in a competitive market system. However, they also assert that there is no one right way to treat an organization as a collective agent, not least in relation to questions of temporal continuity, consistency, and liability.

In their view, BP was a collective agent in the Gulf of Mexico oil spill and liable for the damage caused not because of some pre-institutional form of corporate moral agency but because this interpretation of collective agency best serves the justifying aims of a competitive market system. Similarly, they are critical of the courts' rulings in the controversial *Hobby Lobby* and *Citizens United* cases because religious freedoms and freedom of speech are not relevant to the aims of competitive markets, and these decisions disregard the role of collective agency in wider social activities (for example, freedom of speech in the democratic process, in which the business corporation does not vote and should not partake as it is not a member of society).

PART II OF THE BOOK

In contrast to Part I, the four chapters of Part II are from contributors critical of the idea of corporate moral agency (Hasnas, Maitland, Rönnegard and Velasquez, and Sepinwall).

In "The Phantom Menace of the Responsibility Deficit" (Chapter 5), John Hasnas suggests that the strongest argument for the conclusion that corporations should be held morally responsible for their actions comes from Pettit (2007; also see Chapter 1 in this book). He is ready to assume that Pettit's argument for ascribing moral responsibility is sound and questions instead whether we *should* do so, arguing forcefully that "the ascription of moral responsibility to corporations should be eschewed as an unnecessary, dangerous, and highly illiberal safeguard against a phantom menace" (p. 94).

Pettit argues that we should hold corporations morally responsible because of a possible "responsibility deficit." Hasnas suggests this ignores the potential remedies that exist already without a requirement for moral responsibility, through civil and administrative actions and the prospect of "metaphorical responsibility" (public blame of the corporation resulting in reputational and financial harm). Moreover, noting that moral responsibility is a prerequisite for blame and the possibility of criminal punishment—which advocates of corporate moral responsibility seem to be seeking—Hasnas suggests that this would lead to the punishment of innocent parties (consumers, employees, and shareholders). While acknowledging that this might be effective (in strengthening deterrence of wrongdoing), it would be unjust as a form of vicarious collective punishment.

Ian Maitland, in "How Insiders Abuse the Idea of Corporate Personality" (Chapter 6), examines three ways by which corporate moral agency—which he views as a form of anthropomorphization of the corporation—has been exploited for unwarranted profit or advantage. In his first case, he shows that while the responsibility deficit provides an argument for corporate moral agency, it can not only result in the punishment of innocent parties, as Hasnas argues (Chapter 5), but also shield managers from the legal consequences of their actions. Thus corporate legal responsibility can lead to a different kind of responsibility deficit, evidenced in the prosecutorial shift in focus in recent years at the Department of Justice and the Securities and Exchange Commission, toward prosecuting corporations and not individuals—arguably letting them off the hook. This concern is richly illustrated in the proposed 2009 SEC settlement with Bank of America and the scathing critique of Judge Rakoff. As John Coffee commented, SEC enforcement practices "invite corporate executives to purchase immunity for themselves with their shareholders' money" (p. 110).

Second, Maitland argues that corporate agency was being used (by Justice Stevens) in the *Citizens United* case to potentially disguise a curtailment of constitutional rights of individuals. Thus, in contrast to Hussain and Sandberg (Chapter 4), Maitland supports the majority opinion of the US Supreme Court, suggesting that the ruling was consistent with the necessity at times to "pierce the corporate veil" (p. 115) and acknowledge that, in his view, actions of corporations are the actions of individual members within the corporation who, in this instance, had constitutional rights of free speech that needed to be protected.

Finally, Maitland challenges the entity theory of the corporation wherein, for example, it is said that the corporation owns itself. He considers this view of corporate agency to be inconsistent with shareholder primacy and potentially creating a situation where corporate officers and directors are accountable only to themselves and the property of the corporation can be redistributed from shareholders to stakeholders (for an alternate view, see Smith and Rönnegard 2014). In all three cases, Maitland argues that the anthropomorphization of the corporation is to blame for the abuses he identifies.

In Chapter 7, "On (Not) Attributing Moral Responsibility to Organizations," David Rönnegard and Manuel Velasquez also question the anthropomorphization of the corporation by those who take a "collectivist" position on moral responsibility—in contrast to their "individualist" approach that attributes moral responsibility solely to the members of an organization. They identify six arguments against attributing moral responsibility to organizations, as a separate additional entity. First, while they acknowledge that an organization is more than the sum of its parts, they argue that this does not create some additional entity that is itself an agent separate from the members of the organization and potentially morally responsible and subject to justifiable punishment. Second, they claim that moral responsibility can be attributed to agents only if they possess certain mental states, including knowledge and intentionality, which organizations do not have. They reject, as part of this argument, the idea of a functionalist theory of mind, wherein organizations function as if they had certain capacities, as proposed by Pettit (2007; chapter 1). Third, in a similar vein, they argue that moral responsibility also requires an emotional capacity—an ability to feel guilt and remorse, for example—which organizations do not have.

Rönnegard and Velasquez argue fourthly, that there is organizational action only if its members act. In contrast, collectivists claim that there are many actions of the organization that are not the actions of individual members— just as Steinbeck writes of the banks when their representatives are speaking to the tenant farmers who have lost their land or when we say a team has won a game. Rönnegard and Velasquez suggest that this is again an "as if" attribution and that the actions are still those of individual members of an organization. Their fifth argument questions the punishment of organizations. Consistent with Hasnas (Chapter 5), they view this as morally unacceptable collective punishment that punishes the innocent. Finally, they argue that responsibility requires autonomy that organizations do not have, rejecting arguments about autonomy grounded in organizational procedures.

In conclusion, Rönnegard and Velasquez acknowledge the dominance of the collectivist position but claim that this is the result of wishful thinking. The responsibility deficit, earlier discussed, gives rise in their view to a desire to find someone or something responsible for untoward events, when events can occur for which there are causal but no moral responsibility attributions.

The role of emotion in moral responsibility of organizations is examined in depth by Amy Sepinwall in "Blame, Emotion, and the Corporation" (Chapter 8). She argues that emotions are given insufficient attention in the literature on moral responsibility and yet "emotions are necessary for bringing the morally salient features of the world to light" (p. 145). However, she does not focus on whether a capacity for emotion is necessary for corporate moral agency, she focuses instead on whether corporations are blameworthy. She allows that so-called "recruiting accounts" of corporate moral agency might make a case for corporate capacity for emotion (as a source of knowledge through the organiza-tion's members). On this assumption of corporate moral agency, she then asks whether corporations can be blamed for wrongdoing.

Sepinwall argues that it makes sense to blame only those who can experi-ence guilt. As affect is required to experience guilt and corporations have no capacity for affect, it therefore makes no sense to blame corporations. Here, she argues, the recruiting approach comes up short and cannot be used to justify a claim that corporations are blameworthy because feelings are not delegable—they must be felt directly. She concludes that "we can secure a role for punish-ment of corporations even if, as I have argued, the corporation lacks the capacities for affect that blaming requires" (p. 162). On the basis of her analysis, she also raises broader questions about the role and status of corporations in moral communities.

PART III OF THE BOOK

The two chapters in Part III offer broader and somewhat different takes on the moral responsibility of firms, with a meta-analytic account of the debate on the moral responsibility of firms (Hess) and an argument for positive duties by firms as moral agents, in contrast to the emphasis elsewhere on wrongdoing by firms (Hsieh).

Kendy Hess is a proponent of the idea of corporate moral agency in her published work elsewhere on the topic. In "The Unrecognized Consensus about Firm Moral Responsibility" (Chapter 9), she maintains this position, but chooses to focus on what she sees as the points of consensus across the two camps, demonstrating that there is more in common than we might imagine. First, both camps agree that firms (as collections of individuals or as entities in themselves) should not do things that are morally wrong; second, individuals are not absolved from responsibility for wrongdoing in their roles as members of firms even if the firm as an entity is also responsible; third, our accounts of firm moral action require attention to individuals and to organizational factors. She believes this underlying consensus keeps the debate going, while also, if unacknowledged, potentially allows the debate to be interpreted as "condoning the idea that business is some kind of morality-free endeavor" (p. 185).

From these claims of consensus, Hess argues that the debate is really about how firms exercise their moral agency. She suggests: "Instead of arguing about *whether* firms have moral obligations and moral responsibility, we can shift to a discussion of how best to *account* for the fact that they do" (p. 176). The difficulty lies in what we mean by the firm, as an ontological matter (whether there is a distinct entity—the firm), a metaphysical matter (whether the firm can possess certain properties), a meta-ethical matter (whether it can possess certain sophisticated capacities necessary for moral agency), and as a methodological matter (whether it is better to treat it as if it is a collection of individuals or as an entity and agent in its own right). In this regard, much philosophical debate becomes empirical.

Hess highlights two bad habits in the debate: (1) treating every corporate action as if it is the result of explicit decision-making by some person or group within the organization, when decisions can be distributed across organizations and actions can be the result of "unchosen commitments;" (2) assuming that all moral agency must be like human agency. Hess builds on the latter point to summarize her functionalist account of corporate moral agency, under which moral agency is defined in terms of activities and behavior rather than identity. She concludes that firms should be recognized as moral agents and held responsible for their actions.

In "Corporate Moral Agency, Positive Duties, and Purpose" (Chapter 10), Nien-hê Hsieh focuses on whether firms have positive duties, such as donating medicines to those unable to afford them when this would be inconsistent with the firm's profit-seeking objective. In this way, his attention to corporate moral responsibility focuses on firms doing good rather than bad. He identifies three accounts supportive of such positive duties. First, a rescue account of firm moral duty is found in Dunfee's (2006) treatment of firms with a unique human catastrophe rescue competency. Second, there is a beneficence account, drawing on Smith (2012) who proposed an imperfect duty to take into account the well-being of others, together with Manswell's (2013) claim of a beneficence duty in relation to corporate social responsibility (interpreted as a deontological interpretation of shareholder primacy consistent with the classic account by Milton Friedman). Third, positive moral duties are supported by a justice account drawing on various sources that claim a duty of firms to contribute to bringing about justice in human societies under conditions where states are weak and the firm assumes duties as a secondary agent of justice.

For each account, Hsieh considers whether the firm can be treated as a moral agent—finding that acknowledging business firms as moral agents in their own right helps to underwrite the argument for positive duties of firms. Thus he is less interested in the idea of corporate moral agency per se, than in its implications for positive duties of firms. His purpose "is to further our understanding about how best to theorize about standards that require business firms to engage in activities to benefit parties who would not receive those benefits through routine commercial activity" (p. 189). This is an important project because the need to address the vexing question of the purpose of the for-profit firm is avoided to the extent that such positive duties can be established through firm moral agency.

Finally, in concluding the book, my co-editor Eric Orts richly illustrates how the various positions articulated in the preceding chapters are evident in application to the Volkswagen emissions scandal. He then goes on to show how a legal analysis also sheds important light on the debate about the moral responsibility of firms, including answers to empirical questions about individual responsibility and highlighting questions about who profits and who loses from organizational misconduct and the limited scope for compensation in some cases.

CONCLUSION

With such a rich array of accounts of firm moral responsibility presented here and the depth of scholarship and philosophical thinking on which these accounts are based, there is little reason for me to weigh in with another (and I certainly hesitate to do so). I will admit to being drawn on balance to the arguments in support of corporate moral agency. However, I would describe this as being a narrow and circumscribed form of agency that hopefully avoids anthropomorphization while acknowledging that a firm is more than the sum of its parts. This would then be largely a "functionalist" account consistent in many ways with Hussain and Sandberg (Chapter 4) and Hess (Chapter 9).

I also agree strongly with Hess in her claim that the two camps have much in common and that these consistencies need to be built on, not least if we are to address some of the real challenges posed by firm moral responsibility and corporate accountability more generally. Hopefully, firms are not, as Steinbeck suggests, monsters beyond our control. They are more likely to be brought under societal control through normative pressures if we can better understand the grounds for ascribing moral responsibility for doing good as well as bad (as Hsieh reminds us in Chapter 10) to responsible individuals and the firm, be it as an entity in itself or as a collection of individuals.

REFERENCES

Arnold, Denis G. (2006). "Corporate Moral Agency." *Midwest Studies in Philosophy* 30: 279.

Bratman, Michael E. (2014). *Shared Agency: A Planning Theory of Acting Together.*

Dunfee, Thomas (2006). "Do Firms with Unique Competencies for Rescuing Victims of Human Catastrophes Have Special Obligations? Corporate Responsibility and the AIDS Catastrophe in Sub-Saharan Africa." *Business Ethics Quarterly* 16: 185.

French, Peter A. (1979). "The Corporation as a Moral Person," *American Philosophical Quarterly* 16: 207.

French, Peter A. (2006). *Midwest Studies in Philosophy: Shared Intentions and Collective Responsibility.*

Hess, Kendy M. (2013). "'If You Tickle Us...': How Corporations Can Be Moral Agents Without Being Persons," *Journal of Value Inquiry* 47: 319.

List, Christian and Philip Pettit (2011). *Group Agency: The Possibility, Design, and Status of Corporate Agents.*

Manswell, Samuel (2013). "Shareholder Theory and Kant's 'Duty of Beneficence,'" *Journal of Business Ethics* 117: 583.

Noonan, Laura (2015). "Bank Litigation Costs Hit $260bn: With $65bn More to Come." *Financial Times*, August 23.

Odell, Mark (2015). "Trader Transcripts: 'If You Ain't Cheating, You Ain't Trying'." *Financial Times*, May 20.

Pettit, Philip (2007). "Responsibility Incorporated," *Ethics* 177: 171.

Rönnegard, David (2013). "How Autonomy Alone Debunks Corporate Moral Agency," *Business & Professional Ethics Journal* 32: 77.

Smith, N. Craig and David Ronnegard (2014). "Shareholder Primacy, Corporate Social Responsibility and the Role of Business Schools" (with David Ronnegard), *Journal of Business Ethics* (online first: DOI 10.1007/s10551-014-2427-x).

Smith, Jeffery (2012). "Corporate Duties of Virtue: Making (Kantian) Sense of Corporate Social Responsibility." In *Kantian Business Ethics: Critical Perspectives*, ed. Denis Arnold and Jared Harris.

Tuomela, R. (2007). *The Philosophy of Sociality.*

Velasquez, Manuel G. (1983). "Why Corporations Are Not Morally Responsible for Anything They Do," *Business & Professional Ethics Journal* 2: 1.

Velasquez, Manuel G. (2003). "Debunking Corporate Moral Responsibility," *Business Ethics Quarterly* 13: 531.

Part I

Arguments for Moral Responsibility
of Firms

1

The Conversable, Responsible Corporation

Philip Pettit

This chapter offers a defense of a simple syllogism. First premise: corporations are conversable agents. Second premise: conversable agents are fit to be held responsible for their actions. Conclusion: corporations are fit to be held responsible for their actions. The argument will proceed briskly, since I have defended some of the elements it deploys in previous work, much of it done in collaboration with Christian List.[1] The chapter is in three sections, two devoted to the premises, the third to the conclusion.

FIRST PREMISE: CORPORATIONS ARE CONVERSABLE AGENTS

What Are Corporations?

Corporations—or firms or companies or businesses, as we may also call them—are a species of corporate organization, on a par with clubs, churches, universities, voluntary associations, political parties, and indeed political states. Like such other organizations, as we shall see, they count as agents; that is what distinguishes them from informal groups. But unlike the bulk of other corporate bodies they are commercial, profit-seeking organizations (Orts 2015). And unlike other commercial organizations such as partnerships, they are distinguished mainly by asset lock-in (Kraakman 2009; Ciepley 2013). The members who provide the finance that any corporation will require—the

---

[1] See (Pettit 2003; 2007; 2009; List and Pettit 2011; 2012; Pettit 2014). Particularly important from the viewpoint of this essay is (Pettit 2007), although the line I pursue here is different in character.

shareholders—cannot remove their support at will. They can sell their shares to others, of course, if they can find buyers. But they do not have even the qualified ability to take their capital out of the corporation and use it for their own purposes.

Asset lock-in is of the greatest importance in the organization of a business, since it means that a corporation can rely on retaining the capital at its disposal, so that it is not vulnerable in the manner of the normal partnership. But two other features are also characteristic of the corporation, if not exclusive to it. One is limited liability and the other entity shielding. Limited liability means that the individual shareholders of the company are not personally liable—their personal resources are not at risk—if the company declares bankruptcy. And, complementary to this, entity shielding means that the company is not corporately liable—its corporate resources are not at risk—if individual shareholders declare bankruptcy.

These features of a corporation have the effect of juridifying it. They force us to speak of it as a legal entity separate from the different categories into which members now divide: as an entity that its directors govern, that its shareholders invest in, and that employs its managers and workers. This makes for a contrast with some other corporate bodies. Where we may equate a regular corporate body with the membership as a whole—we may say, for example, that what a club does the membership does—there is no class of members with which we can identify the corporation in the same way; we have little option but to speak about it as an entity apart.

It is worth noting these distinctive aspects of corporations in order to place them in relation to other corporate bodies and to register their special character. But I note them here only to set them aside. The points defended in this chapter do not depend on anything that is exclusive to corporations as such and go through for any kind of corporate body. While my focus is on corporations, then, I shall often indicate that the claims I defend apply to corporate bodies more generally.

The Notion of Agency

The first thing to notice about corporations is that like other corporate bodies, and unlike unincorporated groups, they count in a straightforward sense as agents. But what is an agent? The observation that corporations are agents means nothing in the absence of an answer to this more general question.

In order to answer the question, think about an imaginary, simple artifice and the considerations that might lead us to describe it as an agent (List and Pettit 2011, ch. 1). Imagine a little robot that stands six inches high, has bug-like eyes protruding on stems, can move about on wheels and lift things with little arms at its sides. Suppose that, put on a table top strewn with half a dozen bottles, this object seems to scan its surrounds, with its eyes turning now in this direction, now in that, and responds immediately to a particular stimulus: the appearance, as we take it to be, of a bottle on its side. The stimulus leads it to move to the bottle and, using its arms, to put the bottle upright. Or at least it does this when the lights are on; when there is a real bottle there, and not just the photograph of a bottle; and when the bottle is not so near the edge that the lifting procedure knocks it off the table.

We naturally hold that this robot is an agent—this, in a more or less common sense of the term—because of three things that are true of it. First, we can reasonably ascribe representations to it of its environment, since it reliably reacts over different sorts of stimuli to the appearance of a bottle on its side—even the misleading appearance, as the photograph shows—and does nothing when the bottles are, and presumably appear to be, upright. Second, we can reasonably take it to have the purpose of putting the bottles in its space upright, since it takes steps to make this the case when its representations indicate that some bottles are on their sides and leaves things be when its representations indicate that none are in that position. And third, it more or less reliably acts to realize its purposes—its single purpose, in this case—according to its representations. It forms suitable representations and it performs suitable actions in realizing its purposes, at least when conditions are normal by independently plausible criteria. It occasionally fails to operate at par but only when things are clearly rigged against it: the lights are off, there is a photograph placed to mislead it, or the bottle is near the edge of the table.

Generalizing from this example, we may say that a system is an agent when, in normal, unrigged circumstances, it maintains certain purposes, forms reliable representations of its environment, and acts reliably so as to satisfy its purposes according to those representations. In order to be an agent, then, the system must be evidentially reliable in the formation of representations—this, in the way the robot reliably notices bottles on their sides—and executively reliable in the performance of actions that, according to its representations, are appropriate ways of realizing its purposes. It must exemplify a unified epistemic vision and a coherent practical agenda (Rovane 1997).

In this sense of agency, it should be clear that while trees and plants do not count as agents, non-human animals like birds and cats and dogs certainly do. They have many more purposes than our little robot and many more ways of forming representations: they have many sensory channels, after all, and are capable of integrating the information these convey. But still, they can be said in the same way as the robot to form representations of how things are and to pursue their purposes according to those representations. Or at least they can be said to display such evidential and executive reliability—if you like, such evidential and executive rationality—in presumptively normal conditions.

Corporations Are Agents

Corporations, like other corporate bodies, count as agents in this generous sense. They may fail in the manner of any agents, when things are not normal by plausible criteria. But absent such distorting conditions we can identify various purposes by which they hold, perhaps ordered in a rough hierarchy of importance; we can take them to form reliable judgments or representations about the opportunities at hand or the best means of realizing those purposes; and we find that they more or less reliably act so as to satisfy their purposes according to their representations. Unlike animals, of course, corporations are not biological organisms and unlike robots, they are not electronic systems; they operate on the basis of psychological adjustments among their members, not on the basis of any natural or mechanical infrastructure. But like those other entities they fit the functional profile of agents, and that is all that matters.

The evidential reliability of the corporate body gives us a basis for predicting how its judgments would respond to new evidence, and its executive reliability a basis for predicting how it would act in the event of such a response. In decision-theory terms the organization has a kinematics that governs how it would update in such counterfactual situations, with individual members making the psychological adjustments that support appropriate responses.[2] This kinematics is grounded in a central, decision-making structure, as Peter French (1979) calls it, albeit a structure that may operate via a widely distributed network of sub-structures (Hess 2014).

These observations argue strongly for the view that corporations and other corporate bodies ought to count as agents. Those who reject this view tend to invoke a parallel between markets and corporations, arguing that they each amount to nothing more than a nexus of contracts, as it is routinely put, and that a nexus of contracts cannot exercise agency. The idea, then, is that just as we speak figuratively in saying that markets think and do things—say, think that banking stocks are overvalued and act to put a correction in place—so we speak only figuratively in ascribing attitudes and actions to corporations. On this approach, as one commentator puts it (Grantham 1998, 579), a corporation is just "a collective noun for the web of contracts that link the various participants."

The appeal to the analogy with markets overlooks the presence of a decision-making structure in a corporation and the support this gives to a kinematics. Sure, that structure is grounded in the contractual relations between members but that does not argue in any way against the agential status of the corporate body. Those who invoke the analogy with markets to

---

[2] A system may have a more or less robust kinematics, depending on the range of counterfactual situations where it behaves appropriately. Agency requires an intuitively robust kinematics but it is hard to identify any threshold that a system must reach in order to count as an agent.

deny that status to corporations appear to be moved by the following invalid inference: corporations and markets are both composed out of contracts; but markets are not agents; so corporations are not agents. That argument, of course, is no more persuasive than this blatant non sequitur: animals and trees are both composed out of cells; but trees are not agents; so animals are not agents.[3]

To argue along the lines we have been following so far is to maintain that corporations are interpretable—and, by standard methodological criteria, best interpreted—as having certain purposes, forming certain representations, and acting so as to satisfy those purposes according to those representations. It is to say that like animals and robots they are best seen from within the intentional stance, as Daniel Dennett (1987) calls it (Clark 1994; Tollefsen 2002). But this is not yet to say all that needs to be said about corporations as agents.

Whereas animals and robots are mute beings, corporations are able to speak for themselves and to offer an interpretation of their own purposes, representations, and actions. They are not just interpretable as agents; they interpret themselves as agents. And they do not just interpret themselves as agents; they make a point of communicating that interpretation to their members and to those who interact with them in any way. Corporations speak for themselves in this manner when they rely on authorized spokespersons to speak in their name; these will be individuals or committees recognized under the organization's rules as having the authority, subject to some overall coordination, to express the corporate view in this or that domain. Such spokespersons will give an account of the corporation's goals, long-term and short-term; offer a narrative and usually a justification of its judgments about current market conditions and likely developments; and make sense of what the corporation does in the light of those imputed purposes and representations. And, in specific interactions with other agents—its members or employees, its customers or suppliers, the local government or tax authority—they will declare its intentions, formed on the basis of agreed assumptions, to perform in this or that fashion; in short, they will commit the corporation in a contractual manner.

In speaking for themselves in this way, corporations resemble individual human beings like you and me. And the similarity is important because it means that like you and me, corporations can use words as the means of forming their purposes and representations, not just as signs to report attitudes that are already formed.[4] It means, in a word, that they are *conversable agents*.

---

[3] I cannot consider other, more substantive arguments against the idea that corporations are agents. For two such arguments see, for example, Velasquez (1983) and Rönnegard (2013).

[4] As will become apparent as my argument unfolds in the text, corporations typically form intentional attitudes on the basis of members subscribing to suitable words. Unlike human beings, and of course unlike non-human animals, they do form few intentional attitudes in

The Notion of Conversable Agency

When I ask you about what you believe or desire or intend to do you may speak about yourself as you would about a third person, speculating about precisely what attitude you hold and looking at your past behavior and current intentions in order to help you out in the exercise. But that is not what you or anyone else does in the normal case. What you ordinarily do on being asked whether you believe that such and such is to think about whether you ought to believe such and such—whether the data support the claim that such and such—answering that you believe it, disbelieve it, or have no opinion either way, depending on the evidence at hand (Anscombe 1957; Evans 1982). And equally, on being asked whether you desire or intend to do so and so, what you ordinarily do is to think about whether the prospect is one that you ought to take up in light of the desiderata that weigh with you—your concerns or interests—and, depending on your judgment, answer that you do or do not desire or intend it.

You may have had the relevant belief or intention prior to my asking you about it, of course. But the normal response to the query will still be to check before responding on whether you ought to have it and to form the attitude or to re-form or re-confirm it only in the case of a positive answer. In such a response, then, you do not give a report on your attitude as you might give a report about someone else's. You avow the attitude, as we might say, conveying it in a way that marks your capacity to form, re-form, or indeed unform what you believe and desire, as the relevant data or desiderata require. You speak on the basis of a maker's knowledge of your attitudes, as it used to be said, not a reporter's.

The striking difference between reporting an attitude and avowing it in this sense shows up in the event of your not acting as that attitude would have required or supported. In the case of a reporting a certain belief or intention, or as you might report the belief or intention of another, you can explain and excuse your failure to act appropriately in either of two salient ways. First, by arguing that you changed your mind between the time of reporting and acting; in this case, you may be expected to justify the change of mind by reference to new evidence or other considerations that came to light. Or, second, by arguing that you must have been misled by the evidence about what you believed or intended when you gave your report: this, in the way in which you might have been misled by the evidence about someone else's belief or intention.

Things are very different if you avow the belief or intention rather than reporting it. You might do this by affirming "p" in response to a question as to

---

a sub-personal manner: the only exceptions are those attitudes, like a belief in modus ponens, that are ascribed on the basis of their procedures.

whether you believe that p, or by asserting "I'll be there" in response to the question as to whether you intend to go to a party this evening; in each case the utterance signals that you have made up your mind, not merely that you found you were minded in this or that manner. In the case of such an avowal, you may excuse a failure to act appropriately by the changed-mind excuse but you will not be able to do so plausibly by appeal to the misleading-mind excuse. Because you signal in making an avowal that you are making up your mind rather than just conducting a mind-reading exercise, you cannot plausibly excuse a failure to live up to the words you utter by claiming that you must have gotten your mind wrong; that excuse would only have been available if you had presented yourself as someone reading your mind in the way in which you might try to read the mind of another.

We have good reason as individuals to avow beliefs and desires and intentions rather than just reporting them. By doing so we make our words in expression of those attitudes more expensive; we increase our exposure to a penalty for failure, manifestly depriving ourselves of an excuse whereby we might get off the hook. And by making them more expensive we make them more credible, thereby giving ourselves a better chance of persuading others to rely on us and to enter relationships of cooperation. In putting aside the misleading-mind excuse, we may be said to commit ourselves to the attitudes we communicate; we back ourselves, on pain of penalty, to display those attitudes. And we can also go one stage further in the case of intentions and, putting aside the changed-mind excuse as well as the misleading-mind excuse, commit ourselves in the full-scale manner of making a promise to act in a certain way. This extra commissive move will have the attraction of making our words even more expensive and more credible.

Serving us well in the formation of relationships, self-commitment of the kind involved in avowals and promises is so common that in many contexts we have to go to some trouble to indicate that we are just reporting on ourselves rather than making an avowal, or just making an avowal rather than making a promise. Thus to say "I believe that p" or "I intend to do X" will usually be taken as an avowal rather than a report, and to say "I'll be there" will often be taken as a promise rather than an avowal of intention. In order to signal that you are just making a report in the first case, just making an avowal in the second, you will have to resort to special phrasing. In the first case, you will have to say something like "I think that what I am inclined to believe or prefer or choose is such and such but I may, of course, be mistaken about my attitudes." And in the second, you will have to say: "My intention is to be there but I could yet change my mind."

It is because we understand the meanings of words in common, can look to the demands of reasons in determining what to affirm verbally, and can use words to speak for ourselves in a commissive mode that we count, in my terminology, as conversable beings. We interpret ourselves in words, using them in a conventional sense, and we give that interpretation a unique first-personal authority in our dealings with others by investing the utterances with commissive force. We put our reputation on the line, using the words to invite others to see us in this and that manner: to see us as agents who believe such and such, desire so and so, and intend to do this or that.

We are conversable insofar as our use of words in this interpretive, commissive manner means that we are subjects with whom others can do business. We let them see that we form our attitudes on the basis of the reasons that are relevant, by common consent, to those attitudes. And we give others a powerful basis—one rooted in the interest we have in forming and maintaining certain relations with them—to expect that as we assert things to be, so we will prove to believe them to be; that as we assert that we shall make things be, so we will prove to intend them to be; and so on. Or at least we do this when we do not seek to deceive or manipulate others, trying to get away with masking our real beliefs and intentions. I put aside that complication for the sake of simplicity, although it is clearly relevant in the personal and, to anticipate, in the corporate case.

Corporations Are Conversable Agents

Having spelled out what conversability involves, it should be clear that the agents constituted by corporations, or by any corporate bodies, are conversable in much the manner of individual human beings. The spokespersons who speak in the name of the corporation do not speak just as reporters, as if their job was to take a census on the attitudes of members about any issue they address and then report on what those attitudes seem to be. They speak with the same sort of authority that any one of us assumes when we speak as individuals for ourselves. Where does this authority come from? Very simply, from the fact, long registered in law, that the other members of the corporation ascribe that authority to them, implicitly or explicitly committing themselves as individuals to rally behind the words of their spokespersons on any relevant issue; they treat those words as expressions of attitude that they have to live up to, on pain of corporate failure, in their actions as corporate members.

Thus suppose that the appropriate officers of a corporation enter a contract under which they commit the body to repay a debt on a certain schedule and at a certain rate of interest. Convention and law rule out the possibility that certain members of the corporation—say, a disaffected number of shareholders—might claim that the officers got their intention and promise wrong and that the company is not obligated to meet the terms of the debt. Insofar as the officers acted under the rules of the corporation in accepting and entering the contract—the rules implicitly or explicitly endorsed by members—they made it the case that the corporation formed the required intention and promise; if you like, they made up the mind of the corporation.

You and I have a powerful motive to authorize the words we use in avowal and promise, since this enables us to gain credibility with others and form productive relationships with them. And in the same way the members of a corporate body such as a corporation have a powerful motive to authorize the words of their spokespersons when they make avowals and promises in the corporate name. Unless they authorize those words, being prepared to live up to whatever the words require of them—being prepared, in our example, to go along with the agreed repayment of the debt—they cannot expect to gain the benefits of incorporation. They cannot expect, for example, to be able to persuade any other individuals, or indeed any other organizations, to rely on their corporate word and to cooperate with them in any projects or arrangements that they propose.

That corporations and other such bodies are conversable agents means, in quasi-legal parlance, that they are persons. Not persons in a moral sense—not persons in a sense in which this involves a moral status—but persons in the functional sense of agents who can speak for themselves in a commissive manner. When the idea of the corporate body came to fruition in the high Middle Ages, it was expressed in the claim that such bodies are examples of what Pope Innocent IV cast in a document issued in 1246 as a *persona ficta,* a fabricated person (Kantorowicz 1997). Understanding personhood in a moral sense, the theologians generally took this to mean that the corporation is only a pretend person: a fabrication (Eschmann 1946). But understanding personhood in a functional sense, legal and political thinkers argued, ultimately with more influence, that it meant that the corporation is an artificial person, fabricated in the distinct sense of being made by human hands.

On this interpretation, medieval and later commentators cast the corporate body as a real person but, unlike a natural person, not the bearer of an immortal soul (Woolf 1913; Canning 1980). Thus, as Innocent IV insisted, the corporate body—for example, a body like the University of Paris, the addressee of his 1246 document—could not be excommunicated and consigned for eternity to hell's fires. But, so the lawyers argued, it could be held responsible in law and subjected reasonably to more mundane penalties. I return to the theme in the next section, when I discuss the connection between the conversability of agents and their fitness to be held responsible for what they do.

Corporations Have Minds of Their Own

Before moving on to that section, however, it will be useful to add one further element to our picture of corporate bodies as conversable agents and functional persons. While Thomas Hobbes (1994, ch. 16) also regarded corporate bodies as conversable agents—persons, as he put it, that speak for themselves—he nevertheless held that in comparison with natural persons, they come into existence only by fiction (Skinner 2010). What I take him to mean is not just that they are artificial rather than natural persons—that would have gone without saying—but that they are persons or agents without minds of their own: agents that borrow the attitudes for which they stand from elsewhere rather than forming them for themselves.

This claim is clearly true of the corporate body with a single, dictatorial spokesperson—in effect, a Hobbesian monarch (Pettit 2008; 2014)—since that body borrows from its leader the voice behind which members rally and acts in expression of the leader's mind, not a mind of its own. But Hobbes thinks that all corporate bodies, even ones with a non-dictatorial constitution, are dependent in the same way on recruiting from elsewhere the voice it enacts and the mind it expresses.

Hobbes argues that any non-dictatorial corporate body must authorize the voice of a committee, whether an elite committee or a committee of the whole, and that this voice is determined independently in much the same way as the voice of a dictator. He holds that the committee voice has to be fixed by majority voting, qualified to allow for ties. And, treating this as a voice that is algorithmically determined by majoritarian procedure, he thinks of the group that follows it as an entity that does not have a mind of its own. In following majority voting the corporate body expresses a mind that it recruits, not now from an individual spokesperson, but from a more or less mechanical procedure. And so it does not make up its own mind, as an individual might make up his or her mind, but helps itself to a mind that is independently fixed.

The final element to add to the picture is the observation that Hobbes is mistaken in this line of thought. If a corporate body is to be conversable, and to succeed in getting others to do business with it, then a minimal constraint on the voice it follows, and the mind it expresses, is that it should be sensitive to requirements of consistency; it should display consistency or at least be responsive to evidence of inconsistency, say evidence manifested in the complaints of others. But it turns out that the majority voice of a group on a set of interconnected judgments—even a set as simple, say, as "p", "q" and "p&q"—is liable to be un-remediably inconsistent, as the discursive dilemma shows (Pettit 2001a, b).[5] And it transpires, more generally, that any equally mechanical way of constructing a group voice is subject to similar problems, as the literature on judgment aggregation has established (List and Pettit 2002; List and Polak 2010; List and Pettit 2011).

---

[5] The discursive dilemma is a generalized version of the doctrinal paradox in legal theory (see Kornhauser and Sager 1993; 2004).

The discursive dilemma is readily illustrated for our simple example with "p," "q," and "p&q." Suppose that a group of just three individuals A, B, and C, each with a consistent set of views about those propositions, relies on majority voting to form a group view. It is perfectly possible for the majority voice to support an inconsistent set of views, with the majority supporting each of the simple propositions, for example, but rejecting the conjunction. Table 1.1 illustrates that possibility.

In order for a corporate body to be conversable the members cannot rely on any mechanical rule to determine the body's views; they must institute a system for gaining feedback on the results generated by the protocols they follow, and they must find a way of correcting for any inconsistency produced. The simplest variation on majority voting that would achieve this is the straw-vote procedure (List and Pettit 2011, ch. 2). This would require the members to check after every vote on whether the view endorsed in the vote is consistent with what has already been endorsed and to look for a compromise in the event that it hasn't. Following such a procedure, A, B, and C might agree that as a group they should endorse "p&q," rejecting the majority judgment on that particular proposition. Or of course they might form a different compromise and reject the majority judgment on one of the other propositions instead.

By making the move toward any such compromise the members would cease to look elsewhere to find a voice to follow and a mind to express. They would construct the voice of the corporate body in a way that makes it relatively autonomous from the individual voices of members. And they would make up the corporate mind that their actions as members then go on to express. This holds, not just for the straw-vote procedure of incorporation, but for the myriad alternatives under which a group could allow feedback on the consistency of the attitudes its protocols support, seek to correct for failures, and establish itself as a conversable entity.

Just to illustrate the alternatives possible, those procedures might operate on the outputs, not of voting by members of the group as a whole, majoritarian or otherwise, but on the outputs of different committees on different issues, or indeed on outputs that require the support of distinct committees. And of course corrective adjustment itself might be conducted in different ways: by the membership as a whole, or by a particular committee, or by different

Table 1.1. A discursive dilemma

	Question 1: p?	Question 2: q?	Question 3: p&q?
Person A	P	Not q	Not p&q
Person B	P	Q	p&q
Person C	Not p	Q	Not p&q
The majority	P	Q	Not p&q

committees in different areas. The possibilities are legion and include the sort of mixed constitution—or "mixarchy," as Hobbes called it—that Hobbes himself was anxious, for anti-republican reasons, to resist in the case of the political state (Pettit 2008). As exemplified in the United States, for example, this would require laws to be supported by two houses of Congress as well as the President and would allow the Supreme Court to strike any law down on grounds of being inconsistent with constitutional and other commitments.

PREMISE 2: CONVERSABLE AGENTS ARE FIT TO BE HELD RESPONSIBLE

Holding Agents Responsible

What does it mean to hold agents responsible for doing something? It certainly does not just mean claiming that they were causally at the origin of the effect in question. If it meant this, then we could be said to hold a hurricane responsible when we identify the damage that it did to our neighborhood. There may be a causal sense in which we hold things responsible for their effects, but it is not the sense that is relevant to the question about whether we should hold certain agents responsible: whether they are fit to be held responsible for the action in question.

Perhaps what we mean by holding an agent responsible is illustrated by the regulative stance we take, not to an uncontrollable force like a hurricane, but to our pet dog when we blame it for the wet patch on the carpet or praise it for seeking to go outside when it needs to relieve itself. In this case, by contrast with the case of the hurricane, we recognize that we can train the dog to behave in a certain way and that the best means of doing this is to sanction it by rewards and penalties for how it behaves, praising and petting it when things go well, or wagging our finger threateningly at it when things go badly. Perhaps sanctioning the dog for behaving or not behaving to plan can be usefully taken to exemplify what it means to hold an agent responsible.

This is not satisfactory either. Were I to try to influence you in this conditioning way, the success of the exercise might well depend on my hiding the nature of what I was doing from you; making the project clear would be liable to elicit resentment and reactance in you.[6] That is why we laugh at the cartoon in which the boss leans across his desk and says to a shrinking employee: "They tell me, Jones, that you respond well to intimidation." But

---

[6] Finding it objectionable, you would be likely to prove defiant and counter-suggestible in response to a transparent attempt to condition you, thereby undermining the regulative point of the exercise (Brehm and Brehm 1981; Grabosky 1995).

when I hold you responsible, what I am doing is capable of being made manifest between us and will normally be transparent in that way. And so what I am seeking cannot amount just to the conditioning form of influence that I look for with the dog.

The reason why the sanction-based picture of holding responsible fails the transparency test, plausibly, is that it does not treat the subject who is held responsible as a conversable person. You will have the capacity as a presumptively conversable subject to form attitudes that correspond to the words you are led to endorse under the pressure of relevant reasons, whether of evidence or of interest. And if I want you to behave in a certain manner, the saliently appropriate way of achieving this effect is to appeal to reasons to support the line that I want you to take; only that approach takes account of the very special sort of agent that you are. To seek a conditioning effect, akin to the effect I seek with the dog, would be to try to get in under the radar of conversability. It would be to try to influence you, not as a person in the functional sense of the term, but rather as a slave of stimulus and effect.

This observation points us toward an attractive account of what it is to hold you or any other agent responsible, at least in the special situation where you have spoken about your beliefs, intentions, and the like prior to action. It is to assume that in issuing such words, you were avowing attitudes and promising actions. And then it is to hold you to the expectation, elicited by the utterance of those words, that you will act accordingly: you will live up to those words, proving to display the required attitudes and to perform the required actions.

If you meet that expectation, then I will confirm you in the ascription of conversability and, other things being equal, reward you with my approval, reliance, and cooperation. If you fail to meet that expectation, however, I will respond in either of two ways, one of which puts your capacity to cooperate in question, the other your reliability in exercising the capacity. Thus I may put your very conversability in question, wondering if you have the capacity to understand and honor the import of the words you utter. Or, to take the more likely possibility, I may take you to have that capacity and to have failed to exercise it—to have failed to match words and deeds—in which case, as we generally put it, I will rebuke or censure you. I will rebuke or censure you, at any rate, in the absence of credible and acceptable excuses for the failure. These are excuses that avowals and promises would still leave in place and include ignorance of what was at stake that you were not in a position to notice; pressures, as in prospects or threats of retaliation, that would have made it heroic to live up to the words; or obstacles like a broken leg that got in the way of your being faithful to the words (McGeer and Pettit 2015).

This explanation of what it means to hold you responsible is confined to the sort of case where you utter words in token of what you claim to think or be ready to do and assume responsibility for making your deeds match those words. But I may also hold you responsible in the more general case where you do not explicitly assume responsibility for it. This is the sort of situation where, as a matter of common belief between us, you recognize the expectation on my part that you will conform to common standards, do nothing to cancel that expectation, and then fail—or, as it may be, manage—to meet it. That this is a matter of common belief means that we each believe it, we each believe that we each believe it, and so on in the usual hierarchy (Lewis 1969).

In this more general case, as in the other, you communicate your mind in a commissive way to me and others, but you do so by virtue of what you do not say rather than by virtue of what you do say. Following this pattern, we manifestly or overtly hold you to expectations of non-violence, non-deception, non-coercion, and the like, even when you do not explicitly commit to these. And if you fail to meet those manifest expectations we will hold you just as responsible as if you had explicitly made suitable avowals and promises. You may incur responsibility, even when you do not explicitly assume it.

Fitness To Be Held Responsible

There are three conditions that must be satisfied, intuitively, if you are fit to be held responsible for doing or not doing something, X.[7] They correspond, broadly, with the conditions of grave matter, full knowledge of the guilt, and full consent of the will that were set out in the traditional catechism.

- *Grave matter.* You must have had a presumably non-trivial choice between doing X and not doing X or between doing X and more specific alternatives.

- *Full knowledge of the guilt.* You must have been in a position to gauge standard, presumptively common expectations and to make a normative judgment about the merits of the options, as registered in those expectations.

- *Full consent of the will.* Whatever direction that judgment assumed, you must have had the capacity to choose as that judgment would have required you to choose; and to do this, moreover, because this is what the judgment required.

On this account of fitness to be held responsible for a given deed, it should be clear that you are going to be fit to be held responsible just insofar as you are

---

[7] Notice that as Harry Frankfurt (1969) argues, you may still be held responsible for doing X in a case where you thought you had the alternative of not doing X but were deceived in the matter; unbeknownst to you, you would have been forced to do X, even if you had chosen not to do it. But even in this sort of case you did have two alternatives open. You could have done X voluntarily or you could have tried not to do X. You will choose that second option if you take steps that trigger the force which leads you to do X involuntarily.

a conversable agent. You must have the generic, unimpaired capacity associated with conversability to live up to the expectations you explicitly or implicitly endorse. And that capacity must be unimpeded in the specific choice on hand; it must not be temporarily blocked by ignorance or pressure or obstruction of some kind. Let the generic capacity be absent and you will be exempt from being held responsible from forming or living up to any commitment, explicit or implicit. Let the specific capacity be absent and you will be excused by the factor that impedes it, assuming that you cannot be held responsible on an independent basis for letting that factor get in the way (Gardner 2007). But let both the generic and specific capacity be present and you are firmly on the hook in the case of failure, safely on the podium in the case of success. You will be deserving, as we say, of blame in the one case, praise in the other.

The third condition in this account may seem to require a non-naturalistic free will: a contra-causal capacity, whatever the other factors at work in motivating your decision for or against X, to have set those aside and injected your act of will into the causal chain. Suppose that your capacity to act as your normative judgment requires involves nothing like that sort of free will but consists in a disposition, elicited under natural and cultural pressures, to respond reliably to the normative considerations present; suppose it means that if you do not respond appropriately then that is just a fluke (Smith 2003). If your capacity amounts to nothing more than this, can it really support our holding you responsible, treating you as deserving of censure or praise? The following challenge suggests not.

Suppose you have the generic and specific capacity to do something good, X: you are generally conversable, having the unimpaired capacity to act on normative judgments, and there is no excusing factor that impedes the exercise of that capacity in choosing between X and the alternative. And suppose, as is surely possible, that you fail to exercise your capacity and deliver X, whether because of failing to make the right judgment or failing to act upon it. If your capacity consists just in a disposition to respond reliably to the normative considerations supporting X, then presumably the failure to display that capacity must have been due, at least in the last analysis, to some chance perturbation: perhaps a neural misfiring in your brain. But if the failure was the result of such a misfiring, how can I hold you responsible for it? How can I say, as we do say in such a case, that you could have done otherwise; you could and indeed ought to have responded appropriately to the reasons in favor of doing X? Shouldn't I rather acknowledge that your failure was due to something going awry in the neural works, in which case it would seem inappropriate to lay any blame at your door?[8]

---

[8] For a further development of this challenge, and a more elaborate response, see McGeer and Pettit (2015).

No, I should not dismiss your failure in this way. However transparent and acknowledged, holding you responsible is a regulative practice in which I enjoin you, by virtue of manifesting a certain expectation, to perform in a corresponding manner. And a little reflection on the point of any regulative practice explains why in the case envisaged I should insist that you could have done otherwise and that you are subject therefore to censure.

The point of a regulative practice lies in the presumptive fact that enjoining you to perform appropriately is likely to increase the chance of your doing so. Or at least it is likely to do this insofar as it implies a penalty for non-performance: it takes the form "Do this, or else . . . ." Any injunctive practice will presuppose a generic capacity to comply, as in the presupposition that you are a conversable subject, if it is to serve a regulative function. And any such practice will recognize certain factors—certain excusing factors, as they will seem—such that there is no point in penalizing a failure when it is produced by such a factor. The assumption is presumably that there is little or no hope, in the presence of such excusing factors, of increasing the chance of the person acting as enjoined: the factors in question put the agent beyond the regulative reach of the practice and count for that reason as excuses.

If this is correct, then it should be clear why we should stick to our penalizing instincts in the sort of case envisaged, where you fail to live up to our shared expectations, despite having a specific capacity to have done so. I may freely admit that your failure must have been due ultimately to some misfiring in your makeup—say, some neural glitch—but to give up on censuring you in any case where this is plausible would be to deprive the practice of holding you responsible of any regulative point. It is important with a regulative practice to identify the general capacity it presupposes, and to identify those excusing factors that let the agent off the hook: those factors that make the agent incapable of being regulated profitably. But it would make no sense whatsoever to let the agent off the hook whenever there is some presumptively naturalistic but non-excusing explanation for the failure. It would be to deprive the practice of the regulative role that, by hypothesis, it is meant to serve.[9]

Conversability, Responsibility, and Corporations

What these considerations show is that to be an unimpaired, conversable agent like you or me is to be fit to be held responsible for various actions, in

---

[9] The position sketched here, following McGeer and Pettit (2015), steers a middle course between those on the one side who hold that being fit to be held responsible presupposes that you have a contra-causal free will and those on the other—now an increasing number—who argue that it only presupposes a general capacity to be responsive to the judgments of others: a capacity that implies that the attitudes you have speak to the sort of person you are but not in any demanding sense that you have done otherwise than you did.

particular those in the exercise of which there is no excusing factor that impedes our conversable capacity. But the fact that this is true at the level of conversable subjects like you and me suggests that it should also be true at the level of conversable corporate bodies, including corporations.

Like individual human beings, corporations routinely face decisions on non-trivial matters; in particular, on matters that involve the welfare of ordinary people. Like individual human beings, they are capable as conversable subjects of forming normative judgments on the relative merits of the options before them in any instance. And like individual human beings, they are capable as conversable subjects of letting the normative judgments they endorse constrain what they actually do. Thus we are all in a position to call such a body to account for what it does. More than that, indeed, most of us are in the habit of doing this in a more or less informal way. We would all tend to blame a company for negligence if it put toxic food on the market, for example, or for wrongdoing if it hid fatal design flaws in the motor cars it produces.

But could a corporation not respond to our calling it to account in these ways by maintaining that it was unable to form suitable judgments, or unable to act on the judgments it forms? Could it not claim in that respect to be a special, restricted sort of conversable agent, not an agent like you and me? No, it could not.

Suppose, to take one possibility, that a corporation announced that it was unable to make normative judgments on an issue like whether or not it is wrong to put toxic food on the market or to hide potentially fatal design flaws in the cars it manufactures. In order to make this claim, the corporation would have to have the concepts of what is right and wrong, and the associated capacity to make corresponding normative judgments. And so in making the claim it would presuppose that the content—the proposition asserted—is actually false. It would be guilty of what is known as a performative contradiction. The claim would presuppose that something is so—that it, the corporation making the claim, has a certain capacity—but assert in contradiction of this presupposition, that actually it, the corporation, does not have that capacity.[10]

Or suppose, to take a less radical possibility, that the corporation announced that while it was capable of making such normative judgments, it did not have the capacity or wherewithal to ensure that it lived up to them. It did not have the resources to monitor and police the decisions of its employees so as to reduce the probability of putting toxic food or faulty cars on the market. This claim might not be inconsistent with any presupposition it strictly makes, but it is inconsistent with the manifest fact that even if a corporation lacks such monitoring and policing resources, in most relevant

---

[10] It is akin to the claim: "P; but I don't believe it." The making of this purportedly sincere claim presupposes the belief that p, as our example presupposes certain conversable capacities, but the content of the claim is that this presupposition is unfulfilled.

areas it will have institutional resources sufficient to establish the sort of disciplinary regime required. If the corporation has the capacity to give itself the capacity to live up to the judgments that it is wrong to put toxic food or faulty cars on the market, then it has the capacity to live up to such judgments, period. It might be able to invoke the need for more time to excuse a failure to live up to the judgments on the first or second occasion when it endorses them. But it will have no excuse for not living up to them over the longer haul.

CONCLUSION

My first premise was that corporations are conversable agents—persons, in a functional sense of the term—and my second was that conversable agents are fit to be held responsible. This supports the conclusion that corporations, and indeed corporate bodies more generally, are fit to be held responsible. In particular, since this is where the sharper implications arise, they are fit to be held responsible for actions that breach the common, shared expectations to which we are disposed to hold such entities.

Three points are worth stressing, however, in qualification of this conclusion. The first is that to be prepared to hold corporations responsible is consistent with being prepared at the same time to hold individuals responsible for the things they do in the corporate name. We may think that a corporation should be held responsible for distributing contaminated food, for example, and at the same time argue that certain employees who were negligent in the exercise of their corporate roles should also be held responsible for the part they played. The corporation allows or programs for any such failure, insofar as its procedures make it possible or probable. The individuals who are negligent in the exercise of their roles are in a position where they could have refused to play by the corporation's rules but nonetheless did so. Both are fit to be held responsible in their particular domains of control.

The second point to note is that even if individual members may be held responsible for the part they play in corporate malfeasance, there is still an important point to holding corporations responsible too. This appears in the fact that often the individuals who play a damaging part in a reprehensible corporate act have reasonable excuses for their failure. They may claim that they were not properly informed about the effects of their actions, that they were conforming to widely established precedents, that they operated under constraining expectations, or that they lived in fear of losing their jobs. Suppose we allow individual malefactors off the hook on such grounds, as we often should do. That means that unless we are prepared to blame the corporations they serve—and in effect the memberships who sustain those bodies—as their fitness to be held responsible allows us to do, there will be an avoidable shortfall in the regulatory effects that our responsibility practices are generally designed to achieve. We will leave a loophole for people to incorporate for socially harmful but selfishly rewarding ends, and to do so with relative impunity.

The final point to note is that I have been concerned in this essay mainly with the issue as to whether it is appropriate to hold corporations responsible within our ordinary practices of normative assessment and censure. I believe that their fitness to be held responsible in this way argues for the appropriateness of holding corporations responsible in the criminal law—and not just, for example, in the law of torts—but I have not addressed the issue of criminal responsibility in this particular paper. It is a topic that I would prefer to leave to those better positioned to pronounce on matters of legal and institutional design (Fisse and Braithwaite 1993; Laufer 1994).[11]

REFERENCES

Anscombe, G.E.M. (1957). *Intention.*

Brehm, Sharon S. and Jack W. Brehm (1981). *Psychological Reactance: A Theory of Freedom and Control.*

Canning, J.P. (1980). "The Corporation in the Political Thought of the Italians Jurists of the Thirteenth and Fourteenth Century," *History of Political Thought* 1: 9.

Ciepley, David (2013). "Beyond Public and Private: Toward a Political Theory of the Corporation," *American Political Science Review* 107: 139.

Clark, Austen (1994). "Beliefs and Desires, Incorporated." *Journal of Philosophy* 91: 404.

Dennett, Daniel C. (1987). *The Intentional Stance.*

Eschmann, I. Thomas (1946). "Studies on the Notion of Society in St Thomas Aquinas, 1. St Thomas and the Decretal of Innocent IV Romana Ecclesia: Ceterum." *Medieval Studies* 8: 1.

Evans, Gareth (1982). *The Varieties of Reference.*

Fisse, Brent and John Braithwaite (1993). *Corporations, Crime and Accountability.*

Frankfurt, Harry G. (1969). "Alternate Possibilities and Moral Responsibility." *Journal of Philosophy* 66: 829.

French, Peter A. (1979). "The Corporation as a Moral Person." *American Philosophical Quarterly* 16: 207.

Gardner, John (2007). *Offences and Defences: Selected Essays in the Philosophy of Criminal Law.*

Grabosky, P.N. (1995). "Counterproductive Regulation." *The International Journal of the Sociology of Law* 23: 347.

---

[11] I am grateful for a range of helpful comments received when this paper was presented at a conference at INSEAD in December 2013 and to the legal theory workshop in Columbia University, New York, September 2015.

Grantham, Ross B. (1998). "The Doctrinal Basis of the Rights of Company Shareholders," *Cambridge Law Journal* 57: 554.

Hess, Kendy M. (2014). "The Free Will of Corporations (and Other Collectives)." *Philosophical Studies* 168: 241.

Hobbes, Thomas (1994). *Leviathan,* ed. Edwin Curley.

Kantorowicz, Ernst H. (1997). *The King's Two Bodies: A Study in Mediaeval Political Theology.*

Kornhauser, Lewis A. and Lawrence G. Sager (1993). "The One and the Many: Adjudication in Collegial Courts." *California Law Review* 81: 1.

Kornhauser, Lewis A. and Lawrence G. Sager (2004). "The Many as One: Integrity and Group Choice in Paradoxical Cases." *Philosophy and Public Affairs* 32: 249.

Kraakman, Reiner, et al. eds. (2009). *The Anatomy of Corporate Law: A Comparative and Functional Approach,* 2nd ed.

Laufer, William S. (1994). "Corporate Bodies and Guilty Minds." *Emory Law Journal* 43: 647.

Lewis, David (1969). *Convention.*

List, Christian and Philip Pettit (2002). "Aggregating Sets of Judgments: An Impossibility Result." *Economics and Philosophy* 18: 89.

List, Christian and Philip Pettit (2011). *Group Agency: The Possibility, Design, and Status of Corporate Agents.*

List, Christian and Philip Pettit (2012). "Symposium on Group Agency: Replies to Gaus, Cariani, Sylvan, and Briggs," *Episteme* 9: 293.

List, Christian and Ben Polak (2010). "Symposium on Judgment Aggregation," *Journal of Economic Theory* 145: 441.

McGeer, Victoria and Philip Pettit (2015). "The Hard Problem of Responsibility," in *Oxford Studies in Agency and Responsibility,* vol. 3, ed. David Shoemaker.

Orts, Eric W. (2015). *Business Persons: A Legal Theory of the Firm.* rev. paperback ed.

Pettit, Philip (2001a). "Deliberative Democracy and the Discursive Dilemma," *Philosophical Issues* 11: 268.

Pettit, Philip (2001b). *A Theory of Freedom: From the Psychology to the Politics of Agency.*

Pettit, Philip (2003). "Groups with Minds of their Own." In *Socializing Metaphysics: The Nature of Social Reality,* ed. Frederick F. Schmitt.

Pettit, Philip (2007). "Responsibility Incorporated." *Ethics* 117: 171.

Pettit, Philip (2008). *Made with Words: Hobbes on Language, Mind and Politics.*

Pettit, Philip (2009). "Corporate Responsibility Revisited." *Rechtsfilosofie & Rechtstheorie* 38: 159.

Pettit, Philip (2014). "Group Agents are not Expressive, Pragmatic or Theoretical Fictions," *Erkenntnis* 79 supp. 9: 1641.

Rönnegard, David (2013). "How Autonomy Alone Debunks Corporate Moral Agency," *Business and Professional Ethics Journal* 32: 77.

Rovane, Carol (1997). *The Bounds of Agency: An Essay in Revisionary Metaphysics.*

Skinner, Quentin (2009). "A Genealogy of the Modern State," *Proceedings of the British Academy* 162: 325.

Smith, Michael (2008). "Rational Capacities, or: How to Distinguish Recklessness, Weakness and Compulsion." In *Weakness of Will and Practical Irrationality*, eds. Sarah Stroud and Christine Tappolet.

Tollefsen, Deborah (2002). "Organizations as True Believers," *Journal of Social Philosophy* 33: 395.

Velasquez, Manuel G. (1983). "Why Corporations Are Not Morally Responsible for Anything They Do," *Business and Professional Ethics Journal* 2: 1.

Woolf, Cecil N. Sidney (1913). *Bartolus of Sassoferrato*.

2

The Intentions of a Group

*Michael E. Bratman**

THREE QUESTIONS

In my previous book *Shared Agency* (Bratman 2014), I develop a plan-theoretic model of shared intentions of a group, for example the shared intention of a group to paint the house together, or to rob a bank together, or together to help curb an outbreak of a disease. The model is broadly individualistic in the sense that it sees the proper functioning of a certain structure of the plan-like attitudes of the participants—attitudes with certain contents, certain inter-relations, and in a certain context—as sufficient for forms of social functioning characteristic of shared intention. In the cases on which this model focuses, what makes it true that the group intends, say, to rob the bank is that there is an appropriate inter-connected structure of relevant plan-like states of each of the participants, plan-like states that concern, inter alia, the group's bank robbery. In such cases, if we want to consider the targets of judgments of moral responsibility for robbing the bank, it can seem natural to suppose that those targets are simply the individual participants, though what they are each responsible for might well be affected by the facts underlying the sharing. (One can, for example, be responsible for participating in a conspiracy.) In such cases it can seem natural to understand a judgment that the group is morally responsible for the bank robbery as a summation of judgments about the responsibility of each of the individual participants. After all, insofar as the group intends to rob the bank, what is true is just that each of the participants has relevant intentions—ones that concern,

* Some of the ideas in this essay were presented at the INSEAD–Wharton December 2013 conference on "The Moral Responsibility of Firms: For or Against?" A later version was presented at the University of Copenhagen October 2014 conference on "Thinking (About) Groups." I benefited from comments from participants at both of these conferences. I have also benefited from written comments from Olle Blomberg, Frank Hindriks, and Philip Pettit, and related discussion with Christian List.

inter alia, the bank robbery—and these intentions are, in the context, interconnected in relevant ways.

Matters would seem potentially different, however, if there were cases in which the group has intentions that are not themselves shared intentions. If the group intends, say, to curb the outbreak of a disease in a certain town, and if this is not itself a shared intention of the group, then perhaps there is room for the idea that the group itself is appropriately subject to relevant moral praise (or, in a different case, blame), and in that sense is appropriately held morally responsible for the cited activity.

In saying this I am taking for granted, without argument, the idea that in central cases S's moral responsibility for X is grounded, at least in part, in the role of associated intentions of S concerning X, in S's relevant "quality of will" (Strawson 2003). A second idea that I will take for granted without argument, and that will figure in my discussion below, is that S's intentions provide particularly significant support for such attributions of responsibility when the relevant guidance by those intentions constitutes S's governing her own actions, when the relevant guidance constitutes S's self-governance.[1]

I do not say that the functioning of such self-governance-related intentions suffices for relevant moral responsibility. My assumption is that such intentions are basic to moral responsibility, not that they are the only condition of such responsibility. My focus in this chapter will be on the possibility of group intentions that satisfy this basic condition for group responsibility. I leave open the question whether there are further necessary conditions for such responsibility.

This leads me to the three questions I aim to discuss in this chapter. First, does the plan-theoretic approach to shared intention provide resources for modeling robust group intentions that are not themselves shared intentions? Second, if there are such intentions of a group will their normal functioning at least prima facie help constitute the group's relevant self-governance? Third, what is the implication of our answers to these questions for the possibility of group responsibility?

Concerning my first question, I do not say that a negative answer would establish that there are no group intentions that are not shared intentions. Perhaps there are other routes to a coherent model of such group intentions. Perhaps we can look directly at the overall functional organization of a group. And perhaps when we look directly at that group-level functional organization we can sometimes justifiably ascribe intentions to that group as a part of an overall theory of the group's diachronic functioning that has significant explanatory power.[2] We thereby try to see group intentions as functional (or

---

[1] See T.M. Scanlon's appeal, in his discussion of Strawson's approach to responsibility, to "the capacity for critically reflective, rational self-governance...[a capacity that] is not specifically moral" (Scanlon 2003, 368–9).

[2] This is, broadly speaking, the approach of List and Pettit (2011). As they say, they draw on "a broadly functionalist theory of agency" (id., 75), though in this book List and Pettit focus primarily on beliefs and desires of a group, rather than intentions. See also Pettit (2003).

functionally specified) states within a group-level functioning system. And to do that we need not identify these group intentions with corresponding shared intentions among members.

In contrast, the strategy of *Shared Agency* was to try explicitly to construct relevant forms of sociality and group functioning out of the materials of inter-connected individual planning agency. In that book I tried to show the extent to which we can build characteristic forms of group functioning out of characteristic forms of individual functioning, given distinctive aspects of that individualistic functioning. And my first question in this chapter is whether, in articulating those materials of inter-connected individual planning agency, we thereby have the resources to construct the infrastructure of robust group intentions that are not shared intentions. My answer will be that we do, but that in acknowledging these group intentions we need to give up the idea that such intentions must be embedded in a robust holistic structure of attitudes of that very group.[3] It will sometimes suffice, instead, that the intentions of a group are embedded in a larger structure of attitudes that to a significant extent involves attitudes of the individual participants. And such group intentions can indeed play a central role in the self-governance of the group.

With these results in hand I will turn briefly at the end to their bearing on the possibility of group responsibility.

THE PLANNING THEORY OF SHARED INTENTIONALITY

In the background of my discussion will be the plan-theoretic model of shared intention and shared intentional action that I have developed in *Shared Agency*. So let me briefly sketch relevant aspects of that model here. I begin with the thought that an important feature of individual human agency is that it normally involves complex forms of plan-infused cross-temporal organiza-tion. Given limits in our knowledge and our mental resources, these plans will typically be partial, and will need to be filled in as time goes by. These forms of practical thinking will be guided by an (implicit) acceptance of norms of plan rationality—norms of consistency, agglomerativity, means–end coherence,

---

[3] List and Pettit write: "Let a collection of individuals form and act on a single, robustly rational body of attitudes...and it will be an agent.... [I]t is possible for collections of individ-uals to coordinate their individual contributions so as to achieve this level of functioning. Hence [on the assumption that this possibility is realized] group agents exist." (List and Pettit 2011, 75.) I take it that the "single, robustly rational body of attitudes" to which they appeal is a body of attitudes of the group. So the group's intentions, on this model, would be embedded in a robust holistic structure of attitudes of that very group.

and stability. In this sense there is a distinctive rational dynamics of planning agency. And intentions are states in this planning system.

The next step is to describe inter-related planning structures of participating individuals such that the rational functioning of those planning structures—functioning in accordance with the rational dynamics of individual planning agency—would constitute the rational, social functioning that is characteristic of shared intentional activity. This would be to show that our planning capacities are a common core that lies behind both our capacity for cross-temporal organization in individual intentional agency and our capacity for social organization in our shared intentional activities. (This is a version of the thought that there is a significant parallel between the temporal structure of an individual's life and aspects of inter-personal sociality.) I aim in this way to articulate sufficient conditions for robust forms of shared intentionality in terms of these inter-related, individualistic planning structures; but I leave open the question whether these conditions are strictly necessary for shared intentionality. This is the strategy of sufficiency. And it supports one important aspect of the general thesis of the fecundity of planning agency, the thesis that our capacity for planning agency lies at the bottom of a range of basic practical capacities—in this case, our capacity for shared intentional activity.

In developing this model I suppose that, at least normally, shared intentional activity is explained by a corresponding shared intention so to act. I then describe inter-connected structures of individual planning agency whose functioning in accordance with the rational dynamics of individual planning agency would ensure the social-psychological functioning that is characteristic of shared intention. To specify this social-psychological functioning, I draw on analogies with the roles of individual intentions in organizing individual thought and action. The characteristic social-psychological functioning of a shared intention to X will involve inter-personal coordination of action and planning in pursuit of X and in ways that accommodate the rational agency of each of the participants. It will also involve framing shared deliberation or bargaining concerning how the group is to X. And in the background will be analogous social norms—norms of social agglomeration and consistency, social means-end coherence, and social stability—whose violation would normally undermine these social roles of shared intention.

My proposal is to articulate this structure by appeal, in part, to conditions along the lines of the following:

1. Each intends that we X.

2. Each intends that we X by way of each of our intentions that we X (in this sense these intentions interlock with each other) and by way of X-tracking mutual responsiveness in sub-intention and action, and so by

way of sub-plans of each that mesh with each other. (Plans mesh when they are co-realizable. Plans may mesh even though they do not match.)

3. Each believes correctly that there is persistent interdependence between the intentions in 1.

4. All this is out in the open.

Putting aside some details, what I argue in *Shared Agency* is that when such a public structure of intentions of each functions in accordance with the rational dynamics of individual planning agency, it thereby realizes the roles characteristic of shared intention in part by way of conformity to the associated social rationality norms. Further, when this structure of intentions of each leads to the joint activity by way of relevant mutual responsiveness there is shared intentional activity. I thereby highlight conceptual, metaphysical, and normative continuities with individual planning agency, while also providing the resources to articulate central ways in which shared intentionality goes beyond simple individual planning agency.

A key is the appeal to the *intention* of each in favor of X by way of the other's intention, mutual responsiveness, and meshing sub-plans. It is not just that each intends his part in X and merely expects the other to play her part. So the rational pressure on each to make her plans coherent and consistent ensures rational pressure on each to support the success of the joint activity and the meshing role of the other in that activity. Each is thereby under rational pressure to coordinate with the other—perhaps by way of helping actions—and to avoid ways of acting that are incompatible with the joint activity. These rational pressures on each, pressures grounded in the rational dynamics of individual planning agency, induce, given these distinctive contents and inter-relations, pressures in the direction of social coherence and consistency and associated social coordination and effectiveness.

There can be such shared intentions even though each participates for different reasons. Further, since each intends the joint activity in part by way of the relevant intention of the other, and by way of mutual responsiveness and so meshing sub-plans, each is under rational pressure to seek to ensure that the sub-plans of each, agglomerated together, both are adequate to the shared task and do indeed mesh interpersonally. So, in the absence so far of adequate, meshing sub-plans, a shared intention will tend to structure bargaining or shared deliberation (or the like) in the pursuit of such mesh.

This gives us a plan-theoretic model of those intentions of a group that are shared intentions. A group intends, say, to rob the bank, when its members share an intention to rob the bank together. And the plan-theoretic model of such a shared intention consists of the cited structure of inter-related intentions of the participants, in an appropriate context.

SHARED POLICIES OF WEIGHTS

The next step is to see how this plan-theoretic model can be extended to an important kind of shared policy, namely a shared policy to give certain weights to certain considerations within the group's shared deliberation.

Shared deliberation of the sort of interest here is a shared intentional activity in which the participants bring to bear common standards in their effort to settle questions about how to proceed within a shared intentional activity in which they are engaged. In a central case this will be a matter of bringing to bear shared commitments to weights in the shared deliberation. We might, for example, share a commitment within our shared painting of the house to our giving substantial weight to environmental concerns as we deliberate about which paints to use, and how to dispose of various materials. Or perhaps an academic department has a shared commitment to its giving weight to collegiality, or to issues of sub-field, in its shared deliberations about faculty appointments. Or perhaps a business group has a shared commitment to giving weight to increasing profits, or to satisfying certain environmental concerns, in its shared deliberations.

I argue in *Shared Agency* that while such shared commitments to weights will normally be grounded to some extent in relevant evaluative judgments of the individual participants, sameness of value judgment, even in a context of common knowledge, is neither sufficient nor necessary for a corresponding shared commitment to weights in shared deliberation. And my proposal is that our shared commitments to weights are better modeled as shared intentions that favor our giving certain weights to certain considerations in relevant shared deliberation. Since such shared intentions will normally have a characteristic generality, they will be shared policies of weights—where policies are intentions with suitably general contents. We then extend the plan-theoretic constructivist architecture of shared intention to these shared commitments to weights: a shared commitment to give weight to R is a shared policy to give weight to R in relevant shared deliberation; and this shared policy consists in public, interlocking, and interdependent general intentions, on the part of each, in favor of our giving weight to R in relevant shared deliberation.[4]

Shared policies of weights are policies about how the members of the group are to think together in their shared deliberation. The next step is to consider other kinds of shared policies concerning how those members are to think together.

---

[4] For a more extensive discussion of these matters see Bratman (2014, ch. 7). In Bratman (2007d), I classify such shared policies of weights as a kind of shared valuing.

SHARED POLICIES OF PROCEDURE

Note that shared deliberation can itself be embedded in yet a further structure of shared policies of procedure. A group might have a shared policy to turn to shared deliberation—in contrast, say, with various forms of bargaining—in sorting out issues concerning how it is to carry out a shared project. And such a shared procedural policy might help explain why the group is now engaging in such shared deliberation.

Shared policies of procedure might favor various group decision procedures.[5] A shared policy might favor, say, a majority vote procedure. Or it might favor a consensus procedure characteristic of a Quaker meeting. And so on.

One kind of procedure that might be embraced within a shared policy is a procedure that authorizes a certain sub-group to settle certain issues for the group in its execution of certain shared activities. (Note, though, that such a policy of authorization need not insure legitimate authority.) A philosophy department might have a shared policy of procedure for graduate admissions, one that authorizes a sub-committee to make the decision. And once such procedural policies of authorization are available they can iterate: a sub-group that is authorized by the larger group may have its own policies of authorization of a sub-sub-group, or even just a different group, to make certain decisions that it has been authorized to make.

One can extend a plan-theoretic construction to such shared policies of procedure, including shared procedural policies of authorization. As a first approximation, such a shared procedural policy can be modeled as a public, interlocking, and interdependent structure of relevant policies of each that favor the operation of a given procedure (for example, some voting procedure), where that includes follow-through with the output of that procedure.

Two potential elements in such follow-through can be distinguished. Follow-through may involve further shared intentional activity of the group, shared intentional activity that is guided by the outcome of the procedure. This will involve relevant interlocking, mutual responsiveness, and intended mesh across the group. In contrast, follow-through may be distributed among the activities of certain individuals or sub-groups. Such distributed follow-through need not involve interlocking and mutual responsiveness across the overall group, and so need not involve share intentional activity of the overall group itself.

A shared policy of procedure will normally favor follow-through that to some extent involves further shared activities of the group, shared activities

---

[5] Thomas Hurka highlighted this point in conversation. Appeal to such shared procedural policies is in the spirit of Peter French's work on "Corporate Internal Decision Structures." See French (1984, especially chs. 3–4). Related ideas can also be found in Tuomela (1995, 176–80); Pettit (2003); (List and Pettit 2011, especially ch. 3); Hindriks (2008; 2014); and Ludwig (2014).

that are guided by the outcome of that procedure. However, the shared policy may well also favor follow-through that consists in activities distributed across individuals and/or sub-groups. I will return to this difference below.

GROUP SELF-GOVERNANCE

So the plan-theoretic model can include shared policies of weights and of procedures, including shared policies of authorization. Intended follow-through with the outcomes of procedures favored by such shared policies may be to some extent a matter of further shared activities of the group itself, and to some extent a matter of distributed activities of individuals or sub-groups. This plan-theoretic architecture includes shared policies of weights and/or procedures as structures of relevant, inter-connected policies of each of the participants. Such shared policies of weights and/or procedures are compatible with divergence in the underlying evaluative judgments of the participants and with differences in the reasons for which each participates. Nevertheless, given their central role in the functioning of the group, it is plausible to see such shared policies as speaking for the group on relevant matters. In this way we extend to the group an idea that is important in our understanding of individual agency, namely: that certain attitudes are not merely wiggles in the agent's psychic stew but speak for the agent in the sense that their guidance is, prima facie, the agent's self-governance.[6] And my proposal is that such shared policies of weights and/or procedures will normally be such that when they guide relevant thought and action the group is, in that domain, governing itself.[7]

In a particular case, if we share a policy in favor of weights or a procedure and you knowingly violate that policy, then you are in violation of norms of consistency and coherence on your own intentions and plans. I can appeal to that in criticizing you for your violation. I may also be able to criticize your violation as tending to undermine our group self-governance. Insofar as you yourself value group self-governance, this criticism will engage your own concerns. In this way the connection with group self-governance can help stabilize such shared policies. And this stability of such shared policies contributes to the claim that those policies do indeed speak for the group. So the contribution of such policies to the group's self-governance is

[6] This idea is rooted in work of Harry Frankfurt. See his reflections on "where (if anywhere) the person himself stands" (Frankfurt 1988, 166). For my development of this idea, see Bratman (2007b; 2007c).

[7] This argument also supports the idea that participation in such shared policies ensures membership in the group.

self-reinforcing in the sense that this contribution supports the stability of those shared policies and that stability in turn supports the status of those policies as attitudes whose guidance is, prima facie, the group's self-governance. Or at least this is true for groups whose participants value the group's self-governance.

So the planning model provides for structures of shared policies of weights and procedures whose guidance is, prima facie, the group's relevant self-governance and whose functioning is thereby potentially stabilized in a way that supports the role of those shared policies in the group's self-governance. I now want to argue that such shared policies of procedure can induce group intentions that are not shared intentions.

PROCEDURE-BASED INTENTIONS OF A GROUP

Suppose a group is engaged in a shared intentional activity of providing medical aid in crises around the world. In the face of many claims on its resources it has a shared policy that specifies procedures for deciding whether to provide aid in a specific case. Let's say that this policy authorizes a subgroup to make a decision by way of its own, shared deliberation, followed by a majority vote. Suppose that in a particular case this procedure issues, by way of a split vote on the part of the authorized sub-group, in a decision to provide aid in a certain context C. Given that this is the output of procedures favored by policies that are shared by the participants, this output will be poised to guide relevant follow-through in the sense that given relevant knowledge and rationality on the part of relevant participants, the output would guide such follow-through. This follow-through may simply involve distributed activities of individuals or sub-groups, distributed activities carried out in accordance with the outcome of the procedure. But this follow-through may also involve further shared intentional activities of the group itself, shared intentional activities that are guided by the output of the procedure. In both cases the outcome of the procedure guides thought and action (given knowledge and rationality), but in the second case it guides, in particular, shared thought and action of the group itself.

Now my proposal is that when the output of such a procedure is set to guide (inter alia) further shared intentional activities of that very group, the fact that the procedure has issued in that output ensures that the group itself intends to act in accordance with that output. In the present case, it is likely that the outcome of the procedure is set to guide, for example, further shared deliberations of the group concerning how to coordinate this aid with other aid the group plans to provide (though breakdowns in the guidance remain possible).

If this is true then the group itself intends to provide the aid in context C: this is a procedure-based group intention.

Will this procedure-based group intention be a shared intention? Well, there may be members of the group who judge, at least prior to the outcome of the procedure, that it would be better for the group not to do this. But that does not show that the group's intention to provide aid in C is not a shared intention: a group can share an intention despite such differences in evaluative judgment. What stands in the way of identifying this group intention with a shared intention lies not in such evaluative disagreement but, rather, in the possibility of limited knowledge or rationality. Some members might simply be unaware of the outcome of the procedure. (This will be increasingly common as the group grows in size and complexity.) Given this ignorance, though the group intends to provide medical aid in context C, there may not be a shared intention to provide this aid. Again, suppose some members are aware of the outcome but—because they think that it is a serious mistake—they resist intending that the group provide aid in context C even though they continue to participate in the general shared policies of procedure. This would be a breakdown on their part in plan rationality; but such breakdowns are all too possible. And given such a breakdown there will not in fact be a shared intention that corresponds with the group intention to provide the aid.

So if there is relevant ignorance, or relevant breakdown in individual plan rationality, there may not be a shared intention to provide aid in context C. But such ignorance or rational breakdown may not stand in the way of its being true that the group intends to provide this aid. The outcome of the procedure establishes an intention of the group so long as the outcome would guide relevant shared thought and action under conditions of relevant knowledge and plan-theoretic rationality. So the plan-theoretic architecture can make room, in this way, for procedure-based group intentions that are not shared intentions.

Granted, so long as there is no relevant ignorance or rational breakdown, the procedure-based group intention will correspond to a shared intention.[8] Nevertheless, the procedure-based group intention will not always correspond to an actual shared intention; and the existence of the procedure-based group intention does not depend on the existence of a corresponding shared intention. In this sense procedure-based group intention and shared intention are separable. They are separable even though the infrastructure of procedure-based group intention systematically involves shared intention. The underlying structures and processes that make it true that there is the procedure-based group intention in favor of the outcome of the procedure need not ensure a corresponding shared intention.

---

[8] This point was emphasized in conversation with Olle Blomberg, Brian Epstein, and Arto Laitinen.

Suppose that, in this procedure-based way, the group intends to provide medical aid in context C. What makes it true that the group so intends is a complex structure of shared intentions and policies, actual social procedures and their output, and resulting tendencies toward relevant guidance of (inter alia) relevant shared intentional activities and forms of shared thinking. Appeal to this plan-theoretic structure remains in the spirit of the general thesis of the fecundity of planning agency. But this structure does not itself ensure a corresponding shared intention to provide aid in context C.

GROUP INTENTIONS AND DISPERSED BELIEFS AND PLANS

But now there is a problem. The idea that the group itself intends to provide aid is in tension with a common idea about the holism of the mental. The idea of the holism of the mental is the idea that a mental attitude of S—for example, an intention of S—must be embedded in a substantial, holistically coherent web of related attitudes of S (Davidson 2001; Rovane 1998). In particular, if we ascribe to S an intention to X we are committed to seeing that intention as part of a holistic web of attitudes of S, attitudes that include, for example, beliefs about the nature of X and how it might be done, intentions not to interfere with X and to take needed steps toward X, beliefs about the nature of such needed steps, beliefs needed to have the more immediately implicated beliefs, other pro-attitudes toward X and/or its expected upshots, and so on. But while there may be special cases in which there are sufficiently rich plan-theoretic structures to provide the infrastructure of such a robust holistic web of attitudes of the group, this does not seem to be ensured by the procedure-based infrastructure of the group intention that has been described.

But if the group itself does not have specific beliefs about how to execute its intention to provide aid, and plans about how to do that, how will that intention be effective? The answer is that the efficacy of this procedure-based group intention can involve the operation of a range of related beliefs and plans dispersed among the individual participants. For example, certain participants may know how to prepare and distribute a needed vaccine and have specific plans for doing this in their particular circumstances. It is not necessary to suppose that the group itself has this knowledge or this specific plan for preparing and distributing the vaccine (though it may). Although the group itself has the procedure-based intention to provide the aid, the operation of that intention can draw on relevant beliefs and plans dispersed among relevant participants, beliefs and plans that are responsive to their specific circumstances.[9] We need not suppose that these dispersed beliefs and plans must be beliefs and plans of the group.

Granted, the specific plans of certain participants for preparing and distributing the vaccine are downstream outcomes of the procedures that are supported by relevant shared policies. And I have claimed that the basic outcome of those procedures—an outcome in favor of providing the aid—may be an intention of the group to provide the aid. So why not say that these specific plans are, as well, an element in a procedure-based intention of the group to prepare and distribute the vaccine in this specific way? The answer is that to induce a procedure-based intention of the group an outcome of a procedure needs to be poised to guide shared intentional action on the part of that group. But the cited specific plans for preparing and distributing the vaccine are only poised to guide the thought and action of a sub-set of individuals.

I conclude that the functioning of procedure-based group intentions can draw substantially from a web of dispersed beliefs and plans of individuals or sub-groups that need not be elements in corresponding intentions of that overall group.

This is an extension of an idea implicit in our plan-theoretic treatment of shared intention. Suppose that you and I share an intention to paint the house together. For this shared intention to be effective each will need to have relevant sub-plans, and those sub-plans will need together sufficiently to specify preliminary steps, means, and the like so that in following through with those sub-plans we do indeed paint the house together. But the theory does not insist that all the sub-intentions associated with these sub-plans must be elements in corresponding shared intentions. In intending that our relevant sub-plans mesh we need not intend or expect that our relevant sub-plans match. And aspects of my sub-plans may not themselves be out in the open, or may not involve intentions of mine that interlock with corresponding intentions of yours. For example, my sub-plan for shopping for the paint at Ace Hardware need not be an element in a shared intention in favor of shopping at Ace Hardware. It will many times suffice that you know that some sub-plan or other of mine will solve the problem of how we are to get the paint. You do not need to know what that sub-plan is, nor do you need yourself to have an intention that matches and interlocks with my intention concerning Ace Hardware.

The further web of intentions that supports the efficacy of our shared intention need not be solely a matter of other shared intentions; it can, and normally will, involve as well relevant sub-intentions dispersed among the

---

[9] This is broadly in the spirit of F.A. Hayek's emphasis on "knowledge of the particular circumstances of time and place," knowledge "that is dispersed among many people." See Hayek (1945, 521, 530). For the use of this idea in understanding the distinctive strengths of ancient Athenian democracy, see Ober (2008).

participants, sub-intentions that are not themselves elements in corresponding shared intentions. And the situation with a procedure-based intention of a group is analogous in the sense that the further web of intentions that supports the efficacy of that intention of the group need not be solely a matter of other intentions of the group; it can, and typically will, involve relevant, distributed intentions of the participants, intentions that themselves need not be elements in corresponding intentions of the group. There will be rational pressure for all these various intentions to mesh within a consistent and effective overall web; but they can mesh without themselves being elements in corresponding intentions of the group.

We therefore should not insist that for the group to intend to provide the aid its intention must be embedded in a substantial, holistic web of attitudes of the group. It may suffice that it is embedded in a social context in which relevant attitudes of the participants do a lot of the work.

BETWEEN SHARED INTENTION
AND A ROBUST HOLISM

This may seem to be an unstable result. We do normally expect the intentions of an individual to be embedded in a robust web of relevant attitudes of that individual. But our plan-theoretic construction of procedure-based group intentions allows for group intentions that are not embedded in a holistic web of attitudes of the group. So our plan-theoretic construction of procedure-based group intentions is in tension with a plausible view about the holism of the mental.

In "How to Share an Intention," J. David Velleman addresses an analogous issue. Velleman begins with a Searle-inspired idea that an intention is "a mental representation that causes behavior by representing itself as causing it" (Velleman 2000, 207; see also Searle 1983, ch. 3). Now, Velleman has a distinctive view about why certain representations tend to cause their own fulfillment, a view that appeals to a purported concern with self-knowledge. But I want to put that view aside here and focus on an independent issue, one to which, as Velleman shows, we are led when we see intention as "a mental representation that causes behavior by representing itself as causing it."

Suppose that you and I arrive at a shared intention to walk together, and we arrive at this shared intention by way of a normal conversational exchange in which you say "I will if you will" and I reply "I will." About this pair of interdependent statements Velleman says:

> Our statements . . . combine to form a joint statement saying, in effect, that they will jointly prompt us to take a walk; and they jointly prompt us to take a walk, as

they jointly say. They consequently add up to a single representation that causes our actions by representing itself as causing them—a single token intention that is literally shared between us.   (Velleman 2000, 217–18)

But how could a joint statement literally be an intention? Aren't intentions states of mind? If Velleman is right that this joint statement satisfies his Searle-inspired condition for intention, isn't that an argument against the sufficiency of that condition for intention?

Velleman's response is concessive: "if a commitment's being oral or written entails that it isn't mental, our commitment to taking a walk may not be a mental act or state at all" (Velleman 2000, 219). And the important point for my purposes here is that this opens up the theoretical possibility of intentions that do not satisfy some further condition for being states of mind.

It is this general theoretical possibility—abstracted away from the details of Velleman's theory—that I want to highlight. I have described a plan-theoretic infrastructure of group intentions, one that is set to play standard roles of intention in guiding downstream thought and action of the group even though these group intentions need not ensure corresponding shared intentions. These group intentions may not be embedded in the kind of robust holistic web of attitudes of the group that we may plausibly suppose to be character-istic of mental states of that group. Nevertheless, these group intentions may still be poised to be effective in part because of the way in which they are set to interact with relevant attitudes of the participants. So we should recognize the theoretical possibility of procedure-based group intentions that are neither shared intentions nor embedded in the kind of holistic web of attitudes of the group that we might plausibly suppose is a condition of being a mental state of that group.

We can put the point in terms of the idea of a *subject* of an attitude. In one straightforward sense, if it is true that the group intends to provide the medical aid then the group is the subject of that intention. But there is also a stronger idea of a subject as a unitary locus of a robust holistic web of inter-related attitudes. And in this sense of a subject of attitudes, the group may fail to be a subject of its intention to provide the aid.

In this respect the situation parallels the situation Velleman aims to describe in which (a) there is literally a single intention that is shared, namely the joint statement; (b) this joint statement plays the defining roles of intention; and so (c) we do indeed intend to walk together; but (d) there is no single subject of that intention. (As Velleman says, the "joint making up of minds" that is involved in the joint statement "is not the making up of a joint mind" (Velleman 2000, 219)). Similarly, the procedure-based group intention whose plan-theoretic infrastructure I have tried to describe need not be an intention of a group mind, in a sense of group mind that involves a robust holistic web of attitudes of the group. Nor need it be an intention whose subject (in the strong sense) is the group. So it is a mistake to suppose that a group intention is either a shared intention or an intention of the group that is embedded in a robust holistic structure of inter-related attitudes of that group. Certain procedure-based group intentions occupy the space between these two other possibilities. And the recognition of this intermediate space gives us important theoretical resources.

Even if these procedure-based group intentions are not embedded in such a holistic web of attitudes of the group, and even if the group is not, in a strict sense, the subject of those intentions, these group intentions may still be poised to be effective in part because of the way in which they are set to interact with relevant attitudes and activities of the participants. And, given that the background shared procedural policies normally speak for the group, the functioning of such group intentions will normally be a form of group self-governance.

So we arrive at answers to our first two questions. First, the plan-theoretic approach can model robust group intentions that are not themselves shared intentions; and such group intentions need not be embedded in a holistic web of attitudes of the group. Second, the normal functioning of such group intentions will normally help constitute the group's relevant self-governance.

GROUP RESPONSIBILITY

This takes us to our third question, concerning group responsibility. And here the discussion of our first two questions suggests that procedure-based group intentions are candidates for the kind of intention-based grounding needed for attributions of responsibility to the group. This is because such procedure-based group intentions are set to provide relevant downstream guidance both of the thought and action of the group and of relevant distributed activities of individuals and/or sub-groups, and their playing these roles is, prima facie, the group's self-governance. And I have argued that all this can be true even if these group intentions are neither shared intentions nor embedded in a robust holistic web of attitudes of the group.

But what should we say about those cases in which the group intention does correspond to a shared intention? Well, our main reason for thinking that group intentions can provide the intention-based ground for group responsibility was that such intentions guide thought and action both of the group and of relevant individuals and/or sub-groups, and that their playing these roles can constitute the group's self-governance. Suppose then that a group has a procedure-based intention to X such that this intention plays these roles in its self-governance, but that, because of relevant ignorance on the part of some of the members of the group, there is not a corresponding shared intention. We have in this case the basic intention-based ground for group responsibility. Suppose now that the relevant information newly becomes available to all the members and as a result there newly comes to be a shared intention that corresponds to the procedure-based intention of the group. It does not seem plausible that this change would newly block the group's responsibility, though it might affect the responsibility of relevant individuals. If the procedure-based group intention can provide the intention-based ground for group responsibility in the absence of a corresponding shared intention, then it seems plausible that it can continue to do so even when there is a corresponding shared intention.

So one fundamental condition for group responsibility—a condition of group intention that is poised to be involved in the group's self-governance—can be realized in a procedure-based way. Since there can be such a procedure-based group intention in the absence of a corresponding shared intention, we can resist certain kinds of pressure to reduce relevant judgments of responsibility to judgments solely about the responsibility of each of the participants. And since there can be such a procedure-based group intention that is not embedded within a robustly holistic group mind, we can resist the idea that this basic condition of group responsibility requires such a holistic group mind.

REFERENCES

Bratman, Michael E. (2007a). *Structures of Agency: Essays.*
Bratman, Michael E. (2007b). "Reflection, Planning, and Temporally Extended Agency." In Bratman (2007a).
Bratman, Michael E. (2007c). "Three Theories of Self-Governance." In Bratman (2007a).
Bratman, Michael E. (2007d). "Shared Valuing and Frameworks for Practical Reasoning." In Bratman (2007a).
Bratman, Michael E. (2014). *Shared Agency: A Planning Theory of Acting Together.*
Davidson, Donald (2001). "Mental Events." In Donald Davidson, *Essays on Actions and Events* (2nd ed.).
Frankfurt, Harry (1988). "Identification and Wholeheartedness." In Harry Frankfurt, *The Importance of What We Care About.*
French, Peter A. (1984). *Collective and Corporate Responsibility.*
Hayek, F.A. (1945). "The Use of Knowledge in Society." *American Economic Review* 35: 519.
Hindriks, Frank (2008). "The Status Account of Corporate Agents." In *Concepts of Sharedness: Essays on Collective Intentionality*, ed. Hans Bernhard Schmid, Katinka Schulte-Ostermann, and Nikos Psarros.
Hindriks, Frank (2014). "How Autonomous Are Collective Agents? Corporate Rights and Normative Individualism." *Erkenntnis* 79: 1565.
List, Christian and Philip Pettit (2011). *Group Agency: The Possibility, Design, and Status of Corporate Agents.*

Ludwig, Kirk (2014). "Proxy Agency in Collective Action." *Noûs* 48: 75.

Ober, Josiah (2008). *Democracy and Knowledge.*

Pettit, Philip (2003). "Groups with Minds of Their Own." In *Socializing Metaphysics: The Nature of Social Reality*, ed. Frederick F. Schmitt.

Rovane, Carol (1998). *The Bounds of Agency: An Essay in Revisionary Metaphysics.*

Scanlon, T.M. (2003). "The Significance of Choice." In *Free Will*, 2nd ed., ed. Gary Watson.

Searle, John R. (1983). *Intentionality.*

Strawson, Peter (2003). "Freedom and Resentment." In *Free Will*, 2nd ed., ed. Gary Watson.

Tuomela, Raimo (1995). *The Importance of Us.*

Velleman, J. David (2000). "How to Share an Intention." In Velleman, *The Possibility of Practical Reason.*

3

The Diachronic Moral Responsibility of Firms

Peter A. French

In this chapter, I hope to say something useful about corporate moral responsibility over time.[1] In 1984 I published a paper on responsibility and responsive adjustment in which I argued that the subsequent actions of a person could have a negative or a positive effect on the moral responsibility ascribed to that person for previous bad actions (French 1984).[2] Some philosophers agreed with me

---

[1] A brief historical note: my first attempt to explore the concept of corporate moral responsibility was in a paper I wrote for a conference in 1977 (French 1979). In that and subsequent pieces I provided a functionalist or structuralist account of corporate intentionality and responsibility at the time of an action or event. I made some modifications to my position in the ensuing years by substituting "actor" or "agent" for "person," and clarifying that a corporate and a human agent(s) could be responsible for the same event, a position also defended by Philip Pettit (2007). I also addressed two more substantive measures by replacing my use of the traditional desire/belief model of intention with Michael Bratman's planning model (Bratman 1987, 1999), and responded to the charge made by Deborah Tollefsen (2008) and Mitchell Haney (2004) that my general theory of moral responsibility requires that agents are affective, but I cannot show how corporations can care about the moral quality of their actions by displaying appropriate self-reflective reactive attitudes (French 2012) by arguing that the internal operational mechanisms of many corporations contain conversion rules for the redescription of certain types of utterances by appropriate employees into expressions of corporate self-reflective reactive attitudes that indicate affectivity. For example, when a corporate employee on the telephone says, "We are sorry that we double billed your credit card account," the employee does not regret the corporate act, and is not ashamed or remorseful about what happened. He or she is reading from a script. You, however, are receiving an apology from the corporation because a true description of her reading from that script is "The corporation is expressing regret for what it did." It is as sincere as most apologies go. Recently a Barclays' representative said, "We regret that we did not set honest Libor rates." I take it that he was saying, "Barclays is expressing shame or guilt for its falsification of its London Interbank Offered Rate reports." (I'm not sure what he expressed in his follow-up comments: "We're clean, but we're dirty-clean, rather than clean-clean.") Corporate regret or sorrow or shame is referentially opaque. When it is true that Barclays regrets, it is not necessarily true that the Barclays' spokesperson regrets, though Barclays' expression of regret and the Barclays' spokesperson expressing Barclays' regret are co-referential.

[2] I was not arguing that our gaining certain kinds of information about the action or, especially, the actor's condition or moral status at the time of its occurrence would require

that we might morally reevaluate a person's responsibility based on her subsequent responses to her previous actions, for example, were she to make restitution to someone she had harmed, but they argued that ensuing behavior could never alter a person's responsibility for an earlier action. What I maintained was that one's subsequent behavior might change the truth value of the proposition that one was or was not responsible for an earlier action, so a person's responsibility for the same action or event over the passage of time is not permanently fixed.

Andrew Khoury (2013) has defended a substantial revision of the account I gave of the way responsibility ascriptions may be modified over time by persuasively arguing that the truth of the responsibility ascription that holds the person responsible or not for an action or event at the time of its occurrence (responsibility at T_1 for what was done at T_1) is invariant over time, but that an ascription of responsibility that holds the person responsible or not for the action committed at T_1 at a time later than T_1 (responsibility at $T_1 + n$ for what was done at T_1) may be significantly different with respect to the degree of responsibility ascribed to the person for that previous action.

I am convinced that Khoury's account better captures the way responsibility ascriptions for the same event to the same person are re-evaluated over time than my 1984 account of the Principle of Responsive Adjustment (PRA), though I believe that PRA exposed the crucial fact that a person's responsibility for past behavior is reassessable over time and that his or her subsequent actions and events may play a crucial role in such a reassessment.[3] The degree or amount of blame or responsibility ascribed to the person at the later time for a past event may be more, less, or the same as that ascribed when the event occurred. In other words, the degree of blame (or the intensity of the justified negative participant reactive attitudes directed at the person) at $T_1 + n$ is not limited by the degree of blame justifiably accessed at T_1. The responsibility ascriptions for actions or events at T_1, on Khoury's account that I am now adopting, may be referred to as ascriptions of synchronic responsibility, and those at $T_1 + n$ as diachronic responsibility ascriptions. The latter are

---

altering whether we held the agent responsible. In that paper I focused on cases in which there was insufficient evidence to hold an agent responsible for something untoward at T_1 or even evidence that the agent lacked the appropriate intention at T_1 to support blaming the agent for the event. In such cases, we might be inclined to generosity and let the agent off the hook. But if at a subsequent time the agent repeats the actions of T_1, then our inclination is to blame the agent for the early untoward event, not because we are convinced that the agent at T_1 had the appropriate intention then that motivated the agent's actions, but because at T_2 the agent has acted with intention in a repetitive action.

[3] If no ascription of responsibility to a person for an event is justified at T_1 because of inadequate information regarding the person's intentions or other psychological factors, but at T_2 there is no doubt that the person intentionally repeats the offensive performance, PRA may be used to capture the past event in the present assessment, perhaps in the form of "once again." At the least it reveals character.

assessments of an agent's responsibility or blame (or praise or credit on the positive side) for an action or event after a passage of time typically during which the agent[4] could have undergone psychological or operational changes and/or had opportunity(ies) to rectify, remedy, or redress (or attest to or replicate on the positive side) the agent's action at T_1 in some morally meaningful way. Diachronic responsibility ascriptions are revisitations of moral assessments of an agent's previous actions, but they are not revisions of justified synchronic responsibility assessments. Those remain invariant through time.[5]

Synchronically responsible agents act from internal mechanisms that are moderate reasons responsive (helping myself to the well-known analysis by Fischer and Ravizza (1998)) and affective. They are receptive to reasons, and are at least weakly reactive to those reasons, that is, they display the executive power to do something because of their recognition of a reason to do it, even if they don't actually do it. That is, we assume that such agents at T_1 had certain functional capacities, including the ability to act intentionally, the ability to make rational decisions, the ability to respond to events and criticisms by altering their intentions and resultant behaviors (that is, the ability to appreciate reasons as relevant to act choices and the ability to react to those reasons appropriately), and that they acknowledge ownership of their actions, and evidence the capacity to participate in moral dialogue and address. If in any specific case we discover we are wrong about the agent possessing those functional capacities at the relevant time, we generally retract synchronic responsibility ascriptions and forswear indignation or resentment or hatred of the agent with respect to that case.

The majority of my work on corporate responsibility focused on constructing arguments that the organizational mechanisms of some corporate entities are as capable as the neuro-psychological mechanisms of individual human beings of meeting the functional and structural conditions of being synchronically responsible for actions.[6] From the moral point of view an event or action may not have a single privileged assessment. An individual human may bear responsibility for doing something intentionally that brought about an untoward event, while the firm in which he or she works and that makes possible

---

[4] I switch here from the term "person" to the philosophical term "agent" for reasons that will become clear as the discussion shifts to firms.

[5] Of course, synchronic responsibility ascriptions should be modified if at a later date it is learned they were false, biased, based on insufficient information, and the like. Such modifications are not diachronic responsibility ascriptions as I am using the term. They were simply false or unjustified responsibility ascriptions when made and morally require alteration. Diachronic responsibility ascriptions do not alter synchronic responsibility ascriptions.

[6] There has been considerable debate about whether an account of synchronic responsibility such as I have offered is purely structural and ahistorical. I don't want to get into that argument here and will grant that there may be historical elements, especially in how the subject comes to have the capacity to recognize reasons.

his or her actions with respect to that event also may be held responsible for that event. There also are cases in which a firm, because of its structure, procedures, policies, and so on, bears the responsibility for the event, while no specific individual may rise to the level of individual responsibility with respect to that event.[7] The thrust of my work on this subject has been to try to capture the complexity of the contemporary social/political/economic scene within the ambit of morality. We do not have to settle for excluding powerful elements of that scene from moral scrutiny because they are not individual humans or because those humans working within them cannot be shown to have the appropriate intentional states that support holding them morally accountable for specific untoward events. Consequently, at T_1 a corporation may be an appropriate target, qua corporation, of our moral reactive attitudes, for example blame, resentment, and so on for what it did at T_1. However, that does not mean that at any subsequent time to T_1 it can be justifiably held morally responsible for what occurred at T_1. Although there is often no significant difference between an agent's synchronic and diachronic responsibility for a specific event, there are many types of cases involving both humans and corporations in which the assessments of responsibility for the same event at different times may be at variance.

We may agree that the moral slate isn't scrubbed clean when T_1 turns into T_2.[8] If something untoward occurred at T_1, we are likely to have moral (perhaps legal) reasons to want to know if the agent that was synchronically responsible for it at T_1 is an appropriate candidate at $T_1 + n$ for punishment, blaming, or other forms of still being held to account for it. Diachronic responsibility underlies the ongoing moral and legal appraisal of agents and the continuing use of expressions of reactive attitudes and punishment provoked by their past actions. After all, the very idea of a reactive attitude entails reference to a past event to which one is reacting. Except in the case of the White Queen in *Through the Looking-Glass* (Carroll 1871)[9] punishment is retrospective. Consequently, in ethics and in criminal law we crucially want to be satisfied that the agent under our scrutiny at $T_1 + n$ bears the right relationship to that synchronically responsible agent at T_1 before we bring the weight of morality and law to bear upon it, before we increase or decrease the agent's degree of responsibility gauged in accord with some moral evaluative criteria. It is with the right

---

[7] I have argued this position for many decades (French 1979, 1995, 1996, 2005, 2011).

[8] I make no attempt to specify the length of T_1 or how we know that T_1 has ended and we are now in T_2. I suppose that is a rather important matter to tackle in the metaphysics of time, but I will leave it for another time. For a perplexing version of the problem see Lewis Carroll's *Through the Looking-Glass* (1871) (ch. V) in which the White Queen expounds on the difference between yesterday, today, and tomorrow. It will prove efficacious or it won't.

[9] "'There's the King's Messenger. He's in prison now, being punished: and the trial doesn't even begin till next Wednesday: and of course the crime comes last of all.' 'Suppose he never commits the crime?' said Alice. 'That would be all the better, wouldn't it?' the Queen said" (id.).

relationship that I am primarily concerned and not especially with how the subsequent behavior of an agent may soften or harden our moral appraisal of a past action of that agent.

What is the right relation? The typical answer is an agent at $T_1 + n$ can be held morally responsible for an action performed at T_1 if and only if the agent at $T_1 + n$ is the same agent in all the relevant respects as the agent that performed the earlier action. The assumption, then, is that diachronic ownership issues can be resolved by agent sameness. But how should we understand agent sameness particularly in corporate cases? Conceptions of agent sameness have been proposed from soma-centric ones focused on physical continuity to versions of the Lockean memory criterion and psychological continuity.

Consider the following familiar example. The US Coast Guard's Bureau of Ocean Energy Management Regulation and Enforcement report in September 2011 laid ultimate responsibility on BP (formerly British Petroleum) for the Deepwater Horizon explosion and oil spill and the deaths of eleven rig workers in the Gulf of Mexico. The Coast Guard's report cited BP for a number of illegal and immoral actions and omissions and maintained that "the loss of life and the subsequent pollution of the Gulf of Mexico were the result of poor risk management, last-minute changes to plans, failure to observe and respond to critical indicators, inadequate well control response, and insufficient emergency bridge response training by BP" (Bureau of Ocean Energy Management Regulation and Enforcement 2011, 1–2)). This report can be read as an ascription of synchronic responsibility to BP at T_1 (when the accident occurred in April 2010), but September 2011 was almost one and a half years after the explosion and spill. Was BP as a corporate person or agent at that date diachronically responsible for the Deepwater Horizon disaster? Is it still morally responsible for the Deepwater Horizon disaster today, more than five years since it occurred? That was then, this is now.

A little history will prove useful. From 1954 to 1998 the company today formally called BP Plc was called British Petroleum. In 1998 it became BP Amoco Plc, and in 2001 it was rebranded as BP Plc. In 1967 British Petroleum's tanker *Torrey Canyon* wrecked off the coast of Cornwall causing the UK's largest oil spill to date and massive environmental damage. Suppose that since 1967 the following occurred. (a) The corporation radically modified its organizational structure and operating system regularly, both overtly and tacitly, disassociating itself from its past incarnations. (b) BP Plc omitted references to the *Torrey Canyon* disaster in its internal and external communications. (c) BP Plc's operational structure and its management personnel now share no characteristics or identities with those of British Petroleum of 1967. Thus, although BP Plc is historically and physically continuous with British Petroleum of 1967, BP Plc has no relevant direct operational connections with British Petroleum of 1967. British Petroleum of 1967 satisfied the synchronic conditions for moral responsibility for the *Torrey Canyon* disaster when it occurred, so it was morally synchronically responsible for the *Torrey Canyon* disaster. Is BP Plc that came into existence in 2001 morally responsible for the *Torrey Canyon* disaster? Perhaps not. BP Plc's only connection to British Petroleum of 1967 is an historical and physical continuity thread traceable through the years. (This may be rather like the ship of Theseus: the classical philosophical puzzle of whether something that has had all of its component parts changed over time is still the same thing.) If having an historical continuity (even without identical physical constituents) to British Petroleum were the required diachronic condition, BP would be responsible for *Torrey Canyon*, but my intuition is that merely being able to trace historical or physical continuity in the life of an agent is not the appropriate sameness condition for diachronic ownership of a past action and hence the responsibility of that agent at the later time for that past action of an earlier stage of that agent.

Returning to the Deepwater Horizon case: Is BP today morally responsible for the Deepwater Horizon disaster of April 2010? I think many of us are inclined to say that it is, but BP might argue that though there is a physical and structural historical link between BP in April 2010 and BP today, including its name, it is not the same firm because it fails the test of sameness in crucial respects. Some of its public relations efforts following Deepwater Horizon have taken that approach. BP Plc claims it underwent radical changes in management personnel from the top down (for example, Bob Dudley replaced the infamous Tony Heyward as CEO), as well as nontrivial internal operational structural, procedural, and policy alterations. It may admit to being the same physical entity with a continuous traceable history, but not the same corporation. (Actually it's not even the same physical entity having shed a number of its elements since 2010 by selling off many of its assets to the tune of nearly forty billion dollars, reducing it from the second to the fourth largest oil company in the world.) In a similar vein, as discussed in the philosophical literature on free will and personal identity, we might say that humans who have undergone a drastic brain intervention, despite satisfying standard Lockean criteria of being the same biological human beings, are not the same persons, on Lockean conditions of person identity, if they no longer have the values or memories they had pre-manipulation. We might be persuaded to say, as BP's re-branders would like us to say, that though BP on April 10, 2010 was morally synchronically responsible for the Deepwater Horizon disaster, BP today in 2016, having undergone a substantial managerial and operational manipulation in the interim, is no longer the same corporation, and fails to have diachronic moral ownership of the disaster.[10]

---

[10] In a related vein: the merger of United and Continental Airlines provides a fusion case for identity theorists to mull regarding the moral responsibility of the new entity for my lost luggage on a Continental flight to Cleveland five years ago.

Two of the alternatives to straightforward numerical soma-centric identity for the moral responsibility diachronic ownership condition in the case of humans are discussed in the recent philosophical literature. One is psychological connectedness; the other is narrative coherence. With appropriate modifications, I think either can serve as a satisfactory corporate diachronic moral responsibility/ownership condition that responds to our intuitions regarding when a corporation is diachronically responsible for an event it was synchronically responsible for in a past incarnation, even if it attempts to distance itself from having been responsible for it.

If psychological connectedness is adopted in human cases, diachronic responsibility/ownership for an action at T_1 is dependent on the degree to which and the way in which the subject's current psychology in its neuro-psychological mechanism is connected to the psychology of the agent at T_1 that was the spring of the agent's action at T_1. Psychological connectedness between former and current agents is an intransitive causal relation that comes in degrees. Andrew Khoury writes: "Two psychological states are connected to the degree that they are similar and causally related. Some agent S's psychological state P_1 is psychologically connected to S's later psychological state P_2 if and only if P_1 caused P_2 and P_2 is similar to P_1. Given that psychological connectedness is a relation that comes in degrees (since similarity comes in degrees), when I say that two states are directly connected I mean only to say that they are connected to a high degree" (Khoury 2013, 740).

If psychological connectedness is to be the relevant factor, then justifiable diachronic blaming or the holding responsible and accountable of an agent at T_2 for an action performed at T_1 will be dependent on the degree to which and the way in which identified psychological states and functions of that agent's current neuro-psychological mechanism, such as beliefs, values, desires, and the like, are causally connected to those that were the effective motivational springs in the agent at T_1. If they are psychologically connected to a reasonably high degree in the prescribed fashion, then the agent at T_2 is an appropriate candidate for being held responsible for what was done at T_1. If they are not causally connected to such a degree, then the agent at T_2 is not such a candidate and expressions of the negative participant reactive attitudes directed at that agent because of what was done at T_1 are inappropriate, and should be forsworn.

Translating this argument into the realm of operational mechanisms in which corporations reside, a corporation's diachronic responsibility for a past act is dependent on the degree to which and the way in which the corporation's internal decision structure's policies and procedures that reflect its values, plans, desires, and intentions are causally connected to those that were the effective springs of the past untoward corporate action.

For example, if BP was synchronically responsible for the Deepwater Horizon disaster because of the reasons cited in the Coast Guard's report; if this report provided a true description of underlying operational flaws, policies, and values in BP's organizational mechanism in April 2010; and if BP's organizational mechanism, despite whatever internal personnel and other changes it may have made, continues to evidence those or similar flaws today (it is sometimes said that such things in organizations have a self-sustaining power of regeneration once embedded in an operational mechanism), then BP is diachronically responsible for the Deepwater Horizon disaster in April 2010, perhaps even to the same degree as its synchronic responsibility. The presence of those operational flaws, we may assume, is causally connected to a significant degree to their previous existence in BP's operational mechanism and constitutes adequate evidence of a relevant sufficient degree of agent sameness regardless of what the corporation calls itself or what its public relations firm says about it. It might be further argued that the continued presence of flaws in its operational mechanism is a reason to hold BP today diachronically responsible for the Deepwater Horizon disaster to a greater degree than its synchronic responsibility. Knowing those flaws were cited as causally responsible for the disaster, BP retained the procedures, policies, values, and so on, that led to those flaws or did not significantly ferret them out and alter its operational system to insure against their repetition. If, however, BP has made substantial corrective changes within its organizational mechanism that block the continuation of the offending policies, procedures, and other operational processes, and adopted morally defensible values in their stead, we may assume that despite physical continuity and an historical thread, BP at T_2 is not sufficiently operationally connected or similar to an appropriate degree to BP at the time of the Deepwater Horizon disaster to support a holding of BP at T_2 as diachronically responsible for the disaster as BP was synchronically responsible for it.

The main point is that corporate synchronic responsibility does not limit corporate diachronic responsibility for the same event. Corporate moral responsibility may be enhanced or diminished over time depending on whether there is operational connectedness of its current organizational mechanism (particularly policies and procedures) to the one that was functional at the time of the event. It is the corporation's internal operational mechanism that matters, not the humans working within it. Nonetheless, following Pettit (2007), the humans who were involved in crucial managerial positions in BP in April 2010 are not exempted from synchronic responsibility for the disaster. By the same token, new managers who did not alter defective elements of the firm's operational mechanism (on the supposition above) are not exempt from diachronic moral responsibility for the disaster. Their synchronic and diachronic responsibilities are obviously related to their roles in BP, but are separable matters from the responsibilities of BP.[11]

---

[11] See footnote 3.

To clarify, suppose corporation A at T_1 is synchronically responsible for event E because of its morally deficient internal operational mechanism that includes policy and procedural flaws (embedding certain values) comparable to those cited by the Coast Guard's report in the Deepwater Horizon case. At T_2 suppose that corporation A is transformed into corporation B through a buyout and reorganization, undergoes a change in leadership and the introduction of many new policies and procedures, but does not modify the policy and procedural flaws that led to E. Even though corporation B did not exist at T_1 and being synchronically responsible for E cannot be a part of B's objective past, event E is a part of B's subjective past in that B's current operational mechanism contains the deficiencies that brought about E and are present in B because they were carried over from A.

Corporation A's internal operational mechanism can be described both synchronically and diachronically. What matters with respect to corporation B's diachronic responsibility for E is the degree to which and the way in which B's internal policies and procedures connect to those that were the effective springs of A's causing E and being held synchronically responsible for E at T_1. An additional point worth noting is that the corporatizing of the psychological connectedness or sameness condition is likely to produce more certifiable results than in human cases where philosophers typically arouse the intuitions to which it appeals by fanciful science fiction thought experiments involving scientists intervening in the brains of human subjects. In actual human cases radical psychological nonconnectedness is likely to be more difficult to discern except in the most dramatic dissociative cases. Corporate operational mechanisms are generally more accessible to analysis.

Although I find the corporatizing of the psychological connectedness condition for diachronic responsibility/ownership of an event attractive because it focuses primarily on the functional elements of corporate operational mechanisms, the narrative coherence account of sameness has much to admire when it is corporatized.

In explaining narrative coherence in a human case, Benjamin Matheson writes: "An agent is morally responsible for a past action to the extent that the action coheres with the agent's self-told narrative" (Matheson 2013). The narrative self-constitution position has been articulated by Marya Schechtman (1996) and others.[12] Schechtman maintains that persons "create their identities by forming autobiographical narratives...by coming to think of themselves as persisting subjects who have had experiences in the past and will continue to have experiences in the future" (id. 94).

Human self-told narratives might not be consciously developed. Most human lives, however, are to at least some extent self-told stories in that the

---

[12] For examples see Daniel Dennett (1988, 1989, 1991), Owen Flanagan (1993), Alistair MacIntyre (1981), and Dan McAdams (1993).

autobiographers organize the acts they've performed, the things they've done, and what they plan to do, into intelligibly structured storylines, at least to a reasonable degree, even if they only tell those stories to themselves during reflective interludes. I'm reminded of Ortega y Gasset's comment: "Man…is impossible without the capacity of inventing for himself a life-figure, and of idealizing the person that he will become. Man is the novelist of himself" (1939, 9).

Briefly, the narrative coherence account of diachronic responsibility is that an agent is morally responsible for a past action to the extent that the action coheres with the agent's self-told narrative, as long as that narrative is not delusional or fictional.

On this account, the narrative self, not personal identity or psychological connectedness, is the locus in humans of diachronic moral responsibility. If a past action no longer coheres with one's current self-narrative, it is not something for which one can legitimately be held morally diachronically responsible, for which one can be blamed, punished, or praised. That is one of the reasons for the attractiveness of this position to those puzzling over brain manipulation thought experiments in the free will and personal identity literature in philosophy. This chapter, however, is not the place to discuss the implications of narrative coherence for such things as atonement, contrition, forgiveness, punishment, and the like in individual human cases or how human self-narratives might be objectively vetted.[13]

When we apply the narrative coherence account to the diachronic responsibility of firms we get an interesting result: corporations are responsible at T_1 + n for what they did at T_1 for which they were synchronically responsible, if what they did at T_1 coheres with the corporation's self-narrative at T_1 + n.

First, though, we should ask whether corporations have self-narratives. I think they do, and their self-narratives might be more accessible and lucid to the wider moral community than the self-narratives of most individual human beings. Corporations articulate their narratives in annual reports, in advertising, in legal documents, in internal and external statements of corporate culture, and in policies. The corporate self-narrative is a developmental element of the policy aspects of a corporate internal decision structure.[14] It is the story the corporation continues to tell itself (and others) about itself, but, applying the Schechtman vetting conditions, for this story to function in the criteria of corporate diachronic responsibility it must be internally coherent and, crucially, it must be consistent with reality. So the "bullshit" in advertising and rebranding (Frankfurt 2005), and the delusional elements in corporate literature and communications are necessarily excluded. (So much for BP's claims on its website that "BP pursues energy innovation safely, reliably, and responsibly to help America meet its growing energy needs; BP is dedicated to

---

[13] I have discussed some of these notions elsewhere (French 2014).
[14] See French (1979, 1995, 1996).

ensuring safe and reliable operations; and since 2010, BP has taken major economic and environmental action along the Gulf Coast." Pictures of a white egret on a beach in Louisiana and two pelicans flying over the waves are featured on the site (BP 2016).) Corporate image projection for public consumption should not be confused with a firm's internal reflexive narrative identity.

BP is morally diachronically responsible for the *Torrey Canyon* and the Deepwater Horizon disasters (and the Texas City explosion in 2005 and the Prudhoe Bay spill in 2006) as long as those events are intelligibly part of the corporately self-conceived life story of BP. But should BP cease to be that narrative self by creating or evolving into another narrative self in which the doing of those things does not intelligibly cohere, then BP will no longer be morally responsible for them. It is difficult to conceive of how that might come about and pass the objective vetting tests regardless of whether BP undergoes various forms of corporate fusion or fission. Those historical events, represented as responsibilities of BP, should remain prominently in the BP self-narrative, where, hopefully, they should serve as prompts of operational change. In any event, objective vetting should insure their presence in the BP narratives of the future. Depending on how the story goes, BP will have more, less, or the same degree of diachronic responsibility for them as it had synchronic responsibility when they occurred. As in the case of the operational connectedness alternative, firms that include their misdeeds within their self-narratives and treat them as triggers for reformation typically diminish the degree of their diachronic moral responsibility for those past wrongful deeds.

External and internal reality checks on self-told narratives must ensure that firms, like humans, do not get to whitewash their moral slates by telling delusional stories about themselves. The narratives cannot contain gross errors of significant and publicly observable facts or their interpretation, and the firm's past must help illuminate its present. Ignoring, forgetting, misdescribing, or allowing the firm's public relations department to construct for its own ends the story of the firm's past synchronically responsible misdeeds does not produce a qualifying corporate self-narrative for diachronic moral responsibility purposes.

The amount of illusion, delusion, falsehood, and fabrication in the self-narratives of firms provides a gauge of their corporate moral development. Studies of self-narrative construction in firms could reveal stages of corporate cultural moral maturity. The path to corporate moral maturity may mirror that of human moral maturity during which the comfortable illusions or delusions that shaped a flawed adolescent self-narrative are replaced by cold, hard descriptions of actual events that cohere with reality but lack the magic, charm, and poetry of the fictional versions of callow youth. Autobiographies are not supposed to be romantic novels, despite Ortega's claim.

Consider how we generally treat diachronic responsibility in delusional adult humans. A profoundly delusional human typically is not considered capable of bearing responsibility for past misdeeds, but also not allowed to wander about repeating them. Intervention and regulation are usually employed, and that is how immature, delusional, and stunted corporations (including shell and closely-held ones) should be dealt with morally and legally too.

Of course, narrative coherence issues can be jettisoned if we are satisfied, as I am, that operational connectedness is adequate as a ground for diachronic ownership of past corporate and human actions. However, I am sufficiently intrigued to grant that the self-narrative coherence account of sameness may provide a potentially fruitful anchor of corporate diachronic responsibility. I suspect that it is more likely to do so for corporate agents than human agents for accessibility reasons, though it must be admitted that accessibility is an issue for psychological connectedness in most actual individual human cases. The vetting of corporate self-narratives also may prove a useful task for applied moral philosophers and managerial analysts to pursue whether or not the firms whose narratives they examine employ them. Firms, of course, would be well advised to monitor for coherence and truth the stories they tell themselves about themselves and to avoid being taken in by their marketing and public relations efforts that have distinctly different target audiences and purposes.

REFERENCES

BP (2016). "Gulf Commitment." http://www.bp.com/en_us/bp-us/commitment-to-the-gulf-of-mexico.html.

Bratman, Michael (1987, 1999). *Intention, Plans, and Practical Reason.*

Bureau of Ocean Energy Management, Regulation and Enforcement (2011). "Report Regarding the Causes of the April 20, 2010 Macondo Well Blowout." http://docs.lib.noaa.gov/noaa_documents/DWH_IR/reports/dwhfinal.pdf.

Carroll, Lewis (1871). *Through the Looking-Glass.*

Dennett, Daniel (1988). "Why Everyone is a Novelist." *Times Literary Supplement* (September 22).

Dennett, Daniel (1989). "The Origins of Selves." *Cogito* 3: 163.

Dennett, Daniel (1991). *Consciousness Explained.*

Fischer, John M. and Mark Ravizza (1998). *Responsibility and Control.*

Flanagan, Owen (1993). *Varieties of Moral Personality.*

Frankfurt, Harry (2005). *On Bullshit.*

French, Peter A. (1979). "The Corporation as a Moral Person." *American Philosophical Quarterly* 16: 207.

French, Peter A. (1984). "A Principle of Responsive Adjustment." *Philosophy* 59: 491.

French, Peter A. (1995). *Corporate Ethics.*

French, Peter A. (1996). "Integrity, Intentions, and Corporations." *American Business Law Journal* 34: 141.

French, Peter A. (2005). "Inference Gaps in Moral Assessment: Capitalism, Corporations, and Individuals." *International Social Science Journal* 57: 573.

French, Peter A. (2011). *War and Moral Dissonance.*

French, Peter A. (2012). "Corporate Affectivity and Membership in the Moral Community." Presentation given at Oxford University, http://slideplayer.com/slide/1412408.

French, Peter A. (2014). "Self-Blaming, Repentance, and Atonement." *Journal of Value Inquiry* 48: 587.

Haney, Mitchell R. (2004). "Corporate Loss of Innocence for the Sake of Accountability." *The Journal of Social Philosophy* 35: 391.

Khoury, Andrew C. (2013). "Synchronic and Diachronic Responsibility." *Philosophical Studies* 165: 735.

MacIntyre, Alistair (1981). *After Virtue.*

Matheson, Benjamin (2013). "Compatibilism and Personal Identity." *Philosophical Studies* 170: 317.

McAdams, Dan (1993). *The Stories We Live By: Personal Myths and the Making of the Self.*

Ortega y Gasset, Jose (1939). *Man, as Project* (trans. Samuel P. Moody), http://philosophy.lander.edu/intro/articles/ortega-a.pdf.

Pettit, Philip (2007). "Responsibility Incorporated." *Ethics* 117: 171.

Schechtman, Marya (1996). *The Constitution of Selves.*

Tollefsen, Deborah (2008). "Affectivity, Moral Agency, and Corporate-Human Relations." *American Philosophical Association, Newsletter on Philosophy and Law* 7: 9.

4

Pluralistic Functionalism about Corporate Agency

Waheed Hussain and Joakim Sandberg

People care a great deal about whether we can treat corporations as responsible agents. Most of us want, for example, to hold Union Carbide responsible for the Bhopal gas tragedy in 1984 or to hold BP responsible for the Deepwater Horizon Spill in 2010. At the same time, however, we recognize that business corporations often consist of tens of thousands of individuals, and so, much as in the case of ethnic groups or television audiences, it may not be appropriate to treat these groups of individuals as unified agents in the ordinary sense.

Curiously, most philosophers who discuss corporate agency approach the issue as a "metaphysical" or "pre-institutional" matter. They think of collective agency in general as a property, one that the members of a group possess when the pattern of interaction in the group exhibits a certain structure. Furthermore, these philosophers think that possession of this property makes the members of the group deserving of a certain form of treatment. The main tasks for a theory are then to describe the relevant structural characteristics and to address challenges from more individualistic and atomistic perspectives. According to List and Pettit (2011), for instance, the fundamental question is whether it makes metaphysical sense to speak of "group agents" over and above the individual agents that make up the group. Although they believe that there are important social implications that follow from whether it makes sense to speak this way, the basic idea is that the metaphysics will guide us in answering ethical questions about appropriate forms of treatment. Indeed, most of the authors represented in this book probably hold a similar view.

This chapter takes a different path. We view "metaphysical" or "pre-institutional" accounts of corporate agency in much the same way that many political philosophers view "metaphysical" or "pre-institutional" accounts of moral desert. People sometimes claim that they deserve to be paid more because they possess some natural property or personal characteristic that makes them more deserving—for example, they are smarter, harder working, better educated, and so on (Feinberg 1970; Olsaretti 2004). Many political philosophers reject these arguments because other members of society are not required to pay an individual more simply because she possesses a certain natural property or personal characteristic. Whether a certain payment scheme is normatively required depends on how paying people this way would fit into a wider social practice that answers to substantive moral and political ideals. If paying people on the basis of some property or characteristic would not serve the aims of a wider social practice that answers to everyone's claims to favorable treatment, including the claims of those born without these special talents and abilities, then people with the relevant properties and characteristics have no claim to special treatment (see Rawls 1999; Scanlon 1998). Along similar lines, we argue that the fact that a group of individuals interact with one another in a particular way does not settle the important questions about how we as a society should treat the members of the group. The important questions about appropriate forms of treatment—especially in the case of business corporations—must be addressed by asking what forms of treatment would serve the justifying purposes of a wider social institution or practice.

In this chapter, we develop an account of corporate agency that we call *pluralistic functionalism*. This account holds roughly that questions about the collective agency of business corporations must be answered by asking what forms of treatment for business corporations would serve the justifying aims of the competitive market. This view with respect to the business corporation is based on a wider theory of collective agency which holds that for any group of individuals G, questions about the collective agency of the members of G must be answered by asking what forms of special treatment for the members of G would serve the justifying aims of the wider social practices in which the collective agency of the members of G plays a part. We argue that pluralistic functionalism provides a better account of how to think about the agency of business corporations than rival "metaphysical" or "pre-institutional" accounts. More specifically, we will show that our account can explain a broad range of plausible but seemingly inconsistent judgments that many people hold about the agency of business corporations in different contexts.

COLLECTIVE AGENCY AS A FEATURE
OF SOCIAL PRACTICES

We begin by considering the status of the corporation in the law. One of the most important legal powers that people in contemporary market societies have is the power to establish a corporation. A corporation, at the most basic level, is an organization that the rules of the legal system treat as a legal person: the law treats the organization as having some of the rights, duties, powers, and responsibilities that it typically assigns to natural persons (see Orts 2015). The legal systems in the United States, Canada, and most countries in the world give people the power to establish corporations. If an individual or group in these countries decides to set up a corporation, such as, say, to run a restaurant, the corporation that they set up will have the power to do things like own property (for example the restaurant building) and enter into binding contracts with employees. The corporation will also enjoy other features of the status of a natural person: for example, the corporation can be held liable for harms that result from its activities.

There is no doubt that, from a legal point of view, corporations can act. When a corporation performs an action, it usually does so in virtue of the fact that some natural person performed some action. For instance, when a corporation buys a piece of property, this action occurs in virtue of the fact that some corporate official, usually a natural person, signs her name on a contract, acting in her official capacity. What we want to emphasize, however, is that this relationship between the actions of a corporation and the actions of a natural person does not presuppose any deep "metaphysical" or "pre-institutional" facts about collective agency or group agency. This relationship is simply an implication of the rules of the legal system.

Throughout our discussion, we will refer to various games, practices, and institutions as helpful models for thinking about social life. So here is a helpful way of thinking about the agency of business corporations. Suppose that the Los Angeles Lakers are playing a basketball game against the New York Knicks. When Kobe Bryant scores a basket, that is, he puts a basketball through a hoop, this counts as a basket not just for Kobe, but for the Lakers as a team. From the standpoint of pluralistic functionalism, this relationship between Kobe Bryant's "scoring a basket" and the Lakers' "scoring a basket" involves no robust metaphysical or pre-institutional facts about collective agency: there need be no natural collective agent or group agent that encompasses Kobe Bryant and the other players on the Lakers team. The relationship is simply an implication of the scoring rules in basketball. The rules of basketball are structured so that certain actions on the part of individuals count as both the individual "scoring a basket" and the team "scoring a basket."

Discussions of collective agency or group agency tend to focus on whether a certain internal structure of decision making exists among the members of a group. The assumption is that the presence of some such structure is necessary for the members of the group to have a "collective intention" over and above their intentions as individuals. Moreover, it is assumed that some collective intention of this kind is essential for the group to constitute a collective agent in a morally relevant sense (see Bratman 2014; French 1984; French and Wettstein 2006; List and Pettit 2011; Tuomela 2013). We reject this last claim: a collective intention of the kind that these theorists describe is not essential for the members of a group to constitute a collective agent in a morally relevant sense. In the case of basketball, collective agency hinges on the rules of the game, not the structure of decision-making among the players on a team. Collective agency in this sense can clearly be morally significant insofar as it would be unfair to treat Kobe Bryant's "scoring a basket" as anything other than the Lakers "scoring a basket," given that that the rules of basketball are clear on this point and given that everyone has acted with the expectation that everyone else will follow the rules (see Hart 1984; Rawls 1999; see also Dworkin 1986).

To bring the contrast out more clearly: suppose that we're in the closing minutes of a playoff game and that the intense pressure reduces the Lakers players to bewildered confusion. All coordination among the players on the court breaks down; no one is even trying to coordinate his activities with the others. Suppose, however, that Kobe Bryant, in a magnificent display of individual skill, single-handedly takes on all the Knicks and dunks the ball. According to the rules, this would count not only as Kobe Bryant "scoring a basket," but also as the Lakers "scoring a basket." Yet, by assumption, there is no structure of coordination among the players in Lakers uniforms that could justify the assertion that these players have meshed their intentions, plans, or practical reasoning in such a way that they constitute a collective agent in a "metaphysical" or "pre-institutional" sense (see Bratman 2014; List and Pettit 2011). Seen independently of the basketball game, we would have no special reason to treat the people on the court in Lakers jerseys as a collective agent. The only reason we count the basket as a basket for the team is because (a) the practice—the game of basketball—has a certain scoring rule, (b) the scoring rule serves an important function in the practice, and (c) the practice as a whole is justified.

Just to be clear, we are not denying that there are collective agents or group agents in the "metaphysical" or "pre-institutional" sense. Agents of this kind may exist, and it may even be important in some contexts that agents of this kind do exist. What we are claiming is that when it comes to the important social, moral, and political questions that surround business corporations in contemporary liberal democracies, this metaphysical or pre-institutional sense of collective agency is largely irrelevant. To answer the important questions, we must think of collective agency as a feature of our social practices, one that serves or may serve the goals, aims, and values that justify these practices. We turn now to consider these goals, aims, and values.

PLURALISTIC FUNCTIONALISM ABOUT COLLECTIVE AGENCY

A social practice is a collective enterprise that makes an array of demands on participants, where participants may or may not have good reason to comply with these demands. We follow Ronald Dworkin (1986) in thinking that the requirements of a social practice are not determined by brute sociological facts. From the point of view of participants, the requirements of a practice are meant to serve some underlying goal, aim, or purpose, one that is related to some deeper value or values. As Dworkin rightly argues, the requirements of a social practice are not determined by the conventional understanding of these requirements in a community. Instead, the requirements of a practice are determined by constructive interpretation. To know what a practice requires, you have to formulate the underlying goals, aims, and purposes that the practice is supposed to serve, and then specify the requirements of the practice so that they serve these ends. The interpretation of the underlying goals, aims, and purposes, as well as the specific requirements, should fit with how participants behave and make the practice as worthy of people's compliance as possible.

Social practices in different communities are often best understood as instantiations of a certain category or type. The category or type is understood in terms of a certain abstract structure of requirements and a certain abstract account of the justifying rationale for the arrangement. For example, suppose that you are a professional basketball player who plays in the USA and also competes in the Olympics. When you play in the USA, you, your teammates, the opposing players, referees, officials, and everyone else conform to the rules set out by the National Basketball Association (NBA). When you play in the Olympics, you, your teammates, the opposing players, referees, officials, and everyone else recognize and conform to the rules set out by the Fédération Internationale de Basketball (FIBA). These two social practices are different in the sense that they are distinctive cooperative endeavors that involve different groups of people, and each one imposes a different set of specific requirements on participants.[1] Nonetheless, we can see that these distinct social practices are instantiations of the same abstract type of practice, namely the game of basketball. The rules set out by the NBA and the rules set out by FIBA both define a similar (but not identical) distribution of rights, duties, and responsibilities among players, referees, officials, and so on. Moreover, the underlying purpose of these requirements is understood in terms of similar values, such as the welfare of the players, the entertainment of the audience, and the beauty of the game.

When we survey social life in advanced liberal democracies, the pattern of activity that we see is best understood as consisting of many distinct social practices that are instantiations of different categories or types. One example that we have already considered is the case of basketball. Two more examples will figure prominently in our discussion. One is the practice of electoral

---

[1] For example, a game has four twelve-minute quarters under NBA rules, but a game has four ten-minute quarters under FIBA rules.

democracy. Different countries may have legal rules and social customs that differ in the details, but we can see that these rules and customs are best understood as instantiations of a more abstract practice that we call "electoral democracy." This more abstract practice has certain defining features, including political offices with distinctive powers, political parties that can act independently of the state, and a legal permission for parties to campaign for the election of particular candidates. Moreover, the abstract practice has a certain justifying rationale, where the purpose of electoral democracy is (in part) to realize the ideal of citizen control over the course of public life.

The other practice that will figure prominently in our discussion is the competitive market. Again, different countries will have different specific legal rules and social customs, but we can see that these rules and customs are best understood as instantiations of a more abstract social practice that we call a "competitive market." This more abstract practice has certain characteristic features, including private property rights, firms that operate independently of the state, and a permission to pursue profit. Moreover, the various features of a competitive market are typically understood as having a point or purpose that is related to the value of improving people's quality of life.

As we discussed in the last section, there are many cases where a social practice will direct participants to treat the actions of an individual or group of individuals as the actions of a collective agent. The rules of basketball often direct participants to treat the actions of individual players as the actions of basketball teams. Basketball teams are collective agents, distinct from the specific individuals who are members of the team, and these collective agents have the power to do things like score baskets and win games. In much the same way, the rules of electoral democracy often direct participants to treat the actions of party officials as the actions of the party. Parties are collective agents, distinct from the specific individuals who are members of the party, and these collective agents have the power to do things like adopt party platforms and nominate candidates. Finally, the rules of the competitive market often direct participants to treat the actions of corporate officials as the actions of a business corporation. These collective agents are distinct from the specific individuals who occupy various positions in the organization, and these collective agents have the power to do things like own property, enter into contracts, and declare bankruptcy.

The central contention of pluralistic functionalism is that questions about collective agency are best understood and addressed as questions about the corresponding social practices. To determine whether a group of individuals constitutes a collective agent in a normatively significant sense, we have to ask two questions: (1) Does treating the members of the group as a collective agent serve the goals, aims, and purposes that justify the corresponding social practice? (2) What more precise way of treating these individuals as a collective agent would best advance the justifying aims of the practice?

TWO ILLUSTRATIONS: POLITICAL PARTIES AND BUSINESS CORPORATIONS

To illustrate the central contention of pluralistic functionalism, consider two examples. Take the case of a political party. Political parties are important organizations in advanced liberal democracies, and we often treat the members of a political party as a collective agent in certain ways. For example, we take political parties to have political platforms that consist of various policy commitments, and we treat the members of a political party as collective agents when we regard the policy commitments of the party itself as being conceptually distinct from the policy commitments of the individual members of the party. From the standpoint of our political practices, it is possible that no individual member of a party will actually endorse every plank in the party platform, and it is even possible that no plank in the party platform will actually correspond to the views of a majority of the party membership (see Arrow 1970; Dahl 2006). Although the individual members of the party may determine the party platform together through some voting process, we treat the commitments of the party as a collective agent as being distinct from the commitments that party members hold as individuals.

According to pluralistic functionalism, the collective agency that we accord to political parties is a component feature of a wider social practice. Whether it is appropriate to treat the members of a political party as a collective agent in this way depends on whether treating individuals this way would serve the justifying aims of the wider practice. In the case of political parties, the wider social practice at issue is electoral democracy: the collective agency that we accord to political parties is one component feature of our electoral system. According to one interpretation, the point of electoral democracy is to realize the ideal of citizen control over public life. Assuming that this is the correct way to think about electoral democracy, and assuming also that the practice is justified, treating the individual members of political parties as collective agents is justified insofar as this serves the justifying aims of electoral democracy more generally.

How does collective agency serve the justifying aims of electoral democracy? First, treating parties as having free-standing political platforms facilitates citizen control over public life because this authority structure helps citizens with shared outlooks to form a shared agenda and to coordinate their political activities. Second, treating parties as independent agents facilitates political deliberation: coherent party platforms give individual voters a clear set of choices on a range of policy issues, allowing voters to exercise control over the course of public life (Beitz 1989). Finally, allowing parties to have free-standing political platforms also serves the aims of deliberation because it helps to draw out all of the various reasons and evidence supporting different policy alternatives in public debates (id.).

We treat the members of a political party as a collective agent in the sense that the party has its own policy commitments, distinct from the commitments of its individual members. It seems relatively clear that this form of treatment is justified insofar as it serves the justifying aims of electoral democracy. But now we face a further question: how more specifically should we treat political parties as collective agents in order to advance the justifying aims of this practice?

In order to serve the justifying aims of electoral democracy, the collective agency that we accord to political parties must, among other things, incorporate a temporal constraint. For example, the Democratic Party in the United States was the party of slavery for many decades before the Civil War. It would not make sense for our political practices to hold the party today to be accountable for this past position. This is because holding political parties accountable for positions held in the distant past would interfere with the purposes that political parties are supposed to serve in electoral politics, namely to provide voters with a clear choice between policy agendas in the current election cycle (Beitz 1989). So the collective agency of political parties has an important temporal constraint built into it, one that is justified in light of the purpose that the collective agency of political parties is supposed to serve in the democratic process. It follows also that the collective agency that we accord to political parties may differ in important ways from the collective agency that we accord to other groups of individuals.

We turn now to the case of business corporations. Business corporations are important organizations in contemporary liberal democracies, and we typically treat the groups of individuals who participate in corporations as collective agents in certain ways. To take one example, we treat business corporations as having limited liability. When a corporation enters into contracts with employers, suppliers, customers, lenders, and so on, the law treats these contracts as contracts between the corporation itself and the various counterparties. In the event that the corporation cannot fulfill its financial obligations to one of these counterparties, the law treats the corporation's assets as resources that might be used to fulfill these obligations. But the law does not treat shareholders as personally liable for fulfilling the corporation's obligations. This is because, in the eyes of the law, shareholders have no essential, direct legal relationship to the various parties that enter into contracts with the corporation; it is the corporation itself that stands in these legal relationships.

According to pluralistic functionalism, the collective agency that we accord to business corporations is a component feature of a wider social practice. Whether it is appropriate to treat the participants in a business corporation as having this form of collective agency depends on whether treating corporations this way would serve the justifying aims of the relevant social practice. In the case of business corporations, the relevant social practice is the competitive market. There is a veritable avalanche of different accounts of how the business corporation, understood as a collective agent, serves the justifying aims of a competitive market economy (see Coase 1988; Chandler 1977; Jensen and Meckling 1976; Williamson 1998; Hart 1993; Easterbrook and Fischel 1996, among many others). But here is a simple account that stresses the importance of limited liability. Without limited liability, anyone who pursues a new business venture would have to risk all of her assets, including her house and retirement savings, because if the business venture fails, lenders, suppliers, employees, and other parties would have a financial claim on anything that she owns. Limited liability allows entrepreneurs to limit their financial exposure to just those assets that they invest in a business corporation. This ultimately improves the quality of life for everyone by making it easier for new innovations to come to the market and enrich our lives.

Given that the collective agency of business corporations serves the justifying aims of the competitive market, how more precisely should we understand this form of collective agency in light of these underlying aims? Consider that market actors (especially business corporations themselves) often abuse the power to form a corporation by forming dozens and dozens of nested subsidiary corporations as a way of obscuring their debts from investors and from the wider market. Even if the general practice of treating corporations as independent legal agents can be justified, this particular feature of the practice—that is, the power to form corporations endlessly and for any purpose—does not necessarily serve the underlying purposes of the competitive market. So according to pluralistic functionalism, dummy corporations that simply obscure liabilities from investors do not have independent agency and therefore should not have limited liability in the way that other corporations do.

KEY FEATURES OF PLURALISTIC FUNCTIONALISM

According to pluralistic functionalism, social activity in an advanced liberal democracy is best understood as involving many different social practices, including practices such as professional basketball, electoral democracy, and competitive markets. In the normal case, we treat certain groups of individuals as collective agents because treating these individuals in this way serves an important function in a wider social practice that is justified. This view of collective agency differs from many other contemporary views, and we want to draw attention four distinctive features of pluralistic functionalism.

First, according to our view, there is no pattern of organization or structure of decision-making such that if the members of a group exhibit this pattern, they would have a practice-independent claim to being treated as a collective agent. For example, the mere fact that the members of a certain group have an internal decision-making process that coordinates their activities in a certain way does not give the members of that group a claim to being treated as a basketball team, a political party, a business corporation, or any other type of collective agent. This is roughly analogous to the view, widely held among political philosophers, that the mere fact that someone has a certain property or personal characteristic—for example, being smart or hard working—does not give that person a normatively significant claim on being paid more than others. Whether a certain natural property or personal characteristic constitutes a normatively significant basis for certain forms of treatment depends on whether according the property or characteristic this status would serve the justifying aims of some wider social practice.

Second, pluralistic functionalism denies that there is any encompassing social practice that directs people to treat a group of individuals as a collective agent whenever the relations among the members of this group take a certain form. What we have are various particular practices, such as professional basketball, electoral democracy, and competitive markets, and there are particular forms of collective agency that are appropriate to each practice. The proper way to understand the form of collective agency that applies to a group is to consider the form of collective agency that is specific to the relevant social practice.

Third, pluralistic functionalism regards questions of responsibility that have to do with compensation for harm, restitution, and punishment as questions that must be settled in terms of the justifying aims of particular social practices. There is no encompassing social practice that directs people to treat groups of individuals with certain features as collective agents who must pay compensation, pay restitution, or accept punishment when they perform actions that harm others. Whether a group of individuals must pay compensation, pay restitution, or suffer punishment as a collective entity is a question that must be settled by appeal to the justifying rationale for some specific social practice.

Fourth, pluralistic functionalism implies that the very same group of natural individuals may exercise different forms of collective agency in different social practices. For example, the same group of natural persons may constitute a basketball team from the standpoint of a basketball game, and they may constitute a business corporation from the standpoint of the competitive market economy. The form of collective agency appropriate to this group of individuals may vary depending on whether we are considering the organization from the standpoint of one social practice or another.

VARIABLE STANDARDS FOR CONTINUITY
AND CONSISTENCY

Pluralistic functionalism holds that issues about when and how to treat groups of individuals as collective agents are best understood as interpretive questions about specific social practices. An important implication of this account is that there is no one right way to treat a group of individuals as a collective agent: different forms of treatment are appropriate in different domains and contexts. One form of collective agency will be appropriate for political parties in the electoral process, and another form will be appropriate for business corporations in a competitive market. We want to highlight this feature of the view further by considering three important aspects of collective agency: temporal continuity, consistency, and liability.

Temporal Continuity

One important aspect of agency is temporal continuity. If X is an agent, then we hold X accountable for making commitments in ways that (1) fit with X's past commitments and (2) are sensitive to how the commitments that X makes now will shape the possibilities for commitment that are open to X in the future (see Peter French's Chapter 3 in this book). Although it is certainly true that we sometimes treat groups of individuals as collective agents in this sense, there is a great deal of variation in the ways that we do this. It is an advantage of pluralistic functionalism that it can explain this variation better than rival theories can.

Return again to the case of political parties. As we noted, the Democratic Party in the United States was the party of slavery for many years prior to the Civil War. Most people would agree that there is only one Democratic Party in the United States, a party that has existed continuously from before the Civil War until today. But our political practices do not hold the Democratic Party accountable for its past positions on slavery in the way that we might hold a natural person accountable. For example, even if the Democratic Party never explicitly repudiated its past position, our political practice would not hold the party accountable for this position, so long as it was evident that this position no longer plays a role in the party's current political platform. Our political practices do not hold political parties accountable for positions held significantly far in the past.

The reason for the temporal constraint seems clear. Holding the party accountable for positions held in the distant past would interfere with the purpose that these organizations are supposed to serve in the electoral process. Part of the point of having political parties is that they provide voters in the current election cycle with clear choices between broad legislative agendas, and this ultimately serves the ideal of citizen control by enabling voters to shape the course of public life. Holding a party accountable for coherence in its recent commitments clearly serves the deeper purposes of the democratic process because this is necessary to ensure that parties will fulfill their mandates and voters will get the benefit of a coherent national dialogue over several election cycles. But coherence with positions held in the distant past does not serve any of the purposes of electoral democracy.

Contrast the case of political parties with the case of the Catholic Church. According to pluralistic functionalism, there is greater justification for holding the Catholic Church accountable for its past positions with respect to slavery, insofar as the Church has not explicitly rejected these positions. The reason for this is that the Church is supposed to exercise a particular form of leadership for the global community of Catholics, a community that sees itself as a perpetual association. For an organization whose purpose is understood in this way it makes sense to hold the organization accountable for positions held in the distant past because the organization is supposed to govern in a more or less temporally unconstrained fashion. The difference between the Democratic Party, on the one hand, and the Catholic Church, on the other, does not stem from any differences in the internal structures of these organizations, but from the purposes that these forms of collective agency are supposed to serve in some wider social practice.

Consistency

Another aspect of agency is consistency. If X is an agent, then (1) we hold X accountable for maintaining a consistent set of commitments, and (2) whenever possible, we interpret X's actions and statements as expressions of a consistent set of commitments (again see French's chapter in this book). Although it is true that we sometimes treat groups of individuals as collectively subject to certain norms of consistency, there is a great deal of variation here as well.

Compare the following two cases: (a) a national political party runs candidates in several state elections; and (b) a business corporation defends itself in several lawsuits brought forward in several different states. There is no doubt that in both cases, we are dealing with a single organization or group of individuals, a political party in one case and a business corporation in the other. But our expectations with respect to consistency are quite different. We hold the political party accountable for having a relatively consistent national platform and ensuring that all of its candidates endorse the central elements of this platform. But we have no similar expectation of the business corporation in its legal defense. Suppose that the lawsuit alleges some form of negligent product design: the corporation can advance one theory of what constitutes a safe product design in one jurisdiction and an inconsistent theory of what constitutes a safe product design in another. Our legal practices do not require the corporation to maintain consistency across jurisdictions.[2]

---

[2] Of course, there may be practical considerations that would make it unwise for a corporation to present inconsistent theories in different jurisdictions: after all, the theory that wins a case

Again, the differences in collective agency make sense in light of the fact that collective agency, in each case, is meant to serve a specific purpose in a separate social practice. In the case of political parties, the relevant social practice is electoral democracy. Parties are supposed to structure and organize choices for voters, and consistency across jurisdictions clearly serves this purpose. But the same is not true in the other case.

With respect to the business corporation, the relevant social practice is the competitive market and, in particular, the process of legal adjudication designed to enforce the rules. The point of the legal adjudication process is to ensure that market actors comply with the rules and that any costs imposed on the various parties involved are actually licensed by the rules. A requirement placed on defendants (corporate or otherwise) to have consistent positions across jurisdictions would not obviously serve this purpose. In fact, given that the laws might be different in different jurisdictions, a requirement of consistency might even interfere with the purposes of legal adjudication, forcing a defendant to shape his defense in one jurisdiction to fit with strategic considerations issuing from another.

Variable Standards for Liability

A third aspect of agency is liability for harm. If X is an agent, then we hold X responsible for the damage that X causes in the sense that we require X to pay certain fines, accept certain penalties or pay restitution to the damaged parties (French and Wettstein 2006; Hasnas 2009).

Collective agency varies widely with respect to liability for harm. For example, basketball teams do not have collective liability in the sense just described. Consider that when the players on the Los Angeles Lakers score points and win games, they are clearly acting as a collective agent, that is, a basketball team. But if the Lakers organization cuts corners in building a new arena, and this leads to an accident that hurts some fans, it would be incorrect to attribute the negligence to the basketball team. The negligence is properly attributed to *The Los Angeles Lakers, Inc.*, which is the business corporation that operates the basketball franchise. Basketball teams clearly do not have

---

for the corporation in jurisdiction A might be used against the corporation in jurisdiction B. But our point here is not about strategic considerations of this kind, but about what we expect of different groups, independent of these types of considerations. Even if there were no strategic considerations to prevent a political party from winning elections by running candidates with opposing views in different jurisdictions, we hold political parties to a higher standard that requires a certain form of consistency across jurisdictional lines. The collective agency of business corporations is different in this regard, because absent any strategic limitations, we would not require the corporation to advance consistent theories of product design across legal jurisdictions.

collective liability for harms (or at least certain types of harms) in the way that business corporations do.

Why are business corporations in particular treated as collective agents in the "collective liability" sense? According to pluralistic functionalism, the reason has to do with the competitive market. Market actors may enter into transactions with one another that impose risks on or actually harm bystanders. In order to ensure that the market fulfills its function, which is to improve our overall quality of life, the rules of the market will require market actors to take certain precautions to avoid harming third parties. The rules will also incorporate a system of penalties to ensure that market actors live up to their duties.

It seems clear that a justified system of rules for a competitive market will impose duties and penalties not only on individual market actors, but on corporations as well. The reason for this is not that corporations have a certain internal structure that makes them deserving of punishment: we need not appeal to some collective "bad intention" that must be punished alongside the bad intentions of individuals (see Rönnegard 2013). The reason for imposing duties and penalties on corporations is much more practical. Given that economic activity is incredibly complicated in a modern society, and given the central role that business corporations play in coordinating economic activity, no competitive market system could provide adequate protections to third parties without imposing duties on corporations and imposing penalties on them.

Now some participants in the corporation might complain when we impose penalties on the corporation as a whole: shareholders, for example, might argue that they should not suffer losses because of the bad conduct of corporate officials (see, for example, John Hasnas' Chapter 5 in this book). But this is not a compelling argument. A legitimate system of penalties may sometimes impose costs on certain individuals when this creates an incentive for them to act in a supervisory capacity. For instance, the law might make parents financially liable for the actions of their teenage children as a way of making sure that parents supervise their children vigorously. The justification for these penalties does not stem from any form of agential integration between parents and children, but simply from the need to craft an effective system of protections for other members of the community.

In much the same way, the rules of the market might impose penalties on shareholders as a way of enlisting them in the oversight process. (Notice that this would not be unfair because shareholders have an obvious way to avoid the oversight responsibility: they can sell their shares or invest elsewhere in the first place.) When penalties fall on shareholders because of what corporations or corporate officials do, this is not because the shareholders and other parties involved in the corporation form a collective agent in some "metaphysical" or "pre-institutional" sense. The penalties fall on shareholders simply because this is an effective way of protecting third parties from certain types of harms.

Consider the case of BP and the Deepwater Horizon spill noted at the outset of our chapter. We certainly believe that the various individuals who participate in BP form a collective agent in the sense that the members of the group are collectively liable for the damage that the group causes. But we do not believe that collective liability in this case stems from some "metaphysical" or "pre-institutional" form of group agency. According to pluralistic functionalism, collective liability is a feature of the collective agency of business corporations because the collective agency of business corporations best serves the justifying aims of the competitive market when it includes this feature.

The key ideas are as follows. BP as an organization has certain duties of care with respect to protecting third parties from the risks inherent in its drilling operations. These collective duties give content to the more specific duties of various corporate officials who occupy positions in the BP hierarchy. For example, when we ask what the duties of the CEO of BP are, we can count among these duties a duty to design BP's operations in ways that satisfy the corporate duty to take adequate precautions against harming third parties or exposing them to unacceptable risks. In addition, BP is also subject to certain collective penalties for failing to live up to its obligations, where these penalties can result in costs for corporate officials, shareholders, and even ordinary employees. These costs can be justified as part of an efficient system of oversight.

Some readers (and some other contributors in this book) might want to go further and regard BP as a target for reactive attitudes, such as blame and resentment. Some readers may also regard it as important that BP apologize to its victims and to the wider community for what it has done. We agree that there are important questions to ask here about reactive attitudes. But these are *not* the most important questions that arise with respect to the collective agency of business corporations in the world today. The most important questions about corporate agency are not fundamentally questions about the appropriateness of these types of attitudes. The most important questions have to do with paying compensation, paying restitution, and accepting punishment for unjustifiable harm.

SPHERE DIFFERENTIATION AND THE LEGAL STATUS OF BUSINESS CORPORATIONS

Two recent Supreme Court cases in the United States, *Burwell v. Hobby Lobby* (2014) and *Citizens United v. Federal Election Commission* (2010), have sparked a new debate about corporate agency. The Court decided in each case to alter the status of business corporations so as to grant these organizations certain rights that one normally associates with the status of natural persons: that is, rights of religious expression in one case and rights of political expression in the other. We believe that pluralistic functionalism sheds light on why these decisions are controversial and on the proper way to think about the issues involved.

In *Hobby Lobby*, the question before the Court was whether the state could compel a family-owned business corporation to provide contraceptive services to its employees, even though providing these services would conflict with the family's religious beliefs. The Court ruled that compelling the corporation to provide this care would be inconsistent with the Religious Freedom Restoration Act (RFRA). Part of the Court's reasoning was that business corporations should be treated as persons under RFRA: as the Court put it, "no conceivable definition of the term [persons] includes natural persons and nonprofit corporations, but not for-profit corporations" (*Hobby Lobby*, 25–6).

The *Hobby Lobby* ruling is controversial because it extends certain features of the legal status of natural persons to business corporations. "Metaphysical" or "pre-institutional" approaches to corporate agency have little to say about why decisions such as the *Hobby Lobby* ruling are problematic: after all, on these accounts, either the corporation is an agent and can claim the status granted to other agents, or it is not an agent and cannot claim this status. There is no in between. By contrast, pluralistic functionalism offers a much more nuanced account. The central question, on this view, is not *whether* the corporation is a collective agent, but *what form* of collective agency it possesses. The problem with the Court's reasoning in *Hobby Lobby* is that it does not pay enough attention to the differences between the statuses appropriate to different types of organizations given the roles that they play in distinct social practices.

The feature of the legal status of natural persons that is at issue here is protection for the freedom of religion. On our view, protection for the freedom of religion is justified mainly because of the role that it plays in the civil sphere. The civil sphere is the part of social life in which individuals develop their most fundamental ethical beliefs and commitments, partly through discussion and association with others, and in which people strive to live their lives consistently with their freely formed beliefs and commitments. To pursue these aims effectively, individuals need to have certain forms of protection against discrimination and persecution on the basis of their beliefs: without these protections, employers, retailers, and service providers could use their market power to limit the ability of individuals to form and pursue their ethical, moral, and religious convictions (see Hussain 2012).

The interest that individuals have in developing and pursuing their ethical commitments justifies granting special protections for the freedom of religion not only to individuals in the civil sphere, but also to certain nonprofit corporations, such as churches and mosques. This is because these nonprofit corporations serve as publicly recognized vehicles for people to pursue their ethical commitments in association with others. But the underlying interests of individuals do not justify extending these protections to business corporations as well, even to corporations that are closely held or organized by close-knit families.

A business corporation is not an association in the civil sphere, but rather an association in the competitive market. Business corporations are not like churches and mosques in that they are not publicly recognized vehicles for people to pursue their ethical commitments. Instead, these corporations are meant to serve a function in the competitive market, namely to help individuals to manage business risk and thereby to facilitate socially valuable forms of investment. It is hard to see how granting protections for religious expression to business corporations could be justified in terms of the function that these associations serve in the competitive market. More importantly, treating business corporations as if they were vehicles for people to pursue their ethical commitments would actually *interfere* with the economic purposes that the corporation is supposed to serve. If business corporations were civil associations, like churches and mosques, then employees and managers would have to assess whether they wanted to join in the corporation's religious or ethical project before accepting employment. (Similar considerations would apply to customers as well.) This would clearly interfere with market efficiency, while also depriving us of an important form of civil freedom (see Hussain 2013).

Turn now to *Citizens United*. In this case, the question before the Court was whether the state is constitutionally permitted to place legal limits on when and how corporations, whether for profit or not for profit, may use their general funds for independent political expression in a political campaign. Some background may help to understand the issues. The general funds of a business corporation (for example, Coca Cola) come from its business operations, while those of a nonprofit corporation (for example, the Boy Scouts) come from membership dues and charitable donations. One reason that the law places restrictions on the use of general funds for supporting political expression is that an individual citizen who buys a Coke or joins the Boy Scouts may not want to support the political agenda favored by the leadership of these corporations. In order to separate the economic activities of a business corporation and the civil activities of a nonprofit corporation from the various political activities that these corporations may engage in, the law allows for both types of corporations to establish Political Action Committees (PACs), which are independent organizations that can solicit donations from corporate shareholders, employees, and members for the purposes of supporting a political campaign. The existence of PACs allows members of a corporation to decide for themselves whether to support a political candidate favored by the corporation or not to do so.

Surprisingly, the Supreme Court ruled in *Citizens United* that the First Amendment does not allow the state to impose even modest limits on the corporation's use of its general funds for the purposes of pursuing independent political expression.[3] The central idea is that the freedom of expression as laid out in the First Amendment does not distinguish between the speech of individual citizens or the speech of corporations: the special restrictions on laws that limit expression apply without regard for nature of the speaker.

Pluralistic functionalism can shed light on what is troubling about the *Citizens United* decision. Much as in *Hobby Lobby*, we have a case here that involves the extension of certain aspects of the legal status of natural persons to corporations. And the problem with the Court's reasoning in this case is that it does not distinguish properly between the statuses appropriate to different organizations that are involved in distinct social practices.

The feature of the legal status of persons that is at issue in *Citizens United* is the set of constitutional protections for the freedom of expression. In American constitutional jurisprudence, these protections are justified in part on the basis of the role that the freedom of expression plays in the democratic process (see *New York Times v. Sullivan* (1964)). In order to facilitate open and knowledgeable political dialogue and thereby to hold government officials accountable, citizens who hold different political outlooks need special protections to ensure that they can freely express and elaborate their positions. This rationale clearly supports granting special protections for the freedom of expression of individuals, as well as to political parties and PACs that are expressly established for political purposes. But there is no similar justification for extending these protections to the freedom of expression of business corporations.

Business corporations are organizations that serve a function in the competitive market. Among other things, corporations allow individual market actors to manage their exposure to business risk, which in turn encourages efficient patterns of investment. The special economic function of business corporations is reflected in the fact that—at least in the case of publicly traded corporations—these organizations are imbedded in wider social practices, such as the stock market, which pressure them to act in ways that privilege the pursuit of profit over other objectives. The fact that business corporations are imbedded in these social practices makes it unreasonable to view these collective agents as vehicles of political expression, and moreover, it makes their participation in the democratic process harmful to the underlying ideal of citizens exercising control over the course of public life.

In his dissent in the *Citizens United* case, Justice Stevens makes a very similar point. As he says, "The conceit that corporations must be treated

---

[3] In *Citizens United*, the Court did not change its position that the government may permissibly restrict direct contributions from corporations to political campaigns. In *Buckley v. Valeo* (1976), the Court held that these restrictions are constitutionally permissible because the donor's speech interest is limited (i.e. contributions do not communicate any of the donors underlying reasons for supporting a candidate), while the state interest in avoiding corruption or the appearance of corruption is substantial.

identically to natural persons in the political sphere is not only inaccurate but also inadequate to justify the Court's disposition of this case" (*Citizens United*, Stevens, J., dissenting). He goes on to offer reasons that draw attention to the fact that electoral politics and the competitive market constitute two distinct social practices:

> In the context of election to public office, the distinction between corporate and human speakers is significant. Although they make enormous contributions to our society, corporations are not actually members of it. They cannot vote or run for office. Because they may be managed and controlled by nonresidents, their interests may conflict in fundamental respects with the interests of eligible voters. The financial resources, legal structure, and instrumental orientation of corporations raise legitimate concerns about their role in the electoral process. Our lawmakers have a compelling constitutional basis, if not also a democratic duty, to take measures designed to guard against the potentially deleterious effects of corporate spending in local and national races. (id.)

Justice Stevens is correct to point here to a serious tension between the role that business corporations are meant to play in the market and the role that political organizations are meant to play in the democratic process. Business corporations are neither citizens nor vehicles for the political expression of citizens, so they do not have any obvious claim to participating in the political process. Moreover, various facts about a business corporation's orientation towards profit—for example, the fact that it is often in the corporation's financial interest to distort the truth—make it the case that corporate participation does not serve the justifying aims of electoral democracy. Though it may be true that citizens associate in business and nonprofit corporations, it does not follow that these organizations must be given the same protections that we extend to political parties and to individual citizens. Whether an organization enjoys various features of the status that we accord to a natural person depends on how its having a status with these features would relate to the justifying aims of the relevant social practice.

CONCLUSION

This chapter has outlined an alternative to "metaphysical" or "pre-institutional" accounts of corporate agency. According to pluralistic functionalism, the justification for treating an organization as a responsible agent is not fundamentally tied to the internal structure of the organization, but rather to the aims and purposes of the wider social activity in which this form of collective agency plays a part. We treat basketball teams as collective agents in certain ways because this serves the justifying aims of basketball as a game. We treat political parties as collective agents in certain ways because this serves the justifying aims of electoral democracy.

With respect to the business corporation, the relevant social activity is the competitive market. Questions about when and how to treat the participants in a business corporation as a collective agent are best understood as questions about what forms of treatment would further the justifying aims of this practice. Some indicative answers are that it often makes sense to hold business corporations liable for the damage they cause to third parties, but it does not make sense to require consistency in their legal defenses across jurisdictions. Furthermore, we see little point in granting religious freedom and freedom of political expression to business corporations (assuming that they can form PACs) because the collective agency of business corporations is meant to serve the justifying aims of the competitive market. To treat business corporations as if they were civil associations—like churches and mosques, or political parties— would not serve the justifying aims of the competitive market, the justifying aims of the civil sphere, or the justifying aims of electoral democracy.

REFERENCES

Arrow, Kenneth J. (1970). *Social Choice and Individual Values*, 2nd ed.
Beitz, Charles R. (1989). *Political Equality*.
Bratman, Michael E. (2014). *Shared Agency: A Planning Theory of Acting Together*.
Buckley v. Valeo, 424 U.S. 1 (1976).
Burwell v. Hobby Lobby Stores, Inc., 134 S. Ct. 2751 (2014).
Chandler, Alfred D., Jr. (1977). *The Visible Hand: The Managerial Revolution in American Business*.
Citizens United v. Federal Election Commission, 558 U.S. 310 (2010).
Coase, Ronald (1988). "The Nature of the Firm." In R.H. Coase, *The Firm, the Market and the Law*.
Dahl, Robert A. (2006). *A Preface to Democratic Theory*, expanded ed.
Dworkin, Ronald (1986). *Law's Empire*.
Easterbrook, Frank H. and Daniel R. Fischel (1996). *The Economic Structure of Corporate Law*.
Feinberg, Joel (1970). *Doing and Deserving: Essays in the Theory of Responsibility*.
French, Peter A. (1984). *Collective and Corporate Responsibility*.
French, Peter A. and Howard K. Wettstein (2006). *Shared Intentions and Collective Responsibility*.
Hart, H.L.A. (1997). *The Concept of Law*, 2nd ed.
Hart, H.L.A. (1984). "Are There Any Natural Rights?" In *Theories of Rights*, ed. Jeremy Waldron.
Hart, Oliver (1993). *Firms, Contracts, and Financial Structure*.
Hasnas, John (2009). "The Centenary of a Mistake: One Hundred Years of Corporate Liability." *American Criminal Law Review* 46: 1329.

Hussain, Waheed (2012). "Is Ethical Consumerism an Impermissible Form of Vigilantism?" *Philosophy and Public Affairs* 40: 11.

Hussain, Waheed (2013). "Book Review of Christopher McMahon, *Public Capitalism: The Political Authority of Corporate Executives*." *Notre Dame Philosophical Reviews*. August 17. http://ndpr.nd.edu/news/41657-public-capitalism-the-political-authority-of-corporate-executives.

Jensen, Michael C. and William H. Meckling (1976). "Theory of the Firm: Managerial Behavior, Agency Costs and Ownership Structure." *Journal of Financial Economics* 3: 305.

List, Christian and Philip Pettit (2011). *Group Agency: The Possibility, Design, and Status of Corporate Agents*.

New York Times Co. v. Sullivan, 376 U.S. 254 (1964).

Olsaretti, Serena. (2004). *Liberty, Desert and the Market: A Philosophical Study*.

Orts, Eric W. (2015). *Business Persons: A Legal Theory of the Firm*, rev. paperback ed.

Rawls, John (1999). *A Theory of Justice*, rev. ed.

Rönnegard, David (2013). "How Autonomy Alone Debunks Corporate Moral Agency." *Business & Professional Ethics Journal* 32: 77.

Scanlon, T.M. (1998). *What We Owe to Each Other*.

Tuomela, Raimo (2013). *Social Ontology: Collective Intentionality and Group Agents*.

Williamson, Oliver E. (1998). *The Economic Institutions of Capitalism*.

Part II

Arguments against Moral Responsibility of Firms

5

The Phantom Menace of the Responsibility Deficit

*John Hasnas**

At least since the publication of Peter French's seminal work, *The Corporation as a Moral Person* (French 1979), academic debate has raged over whether it is appropriate to attribute moral responsibility to corporations as collective entities.[1]

Most theorists who consider the matter argue that corporations can bear moral responsibility (see, for example, De George 1981; Donaldson 1982; Goodpaster 1983; Manning 1984; Werhane 1985; Ozar 1985; Phillips 1992; Seabright and Kurke 1997; Moore 1999; Soares 2003; Pettit 2007; Dubbink and Smith 2011), but powerful arguments to the contrary have been produced by the minority who disagree (see, for example, May 1983; Velasquez 1983; Danley 1990; Velasquez 2003; Rönnegard 2013).

In my judgment, the strongest argument for the conclusion that corporations should be held morally responsible for their actions has been advanced by Philip Pettit (2007). Pettit provides a forceful and lucid two-step argument for this conclusion; arguing first that corporations are fit to be held morally

* The author wishes to extend his sincere thanks to Eric Orts and Craig Smith for inviting him to the conference on *The Moral Responsibility of Firms: For and Against?* at INSEAD at which this paper was originally presented and to Michael Bratman, Philip Pettit, and Kendy Hess for their helpful critical comments. The author also wishes to thank Ann C. Tunstall of SciLucent LLP for her comments on a draft of this article and Annette Hasnas of the New School of Northern Virginia and Ava Hasnas of the Oakwood School for providing first-hand experience regarding the injustice of collective punishment.

[1] For purposes of concision, I will employ the term "corporation" to refer not merely to businesses that have gone through the formal process of incorporation, but to business organizations generally, regardless of their legal form. With regard to the attribution of moral responsibility to collective entities, there is nothing special about corporations and no reason to distinguish them from partnerships or other forms of business organizations. I employ the term "corporation" in this generic sense purely for purposes of expressive convenience.

responsible, and second that, given this fitness, they should be. (See also his argument in Chapter 1 of this book.)

Virtually all discussion of Pettit's argument has concerned its first step. The debate has almost exclusively focused on whether corporations are the type of entities that can bear moral responsibility.[2] In this chapter, I propose to focus on the second step of the argument. I will assume that Pettit has established that corporations *can* be held morally responsible, and then ask whether they *should* be. I will argue that the answer to this question is a resounding "No." Given the criteria that Pettit himself supplies for making this decision, it would be inappropriate to ascribe moral responsibility to corporations.

PETTIT'S ARGUMENT

Pettit provides a clear and concise account of the argument for corporate moral responsibility in his article, *Responsibility Incorporated* (Pettit 2007). Using this as a source, I examine both steps in his argument.

Step 1: Corporations' Fitness To Be Held Morally Responsible

Pettit identifies three conditions that must be met for a person or entity to be a bearer of moral responsibility–conditions he calls value relevance, value judgment, and value sensitivity (Pettit 2007, 175). Value relevance requires that the person or entity be "an autonomous agent [that] faces a value-relevant choice involving the possibility of doing something good or bad or right or wrong" (id.). Value judgment requires that the person or entity have "the understanding and access to evidence required for being able to make judgments about the relative value of such options" (id.). Value sensitivity requires that the person or entity have "the control necessary for being able to choose between options on the basis of judgments about their value" (Pettit 2007, 175). For purposes of concision, Pettit's three conditions could be condensed into the statement that moral responsibility requires a person or entity to possess autonomy, judgment, and the capacity for self-control.

Pettit contends that corporations satisfy the value relevance condition because they can act autonomously. They can *act* because groups qualify as agents "when members act on the shared intention that together they should

---

[2] This is not unique to Pettit's argument. Virtually all debate over all arguments in support of corporate moral responsibility has been over whether corporations *can* bear moral responsibility. Little, if any, has concerned whether they *should*.

realize the conditions that ensure agency" (Pettit 2007, 179).[3] And they can act *autonomously* because the attitudes of corporations "cannot be a majoritarian or nonmajoritarian function of the corresponding attitudes among individuals, and, as follows under some plausible assumptions, . . . they cannot even be fixed by a mix of such functions" (id., 184). Thus, the autonomy of the corporation "is intuitively guaranteed by the fact that on one or more issues the judgment of the group will have to be functionally independent of the corresponding member judgments, so that its intentional attitudes as a whole are most saliently unified by being, precisely, the attitudes of the group" (id.).

Pettit further contends that corporations satisfy the value judgment condition because their internal structure specifies a deliberative decision-making procedure. "A group will form a judgment or other attitude over a certain proposition when the proposition is presented for consideration and the group takes whatever steps are prescribed in the constitution for endorsing it . . . " (Pettit 2007, 186). Thus, a corporation "will be able to form a judgment over any proposition that members are capable of presenting for consideration and of adjudicating by means of a vote or something of the kind" (id., 187).

Finally, Pettit contends that corporations can satisfy the value sensitivity condition—that corporations can exercise self-control as collective entities. He recognizes that to establish this, he must overcome the problem raised by the fact that "[w]hatever a group does is done by individual members on behalf of the group and is done intentionally by those individuals" (Pettit 2007, 188). This makes it appear that control of corporate actions lies not with the collective entity, but "entirely with . . . the members who act in its name [and] have exclusive control over what is done and exclusive responsibility for doing it" (id.). However, Pettit argues that corporate control is compatible with individual control in the sense that the corporate body controls the programming that produces the individually controlled actions that implement that programming. The corporation "can share in that control, so far as it relates as a programming factor to the implementing factor represented by the active individual" (id., 191). Thus, the corporation:

> may control in a reason-sensitive way for the performance of a certain action by some members . . . by maintaining a constitution for the formation and enactment of its attitudes, arranging things so that some individual or individuals are identified as the agents to perform a required task, and other individuals

---

[3] Pettit explains that groups act as an agent when the members "each intend that together they mimic the performance of a single unified agent" (Pettit 2007, 179). In such cases,

> [t]hey will each intend to do their bit in the pattern of coordination required for this performance. They will each be motivated to do this by the belief that others intend to do their bit too. And all of that will be above board, as a matter of shared awareness: each will believe that those conditions obtain, believe that each believes this, and so on. (id.)

are identified as agents to ensure that should the performers fail, there will be others to take their place as backups.   (id., 192)

Through this chain of reasoning, Pettit has constructed a strong argument for the conclusion that corporations can be the bearers of moral responsibility. Nevertheless, several serious objections to its basic premises have been raised. For example, Manuel Velasquez (2003) has argued forcefully that corporations can neither act nor have intentions, and David Rönnegard (2013) has produced an interesting analysis designed to show that they cannot possess autonomy. (See also Chapter 7 in this book co-authored by these scholars.) However, it is not my intention to attempt to resolve such matters here. For purposes of this chapter, I will assume that Pettit has established that it makes sense to ascribe moral responsibility to corporations. On that assumption, the question now becomes whether we should.

Step 2: The Point of Holding Corporations Morally Responsible

Having claimed to show that corporations can bear moral responsibility, Pettit realizes that his job is not done. As he explains:

> The argument so far shows that group agents can meet the three conditions for being thought and held responsible. But it is one thing to say that there is no bar to holding group agents responsible, given that they can satisfy the conditions reviewed. It is quite another thing to argue that there is a point to this exercise. Someone might maintain, after all, that so long as we hold members responsible for their individual contributions to the doings of a group agent, there will be no practical gain, and there may even be a disadvantage, in going on to hold the group as a whole responsible as well.   (Pettit 2007, 192–3)

To show that "there is a point to this exercise"—that we *should* assign moral responsibility to corporations—Pettit argues that doing so is necessary to avoid the "danger of a responsibility deficit."[4] He explains that:

> even when all the relevant enactors in a group action have been identified and held responsible, still it may be important to hold the group agent responsible as well. The reason for this, very simply, is that it is possible to have a situation in which there is ground for holding the group agent responsible, given that it satisfies the three conditions listed, but not the same ground for holding individual enactors responsible. The responsibility of enactors may leave a deficit in the accounting books, and the only possible way to guard against this may be to

---

[4] This phrase is taken from Pettit's remarks and their accompanying handout at the conference on *The Moral Responsibility of Firms: For or Against?* held at INSEAD on December 13, 2013. For the final version of these remarks see Chapter 1 in this book.

allow for the corporate responsibility of the group in the name of which they act.   (Pettit 2007, 194)

A responsibility deficit can arise whenever a corporation takes an action for which no set of individuals bear full responsibility. Thus:

> collections of agents may act in a way that predictably brings about bad results, without the members of the collection being individually or distributively culpable, or at least not in a serious measure. It may be that the individuals are ignorant, and blamelessly ignorant, of the harm that they together bring about. It may be that they each take themselves not to make a pivotal difference to a harm done, as with the firing squad in which members each treat the behavior of the others as fixed. It may be that they take themselves to make a difference, but not the right sort of difference, in particular not the sort that increases the harm; for example, each driver in a group of dangerously speeding cars may see that he or she dare not slow down, for fear of making a bad outcome worse. Or it may be that while each is aware of the harm done, and aware of making a difference, even the right sort of difference, still they each act under such felt pressure—perhaps pressure from one another—that they cannot be held fully responsible for the contribution they make to a bad outcome; they can each reasonably argue that the circumstances mitigate the degree of their personal responsibility.   (id., 195)

Pettit finds such responsibility deficits—such "[s]hortfalls of individual responsibility"—to have "a distressing aspect in the case of the *unincorporated* collection, since they mean that although the individuals do something bad together, there is no one to hold responsible" (id., 196) (emphasis added). He regards it as fortunate that this untoward result may be avoided in the case of corporations.

> But the failures of individual responsibility in the case of the *incorporated* group may leave us with someone to hold responsible: the group agent itself.... And the fact that enactor responsibility can fall short in the ways illustrated means that there may be very good reason to hold the group responsible in addition to holding the enactors responsible. (id.)   (emphasis added)

This is especially important because:

> the failure to impose a regime of corporate responsibility can expose individuals to a perverse incentive. Let human beings operate outside such a regime, and they will be able to incorporate, so as to achieve a certain bad and self-serving effect, while arranging things so that none of them can be held fully responsible for what is done.   (Pettit 2007, 196)

Pettit illustrates the danger of the responsibility deficit with the case of the *Herald of Free Enterprise*, a ferry that sank in the English Channel in 1987, drowning nearly 200 people. In that case, the company operating the ferry failed to exercise proper safety precautions and "was extremely sloppy, with poor routines of checking and management" (id., 171). Pettit complains that in that case "the courts did not penalize anyone in what might seem to be an appropriate measure" because they were unable "to identify individuals in the company or on the ship itself who were seriously enough at fault" (id.).

Thus, Pettit concludes that the ascription of moral responsibility to corporations is justified by the need to counteract the perverse ramifications of the responsibility deficits that would otherwise result.

> I conclude that not only is it going to be possible to hold group agents responsible, as their satisfaction of our three conditions ensures, it is also likely to be desirable. Let group agents be freed from the burden of being held responsible, and the door will open to abuses: there will be cases where no one is held responsible for actions that are manifestly matters of agential responsibility.   (id., 196–7)

THE PHANTOM MENACE

As much as I admire the quality of Pettit's reasoning, the second step of his argument does not establish its conclusion. Pettit himself recognizes that even under the assumption that "there is no bar to holding group agents responsible," it is possible that "there will be no practical gain, and there may even be a disadvantage" in doing so. This is precisely the case. As a practical matter, the responsibility deficit poses no danger that needs redressing—it produces no perverse incentives that are not already adequately addressed and does not open the door to the type of abuse that Pettit fears. Hence, there is no practical gain to be had from assigning moral responsibility to corporations. There is, however, an extremely serious *ethical* disadvantage to doing so because the consequences it entails are antithetical to the fundamental tenets of liberalism. Contrary to Pettit, I contend that the ascription of moral responsibility to corporations should be eschewed as an unnecessary, dangerous, and highly illiberal safeguard against a phantom menace.

A. No Practical Gain

Let us begin by examining why the responsibility deficit does not pose the danger that Pettit thinks it does. Keep in mind that the responsibility deficit is a deficit of *moral* responsibility. Hence, it can have no effect on any potential safeguard against corporate wrongdoing that does not require moral responsibility for its implementation.

Pettit's fear is that:

> the failure to impose a regime of corporate responsibility can expose individuals to a perverse incentive. Let human beings operate outside such a regime, and they

will be able to incorporate, so as to achieve a certain bad and self-serving effect, while arranging things so that none of them can be held fully responsible for what is done.... Let group agents be freed from the burden of being held responsible, and the door will open to abuses: there will be cases where no one is held responsible for actions that are manifestly matters of agential responsibility.

(Pettit 2007, 196–7)

This would certainly be a problem if the inability to assign *moral* responsibility to corporations precluded the assignment of *any kind of* responsibility to corporations. But this is patently not the case. Moral responsibility is not a prerequisite for the assignment of civil, administrative, or "metaphorical" responsibility.

Consider civil liability, which holds corporations responsible for providing financial restitution for harm that results from the wrongdoing of their employees. Restitution does not require the party making the payment to be morally responsible for the harm suffered by the recipient. One who finds a lost item or innocently receives stolen property is obligated to return it to its owner even though he or she is not responsible for the owner's loss. The Anglo-American system of civil liability requires parties that do not exercise the required level of "reasonable" care to pay compensation to those they have injured even though they have done the best that they personally can to avoid the harm and are not morally blameworthy. (See *Vaughan v. Menlove* (1837); Holmes 1881.) For harm caused by commercial products and by certain abnormally dangerous activities, compensation is required even though the manufacturer or individual actor is completely blameless. (See *Rylands v. Fletcher* (1865); American Law Institute 1977, §402A.) Employers are required to pay compensation for the harm done by their employees even though the employer had no part in causing the harm and was not at fault in hiring the employee. Indeed, the principle of vicarious liability (*respondeat superior*) guarantees that corporations will have to pay restitution for the wrongs done by their employees regardless of whether they are morally responsible entities (American Law Institute 2006, §2.04; Orts 2015, 139).

Further, corporate moral responsibility is not necessary for corporations to be liable for exemplary damages—payments beyond those necessary to compensate the injured party—in civil lawsuits. Although such damages are usually referred to as "punitive" damages, they are not punitive in the sense of requiring a finding of morally blameworthy conduct to be awarded. When applied to corporations, such damages are justified on the basis of their regulatory effect, and are awarded to create an incentive for corporations to undertake efforts to prevent their employees from engaging in recklessly dangerous behavior or acts of intentional wrongdoing (Keeton 1984, 13).

Next consider administrative responsibility. Corporate moral responsibility is not required for corporations to be subject to sanctions for violating administrative regulations.[5] Administrative regulations are imposed on individuals and businesses to cause them to behave in ways that the regulators believe to be conducive to the common good. To be effective—that is, to successfully regulate the market to achieve the desired social outcome—administrative regulations must apply to all market actors, not merely those that are capable of bearing moral blame. Thus, corporations will be restrained by administrative regulations whether they are morally responsible entities or not.

Finally, and perhaps most importantly, actual corporate moral responsibility is not required for corporations to be subject to what may be called metaphorical responsibility. Human beings (with the possible exception of those who would read a book like this one) routinely anthropomorphize corporations. The general public (including the media) continually speaks as though corporations were corporeal entities capable of acts of judgment and will in the same manner as ordinary human beings. As a result, whenever the employees of a corporation are negligent or otherwise engage in wrongdoing, the public excoriates the corporation *as though* it were the author of its employees' actions. Regardless of what philosophers think about whether corporations are morally responsibility entities, corporations are always subject to such metaphorical ascriptions of responsibility. But metaphorical corporate responsibility is just as damaging to a corporation's reputation and just as destructive to its financial bottom line as actual moral responsibility would be. Thus, market forces provide a strong financial incentive for corporations to do all that they can to curtail wrongdoing by their employees—one that cannot be enhanced by conjoining the actual ascription moral responsibility to the metaphorical one.

Given that corporations are subject to civil, administrative, and metaphorical responsibility with their corresponding threats of damage payments, administrative fines, and market sanctions, it is difficult to see how a deficit of *moral* responsibility will enable individuals "to incorporate, so as to achieve a certain bad and self-serving effect, while arranging things so that none of them can be held fully responsible for what is done" or that "there will be cases where no one is held responsible for actions that are manifestly matters of agential responsibility" (Pettit 2007, 196–7). Especially in the contemporary legal environment in which there is an insistent call for tort reform—in which the civil liability system is under attack for placing unreasonable demands on corporations to behave responsibly—a concern that the absence of corporate moral responsibility will produce irresponsible behavior seems out of place.

Indeed, Pettit's own chosen example of the *Herald of Free Enterprise* belies his point. This was not a case in which the responsibility deficit allowed a corporation to escape deserved liability. Pettit's characterization of the case as

---

[5] This is evidenced by the fact that administrative violations are typically strict liability offenses that require no consciousness of wrongdoing.

one in which "the courts did not penalize anyone in what might seem to be an appropriate measure, failing to identify individuals in the company or on the ship itself who were seriously enough at fault" is, at best, somewhat misleading. Both the negligent employees and the company that operated the ferry, P&O European Ferries (Dover) Ltd. (P&O), were subject to *civil* liability for the wrongful death of the passengers. Furthermore, P&O was liable to criminal punishment for any and all crimes committed by its employees. The only controversial aspect of the case was whether P&O could be convicted of manslaughter even though none of its employees had the mental state necessary for such an offense (Colvin 1995).[6]

At the time, British criminal law attributed the crimes of a corporation's employees to the corporation, but lacked the "collective knowledge doctrine" that is an element of United States federal criminal law and allows the facts known to individual employees to be aggregated into the knowledge of the corporation. As a result, the manslaughter prosecution against P&O was dismissed (Pieth and Ivory 2011). This feature of British law was subsequently changed by the Corporate Manslaughter and Homicide Act (2007), which greatly expanded the basis for corporate criminal liability (Beale 2009, 1495–6).

This is all beside the point, however. The inability to convict P&O of manslaughter was due to the UK's legal definition of corporate *mens rea*, not to any deficit in moral responsibility. Further, even if P&O had been subject to criminal conviction for manslaughter, its punishment, which in the case of corporations necessarily consists in a financial penalty, would have been an order of magnitude lower than the expected civil damages. It is unreasonable to believe that the absence of a relatively small criminal fine in the presence of a massively large civil damage award constitutes a situation in which the corporation is "freed from the burden of being held responsible" such that "no one is held responsible for actions that are manifestly matters of agential responsibility."

In sum, given the existence of several overlapping and effective mechanisms for ensuring that corporations are held responsible for any and all wrongdoing on the part of their employees, it is unreasonable to believe that a deficit in *moral* responsibility can have a pernicious impact on corporate behavior. Hence, there is no *practical* gain to be derived from attributing moral responsibility to corporations.

B. The Disadvantage

Corporate moral responsibility is not necessary for us to hold corporations civilly, administratively, or metaphorically responsible for the actions of their

---

[6] I cite this source because it is the source cited by Pettit as the basis for his assertion.

employees. What, then, would be the effect of remedying the responsibility deficit? What would change in the world if we decide to treat corporations as morally blameworthy entities?

I contend that only one thing would change. It would be proper to subject corporations to criminal punishment.[7]

Moral responsibility is a prerequisite for blame.[8] Blameworthy action is action that merits punishment. The point of asking whether a person or entity is morally responsible is usually to determine whether that person or entity is liable to punishment. Indeed, the reason why the corporate moral responsibility debate is such a lively one is that most of the advocates of corporate moral responsibility believe that it is important to be able to impose punishment on corporations as collective entities, and they recognize that moral responsibility is necessary for such punishment.

Punishment is the infliction of a harm or penalty on a party in response to a transgression. In most circumstances, inflicting harm on others is a wrong. When punishment is involved, this is not the case. Punishment implies that the infliction of harm is justified, and hence not wrongful. The thing that justifies the punishment is the claim that the party being punished is a morally responsible agent who has engaged in proscribed conduct. Punishment is not designed to compensate injured parties or facilitate the achievement of some social good. It is designed to balance the moral account books.

Criminal punishment consists of the imposition of a penalty prescribed by law for the commission of a criminal offense. A just legal system imposes criminal sanctions only on morally responsible agents. Therefore, moral responsibility is (or should be) a prerequisite for criminal punishment. If corporations are morally responsible agents, then they are properly eligible for criminal punishment; if they are not, then, in justice, they should not be.

Pettit himself explicitly recognizes that corporate moral responsibility is a necessary condition for the application of the criminal sanction to corporations as collective entities, stating:

> I argue that corporate bodies are fit to be held responsible in the same way as individual agents and this entails that it may therefore be appropriate to make them criminally liable for some things done in their name; they may display a guilty mind, a *mens rea*, as in intentional malice, malice with foresight, negligence, or recklessness.   (Pettit 2007, 176)

---

[7] Corporations are, as a matter of fact, subject to criminal punishment at present. This fact does not imply that it is proper to subject corporations to criminal punishment any more than the fact that Jim Crow laws mandated the segregation of African-Americans implied that it was proper to segregate African-Americans.

[8] It is, of course, also a prerequisite for praise, but that is not relevant in the present context, and so will be ignored.

This helps explain his selection of the *Herald of Free Enterprise* case as an illustrative example because the only conceivable responsibility deficit in that case was the court's dismissal of the criminal manslaughter charge against P&O on the ground that British criminal law did not recognize the existence of an independent corporate *mens rea*. Indeed, Pettit's selection of this case suggests that he, like most other commentators, sees the main point of assigning moral responsibility to corporations to be to ensure that corporations are subject to criminal punishment as collective entities.

But here we confront the disadvantage of assigning moral responsibility to corporations. For to the extent that doing so renders corporations liable to criminal punishment as collective entities, it contravenes the most fundamental principles of a liberal society.

To see why, consider what it means to punish a corporation. A corporation is not a thing that can experience harm or pain in itself. Rather, it is a complex network of constantly changing human beings who are related to each other through certain formal and informal arrangements. The difficulty in attempting to punish a corporation is that there is no definite object present to absorb the punishment. Any punishment directed toward a corporation necessarily passes through its nominal facade to fall on some set of human beings.

As mentioned above, any criminal punishment directed toward a corporation is necessarily financial in nature. Corporations cannot be incarcerated. They may be fined, which constitutes the direct application of a financial penalty. They may have licenses revoked or otherwise have their freedom to transact business restricted, but such measures merely constitute the indirect application of a financial penalty—they are punitive only to the extent that they reduce the corporation's profitability. They may be liquidated, which can be thought of as a corporate death sentence. But since corporations are not literally living things, any "execution" is entirely metaphorical. Liquidation is to be feared only because of the financial losses individuals suffer as a result of it.

Who pays when any such punitive financial loss is imposed upon a corporation? To the extent that the loss can be passed along through increases in the price of the corporation's products, it is the consumers who pay. To the extent that the corporation can assimilate the loss by reducing labor costs, it is the employees who pay. And to the extent that the corporation is unable to pass along the loss to either of these groups, it is the owners of the corporation, the shareholders, who pay.

The characteristic that all of these stakeholder groups share is that their members are usually innocent of personal wrongdoing. Consumers obviously play no role in any wrongdoing by corporate agents. The employees who lose their jobs due to corporate retrenchment may have had nothing whatever to do with the wrongdoing and been completely unaware of it. And given that the defining characteristic of the modern corporation is the separation of ownership and control, the shareholders had no knowledge of or control over the behavior of the employees who engaged in the wrongdoing. Corporate punishment necessarily falls indiscriminately on the innocent as well as or, more frequently, in place of the guilty. Corporate punishment is inherently vicarious collective punishment.

It should be clear that such punishment is inherently unjust. As noted above, the thing that distinguishes punishment from the naked infliction of harm is that punishment is deserved. Punishment is punishment only when it is imposed in response to some transgression on the part of the party being subjected to it. Unless this is the case, "punishment" is nothing more than coercion. That is why, on the international level, collective punishment is considered a human rights violation (see, for example, American Convention on Human Rights (1969), Art. 5(3); African Charter on Human and Peoples' Rights (1981), Art. 7) and is banned as a war crime by the Geneva Convention (Geneva Convention IV Relative to the Protection of Civilian Persons in Time of War (1949), Art. 33(1)). Although the wrong of imposing financial collective punishment on a corporation's stakeholders may be an order of magnitude less severe than that of the war crimes addressed by the Geneva Convention, it is not distinguishable from it in principle.

Consider that a handful of the employees at Arthur Andersen engaged in conduct that the United States government believed to constitute obstruction of justice. Each of these employees was subject to indictment, conviction, and punishment for the offense as individuals. The government nevertheless chose to indict the firm as a collective entity. The result was the collapse of the company, which cost 85,000 employees in 390 offices around the world their jobs (Ainslie 2006, 107). Virtually all of these employees were personally innocent of wrongdoing. It is difficult to see how assigning punishment to corporations can be ethically justified if the practical consequence of doing so is that secretaries in France get fired for the conduct of executives in Texas.

Advocates of corporate moral responsibility often attempt to justify punishing corporations as collective entities on grounds of deterrence. They argue that the ability to impose criminal punishment on corporations can motivate managers to institute compliance programs and make efforts to maintain a good corporate ethos that can reduce wrongdoing by employees. But it is far from clear that this is correct. Given the existence of potentially massive civil damages, administrative fines, and loss of public good will that corporations suffer as a result of wrongdoing by their employees, it is difficult to see how the threat of additional, comparatively small criminal penalties would add any noticeable deterrent effect. But even under the assumption that it would—even under the assumption that there are circumstances in which the desire to avoid the stigma associated with a criminal conviction is a stronger motivation than the desire to avoid economic loss—deterrence cannot justify collective punishment.

This is because the objection to collective punishment has nothing to do with its effectiveness. Indeed, the threat of collective punishment usually *is* an effective way to motivate people to suppress undesirable conduct by others. That is almost always its purpose. The problem with collective punishment is not that it is ineffective. It's that it is unjust.

Deterrence can, of course, be a legitimate purpose of punishment. There is nothing ethically objectionable about imposing punishment on a *wrongdoer* to discourage others from behaving in a similar way. By associating punishment with transgression, we hope to cause others to refrain from transgressing for fear of a similar sanction. But this form of deterrence is distinct in kind from the form that consists of threatening to punish those who are innocent of wrongdoing to pressure them into suppressing the undesirable conduct of their fellow citizens.

The world would be a better place if we could more effectively deter crimes committed by teenagers. And we undoubtedly could do so by threatening to punish the teenagers' parents for their children's offenses. We do not do so because we recognize that such punishment is no different in principle from the more venal and obviously unacceptable practice of the Nazis who sought to deter acts of resistance by punishing innocent members of the communities in which such acts occurred. Threatening the innocent stakeholders of a corporation with punishment for the wrongdoing of culpable employees in order to force corporate managers to engage in more intensive self-policing is not ethically distinct from threatening to punish the innocent members of a family or a community for the wrongdoing of their relatives or fellow community members.

Note that the punishment that falls on the innocent stakeholders as a result of punishing the corporation is not some unfortunate side effect, but the very point of the exercise. The situation we are considering is not analogous to one in which a parent's conviction of a crime imposes financial and emotional hardships on his or her innocent children. Children suffer harm when their parents are punished. But such harm is incidental to the punishment of the parent, and is regarded as a regrettable byproduct that should be minimized as much as possible. In contrast, when a corporation is punished, the harm falls on innocent stakeholders as principals, not as third parties. They are the first to feel the effects of the punishment, not the dependents of others who are being properly punished for wrongdoing. Further, this is the intended, not a regretted, result. Inflicting punishment on the corporation's stakeholders is the whole point of punishing the corporation. The purpose of threatening such punishment is to motivate the corporation to engage in greater efforts at self-policing. No effort will be made to minimize the harm suffered by the innocent corporate stakeholders because doing so would defeat the purpose of imposing the punishment in the first place.

The "disadvantage" of attributing moral responsibility to corporations is that, to the extent that it authorizes the punishment of corporations, it authorizes vicarious collective punishment. But collective punishment is inherently unjust. And such punishment cannot be redeemed by arguing that it has deterrent value. For collective punishment involves punishing the innocent to attain a desired societal end, and as such is incompatible with the Kantian insight that lies at the heart of any liberal society, namely, that individuals may not be used merely as means to the ends of others or of society as a whole.

I submit that introducing such an illiberal protection against the non-existent danger of the responsibility deficit is no small disadvantage. Rather, it is an overwhelmingly strong reason for concluding that even if there is no logical inconsistency in attributing moral responsibility to corporations, we should not do so.

C. An Important Caveat

My argument against attributing moral responsibility to corporations rests on the inherent injustice of collective punishment. But it is worth noting that although the existence of corporate moral responsibility authorizes the punishment of corporations, it does not mandate it. It is perfectly consistent to argue both that the attribution of moral responsibility to corporations is important because it authorizes the moral condemnation of corporations as collective entities and that corporations should nevertheless not be subject to punishment. Blameworthiness does not entail liability to punishment, and it makes perfect sense to say that although corporations have acted in a blameworthy manner, they should not be punished for it. Thus, if there were some way of ensuring that the attribution of moral responsibility to corporations would not lead to corporate punishment, corporate moral responsibility would be ethically unobjectionable.

Note, however, that even if this were the case, corporate moral responsibility would still carry no *practical* significance. As noted above, corporations are always subject to metaphorical responsibility—they will be treated by the public as though they are morally responsible entities whether they are or not. If the first step in Pettit's argument establishes its conclusion, it would provide a reasoned grounding for this common practice. But it would not enhance or augment the practice itself. In the current cultural milieu, corporations will be subject to moral censure as collective entities regardless of the state of academic debate over corporate moral responsibility.

Of course, there is no way of ensuring that the attribution of moral responsibility to corporations will not lead to corporate punishment. The point of Pettit's selection of the *Herald of Free Enterprise* as his illustrative case was to argue for an expanded definition of corporate criminal liability. The number of theorists who argue for corporate moral responsibility in order to be able to blame *but not punish* corporations must be vanishingly small.[9] Although it is not logically necessary, in the contemporary environment, blaming corporations for the actions of their employees inevitably leads to calls to inflict punishment on them. Sufficient evidence for this assertion can be supplied simply by pointing at BP (an example used in Peter French's contribution in Chapter 3). If we are to avoid the illiberal consequences that can arise from attributing moral responsibility to corporations, prudence cautions us to refrain from attempts to draw subtle distinctions between blameworthiness and punishability, and eschew corporate moral responsibility entirely.

CONCLUSION

In the much derided first episode of the Star Wars saga, *The Phantom Menace*, the freedom of the Galactic Republic is lost when its representatives are persuaded to adopt illiberal measures due to their fear of a non-existent threat. This is an apt analogy for the situation in which we contemplate attributing moral responsibility to corporations. The responsibility deficit we fear is a non-existent threat—a phantom menace. Yet to protect ourselves against it, we contemplate authorizing a form of collective punishment that targets the innocent as a means of expressing our outrage over the actions of the guilty. But collective punishment—imposing punishment on a group for the wrong-doing of one or more of its members—is antithetical to the respect for the individual that lies at the heart of a liberal society.

The question addressed by the first step in Pettit's argument—the question of whether corporations are the type of thing that can bear moral responsibility—is the subject of a contentious and ongoing debate among philosophers. However, we need not await a definitive resolution of that debate to know the answer to the question addressed by the second step in Pettit's argument—the question of whether we should attribute moral responsibility to corporations. Because doing so provides no practical benefit while furnishing a ground for punishing the innocent, the answer is a resounding "No."

---

[9] Small, but not zero, because Michael Bratman indicated his willingness to adopt this position at the conference at which the paper for this chapter was originally presented. For the final version Bratman's contribution, see Chapter 2 of this book.

REFERENCES

African Charter on Human and Peoples' Rights (1981). OAU Doc. CAB/LEG/67/3 Rev. 5.

Ainslie, Elizabeth K. (2006). "Indicting Corporations Revisited: Lessons of the Arthur Anderson Prosecution." *American Criminal Law Review* 43: 107.

American Convention on Human Rights (1969). 1144 UNTS 123.

American Law Institute (1977). *Restatement (Second) of Torts.*

American Law Institute (2006). *Restatement (Third) of Agency.*

Beale, Sara Sun (2009). "A Response to the Critics of Corporate Criminal Liability." *American Criminal Law Review* 46: 1481.

Colvin, Eric (1995). "Corporate Personality and Criminal Liability." *Criminal Law Forum* 6: 1.

Corporate Manslaughter and Homicide Act (2007). http://www.legislation.gov.uk/ukpga/2007/19/contents.

Danley, John (1990). "Corporate Moral Agency: The Case for Anthropological Bigotry." In *Business Ethics*, ed. W. Michael Hoffman and Jennifer Mills Moore, 2nd ed.

De George, Richard T. (1981). "Can Corporations Have Moral Responsibilities?" *University of Dayton Review* 5: 3.

Donaldson, Thomas (1982). *Corporations and Morality.*

Dubbink, Wim and Jeffrey Smith (2011). "A Political Account of Corporate Moral Responsibility." *Ethical Theory and Moral Practice* 14: 223.

French, Peter A. (1979). "The Corporation as a Moral Person." *American Philosophical Quarterly* 16: 207.

Geneva Convention IV Relative to the Protection of Civilian Persons in Time of War. (1949). http://www.encyclopedia.com/article-1G2-3434600393/geneva-convention-iv-civilian.html.

Goodpaster, Kenneth (1983). "The Concept of Corporate Responsibility." *Journal of Business Ethics* 2: 1.

Holmes, Oliver Wendall (1881). *The Common Law.*

Keeton, W. Page et al. (1984). *Prosser and Keeton on Torts*, 5th ed.

Manning, Rita C. (1984). "Corporate Responsibility and Corporate Personhood." *Journal of Business Ethics* 3: 77.

May, Larry (1983). "Vicarious Agency and Corporate Responsibility." *Philosophical Studies* 43: 69.

Moore, Geoff (1999). "Corporate Moral Agency: Review and Implications." *Journal of Business Ethics* 21: 329.

Orts, Eric W. (2015). *Business Persons: A Legal Theory of the Firm*, rev. paperback ed.

Ozar, David T. (1985). "Do Corporations Have Moral Rights?" *Journal of Business Ethics* 4: 277.

Pettit, Phillip (2007). "Responsibility Incorporated." *Ethics* 117: 171.

Phillips, Michael J. (1992). "Corporate Moral Personhood and Three Conceptions of the Corporation." *Business Ethics Quarterly* 2: 435.

Pieth, Mark and Rhadha Ivory (2011). "Emergence and Convergence: Corporate Criminal Liability Principles in Overview." In *Corporate Criminal Liability: Emergence, Convergence, and Risk*, ed. Mark Pieth and Rhadha Ivory.

Rönnegard, David (2013). "How Autonomy Alone Debunks Moral Agency." *Business and Professional Ethics Journal* 32: 77.

Rylands v. Fletcher, 159 Eng. Rep. 737 (1865).

Seabright, Mark A. and Lance B. Kurke (1997). "Organizational Ontology and the Moral Status of the Corporation." *Business Ethics Quarterly* 7: 91.

Soares, Conceição (2003). "Corporate Versus Individual Moral Responsibility." *Journal of Business Ethics* 46: 143.

Vaughan v. Menlove, 132 Eng. Rep. 490 (1837).

Velasquez, Manuel G. (1983). "Why Corporations Are Not Morally Responsible for Anything They Do." *Business and Professional Ethics Journal* 2: 1.

Velasquez, Manuel G. (2003). "Debunking Corporate Moral Responsibility." *Business Ethics Quarterly* 13: 531.

Werhane, Patricia H. (1985). *Persons, Rights, and Corporations*.

6

How Insiders Abuse the Idea of Corporate Personality

Ian Maitland

"The price of metaphor is eternal vigilance"—Arturo Rosenblueth and Norbert Wiener

Lewontin 2001

It is a truism that any act performed by a corporation is really an act performed by one of its managers or employees on its behalf. Nevertheless in our everyday speech we regularly attribute responsibility for those acts to the corporation itself. This practice may be unavoidable. As F. W. Maitland noted in 1900, calling a particular type of contractual relationship a "corporation" is "a mere labour-saving device like stenography or the mathematician's symbols" (Hessen 1979, 42). But despite sound practical reasons for our linguistic and legal conventions, we should not blind ourselves to their dangers, some of which I propose to explore here. I examine three cases where I believe the anthropomorphization of the corporation has become a source of mischief, manipulation, or abuse.

I am not the first person to make this argument about the dangers of treating the corporation as a moral agent. The issue is part of an ongoing debate among business ethicists about corporate moral agency. Manny Velasquez's (2003; see also 1983) warning deserves special mention because of the great care and lucidity with which he debunked the idea that corporations can be morally responsible for their acts and his vivid account of wrongdoing at Santa Clara-based National Semiconductor.

As Velasquez relates, National Semiconductor designed and manufactured computer chips. In 1984, the US Department of Defense charged that, over three years, the company had sold it some 26 million computer chips that had not been properly tested and had then falsified records to cover up the fraud. These potentially defective chips had been placed in aircraft guidance systems, nuclear weapons systems, guided missiles, and other critical systems. Potentially, more than one hundred employees participated in the cover-up. National

Semiconductor agreed to pay $1.75 million in penalties, but it refused to turn over the names of any of the individuals who had carried out the illegal actions.

In defense of this settlement, the company's CEO, Charles Sporck, resorted to the argument that I criticize here. He stated that the responsibility for the wrongful actions belonged to the company, not to any individual executives or other employees: "We have repeatedly said that we accept responsibility as a company and we steadfastly continue to stand by that statement." A spokesman for the company said: "We will see [that company employees] are not harmed. We feel it's a company responsibility, [and this is] a matter of ethics" (Velasquez 2003, 534–5). This chapter shows that, despite its veneer of academic respectability, this argument is nothing more than a subterfuge to protect the guilty from the legal consequences of their actions.

Corporations are complex structures. It is hard to determine which managers or employees bear the actual responsibility for an act of the corporation. It is also hard to predict how different constituents of the firm will be impacted by regulatory or legal actions against the firm. And it is hard for an outsider to discern the actual relationships, rights, and duties of the parties or constituencies that make up the corporation. The practice of attributing moral or legal agency to the corporation has the great virtue of simplifying discourse about the corporation. But like all simplification, it distorts the truth. It makes the actual workings of the corporation more opaque. Worse, it creates complacency about our understanding of what is going on in the black box of the corporation and where moral and legal responsibility actually lies. As a result, as has been said about the London *Times*, the rarefied jurisprudence of the corporation or esoteric discourse about corporate ontology are an example of the upper classes talking to one another without being overheard. The resulting confusion creates temptations for insiders to exploit outsiders. The idea of corporate agency or responsibility, in skillful hands, can be used to deepen this confusion for profit or other advantage.

In this chapter, I examine three ways in which the idea of corporate responsibility has been exploited for this purpose. First, I illustrate how it has been used to shield the people responsible for acts from the legal consequences of those acts. Second, I describe how it has been used to try to disguise the abridgment of constitutional rights. And, finally, I show how it can be used to dispossess or expropriate the shareholders of corporations.

HOW CORPORATE LEGAL RESPONSIBILITY CREATES A RESPONSIBILITY DEFICIT

In the United States, for over a century, corporations have been subject to criminal as well as civil liability for the wrongful actions of natural persons they employ. In a recent study of prosecutions of corporations, Brandon

Garrett (2014) notes that "few foreign countries have anything like the broad standard for corporate criminal liability that the United States has long had in federal courts." Corporate criminal liability is thus a form of American Exceptionalism. Most countries in Europe and the world lack corporate criminal liability and have only recently enacted a handful of specific corporate crime statutes. Foreign countries impose civil regulatory fines and individuals may be prosecuted, but firms rarely face prosecution (Garrett 2011, 1777–8).

Another case of American Exceptionalism is the discretion enjoyed by federal prosecutors. They "possess extraordinarily wide discretion as compared to their counterparts around the globe" (id., 1778).

Many business ethicists applaud the trend for corporations (qua corporations) to be held criminally liable for the actions of their employees as well as vicariously responsible for their employees' acts in non-criminal cases. They are also attracted to the related idea of corporate moral agency and responsibility, though perhaps mostly for pragmatic reasons. Sometimes, because of the complexity of the corporation, it is difficult to pin down who in the corporation actually made and/or carried out illegal and unethical decisions. Therefore, to use Patricia Werhane's phrase, the corporation may be let off the "moral hook" (Werhane 1989, 821). Part of the appeal of the idea that a corporation, as distinct from its managers and employees, can be morally responsible arises from a perceived *responsibility deficit* when no responsibility can be assigned to individual members of the corporation (Rönnegard 2013, 95).

The US practice of holding corporations criminally and civilly liable for wrongdoings of their managers or employees provides a natural experiment for assessing whether corporate responsibility cures—or aggravates—this responsibility deficit. In this section, I argue that this innovation, corporate criminal and civil liability, rather than achieving its goal of holding corporate officials accountable for their misdeeds by giving prosecutors more weapons or tools for law enforcement, has had the perverse result of making corporate officials less accountable. The prosecution of the corporation has become an alternative to the prosecution of individual wrongdoers rather than a means of strengthening or supplementing it. Effectively, the practice of holding corporations liable for the wrongdoing of their executives has created a scapegoat which diverts legal responsibility from the executives, managers, and employees who have committed wrongful acts. We have fallen into the trap that Velasquez (2003, 15) warned of: "[I]f we accept the view that moral responsibility.... rests with the corporation, we will be satisfied with blaming and punishing only the corporate entity."

Over the past two decades or longer, there has been a shift in the focus of US Department of Justice and the Securities and Exchange Commission (SEC) away from prosecuting managers to prosecuting companies and other institutions.[1] As US District Judge Jed S. Rakoff (2014) says, "It is true that prosecutors have brought criminal charges against companies for well over a hundred years, but until relatively recently, such prosecutions were the exception, and prosecutions of companies without simultaneous prosecutions of their managerial agents were even rarer." He told the *Wall Street Journal* that when he was a prosecutor in the 1970s companies were almost never charged (Rothfeld 2014). "It was considered a failure if you thought a crime was committed not to be able to prove it against the individual." He said the deterrence of crime achieved by charging companies "doesn't remotely compare" with "putting people in jail."

This trend to prosecuting companies passed largely unremarked until September 2009, when the same Judge Rakoff created a sensation by refusing to rubber stamp a settlement reached between the SEC and Bank of America. The SEC had charged Bank of America with defrauding its shareholders. According to the SEC, when Bank of America took over Merrill Lynch and Washington Mutual, its proxy statement said that it would bar Merrill from paying discretionary year-end bonuses. Nonetheless, in violation of this promise, Bank of America permitted Merrill to pay up to $5.8 billion in bonuses. After negotiations, the SEC announced a settlement with Bank of America under which Bank of America paid a $33 million civil penalty, and no officer or employee paid anything or was otherwise disciplined (Coffee 2009).

In a stinging rebuke to the SEC, Judge Rakoff rejected the settlement and sent it back to be amended. He declared that he could not certify that the settlement was fair and reasonable or in the public interest. He said the parties' submissions to the Court "leave the distinct impression that the proposed [settlement agreement] was a contrivance designed to provide the SEC with the facade of enforcement and the management of the Bank with a quick resolution of an embarrassing inquiry—all at the expense of the sole alleged victims, the shareholders" (*Securities Exchange Commission v. Bank of America Corp.* (2009), 510).

It is worth reviewing Rakoff's objections to the practice of bringing actions solely against the corporation. He was particularly scathing in his comments on the settlement's treatment of shareholders who, after all, were the supposed victims of Bank of America's behavior. The settlement, he declared, was effectively a "proposal to have the victims of the violation pay an additional penalty for their own victimization" (id., 508). He said that the settlement was "not fair, first and foremost, because it does not comport with the most

---

[1] "Between 2001 and 2012, no individuals were charged in 65% of 255 cases in which the Justice Department reached deferred-prosecution agreements or nonprosecution agreements, which allow firms to avoid criminal convictions.... At the same time, no employees were charged in 75% of 125 cases in which public companies were charged and convicted or reached plea agreements over that period...." (Rothfeld 2014, citing Garrett 2014).

elementary notions of justice and morality, in that it proposes that the shareholders who were the victims of the Bank's alleged misconduct now pay the penalty for that misconduct. The SEC admits that the corporate penalties it here proposes will be 'indirectly borne by [the] shareholders....." (id., 509).

The agency defended the settlement against the charge that it was unfair to shareholders. This was justified, the SEC said, because "[a] corporate penalty.... sends a strong signal to shareholders that unsatisfactory corporate conduct has occurred and allows shareholders to better assess the quality and performance of management" (id., 508, quoting SEC). Rakoff subjected this defense of the settlement to withering scorn: The "notion that Bank of America shareholders, having been lied to blatantly in connection with the multi-billion-dollar purchase of a huge, nearly-bankrupt company, need to lose another $33 million of their money in order to 'better assess the quality and performance of management' is absurd," he said (id.).

Rakoff also criticized the SEC's decision not to prosecute the individual managers and executives who made the decisions in question. He noted that the settlement "would effectively close the case without the SEC adequately accounting for why, in contravention of its own policy.... it did not pursue charges against either Bank management or the lawyers who allegedly were responsible for the false and misleading proxy statements." Rakoff questioned the propriety of allowing "the very management that is accused of having lied to its shareholders to determine how much of those victims' money should be used to make the case against the management go away" (id., 510). He complained that, under the settlement, "the parties were proposing that the management of Bank of America—having allegedly hidden from the Bank's shareholders that as much as $5.8 billion of their money would be given as bonuses to the executives of Merrill who had run that company nearly into bankruptcy—would now settle the legal consequences of their lying by paying the SEC $33 million more of their shareholders' money" (id., 508).

Another critic of the settlement, Professor John Coffee (2009), was even blunter. He labeled the whole process a "de facto sale of indulgences" and said SEC enforcement practices "invite corporate executives to purchase immunity for themselves with their shareholders' money."

Rakoff's peroration in another similar case deserves to be quoted in full:

> Finally, in any case like this that touches on the transparency of financial markets whose gyrations have so depressed our economy and debilitated our lives, there is an overriding public interest in knowing the truth. In much of the world, propaganda reigns, and truth is confined to secretive, fearful whispers. Even in our nation, apologists for suppressing or obscuring the truth may always be found. But the SEC, of all agencies, has a duty, inherent in its statutory mission, to see that the truth emerges; and if fails to do so, this Court must not, in the name

of deference or convenience, grant judicial enforcement to the agency's contrivances. (*Securities and Exchange Commission v. Citigroup Global Markets Inc.* (2011), 335)[2]

The key takeaway from these cases is captured by Rakoff's words—"facade of enforcement," "contrivances," and "propaganda"—all versus the *truth*. The SEC pretended to prosecute the malefactors, and the malefactors pretended to pay a penalty.[3] The whole transaction reeked of a fraud using the judicial system as a proxy. This fraud was possible only because of public confusion about who would actually bear the cost of the penalty.

It is true that the SEC was understaffed. It had a vast caseload. An angry public was baying for bankers' blood. The agency knew that lawsuits against individuals would be hard-fought and would tie up resources. If the SEC were to just pursue cases against individuals, according to one of its former chairmen, Harvey Pitt, "they will be getting far less settlements, which means they will have to litigate more cases, which means they will bring less cases" (Sorkin 2010; see also Rakoff 2015). It is easy to sympathize with the SEC, but impossible to excuse its behavior. The SEC chose to provide the pretense of enforcement rather than the real thing.

Of course, the fact that the SEC and the Bank of America were play-acting didn't mean that no one was harmed. As Rakoff (2014) pointed out, "from a moral standpoint, punishing a company and its many innocent employees and shareholders for the crimes committed by some unprosecuted individuals seems contrary to elementary notions of moral responsibility." This is an open secret. Thirty-five years earlier, Professor Coffee (1981, 406) had pointed out that: "Axiomatically, when corporations do not bear the ultimate cost of the fine; put simply, when the corporation catches cold, someone else sneezes." "Only the most obtuse judge can fail to understand that such penalties will

---

[2] In this case, decided in 2011, Judge Rakoff rejected a similar settlement, or "contrivance," as he called it. The SEC had proposed a $75 million settlement with Citigroup for failing to inform its shareholders of more than $40 billion of subprime mortgage investments. This time, the SEC pierced the corporate veil and went after two former officers of Citigroup. The former officers settled. Gary Crittenden, who made $32 million in 2007–8, agreed to pay $100,000, and another former officer agreed to a fine of $80,000. Rakoff noted that the settlement "leaves the defrauded investors substantially short-changed" (*Securities and Exchange Commission v. Citigroup Global Markets Inc.* (2011), 334). As Aaron Ross Sorkin wrote, "On its face, the settlement looked like a victory for the good guys. The SEC was finally holding Wall Street responsible for misleading shareholders." "But take a step back and ask this question: Who is paying the $75 million fine?" Sorkin supplied the answer: "The answer is Citigroup's shareholders—the same people who were arguably defrauded by its failure to disclose its exposure to subprime mortgages in the first place" (Sorkin 2010). In June 2014, the Court of Appeals for the Second Circuit in New York slapped Judge Rakoff's wrist saying he had "abused" his discretion (Protess and Goldstein 2014), but Rakoff had made his point.

[3] I call them "malefactors," but the truth is that we will never know whether they acted illegally. That is another price we pay for the SEC's practice of giving a get out of jail free card to top executives. With a lot of justice, the *Wall Street Journal* (2015) has called many of these prosecutions "Washington shakedowns." The editorial page has argued that the settlements were extorted from banks anxious to avoid "unpleasant publicity and a juror pool angry about bank bailouts."

ultimately fall on innocent parties" (id.). Velasquez (2003, 12) said that "in fact it is not possible to impose blame or punishment upon an organizational structure without having that blame or punishment fall on the shoulders of the corporation's members." And as John Hasnas writes in Chapter 5 of this book, "Any punishment directed toward a corporation necessarily passes through its nominal facade to fall on some set of human beings." This point is obvious to most legal scholars and philosophers, but it is much less apparent to a normally rationally ignorant public "in one of its periodical fits of morality" (Macaulay 1831, 547).

It is not just the shareholders who were harmed. Another innocent by-stander that was hurt by this transaction is the rule of law. It seems reasonable to speculate that the punishment meted out by the SEC to Bank of America will have little deterrent effect because the decision makers were not punished. That is Rakoff's (2014) view: "Although it is supposedly justified because it prevents future crimes, I suggest that the future deterrent value of successfully prosecuting individuals far outweighs the prophylactic benefits of imposing internal compliance measures that are often little more than window-dressing" (though it is true that Rakoff's primary target here is a related practice of deferred prosecutions). Nor is it likely that the punishment will be sufficient to induce shareholders to rein in management (see also Kraakman 2000, 672). The last word in this section belongs to Rakoff (2014): "Just going after the company is also both technically and morally suspect. It is technically suspect because, under the law, you should not indict or threaten to indict a company unless you can prove beyond a reasonable doubt that some managerial agent of the company committed the alleged crime; and if you can prove that, why not indict the manager?"

SILENCING SPEECH BY INDIRECTION

The last section showed how corporate managers can avoid their personal legal liability by shifting it to the corporation. This section explains how the legal rights of natural persons can be restricted by imputing those rights to a corporation. The example I discuss here is the First Amendment's bar on Congress restricting freedom of speech. In the well-known *Citizens United* case, the Supreme Court ruled by a bare five to four majority that corporations could not be prevented by law from engaging in election-related speech, for example, expressing views in a Presidential or Congressional race.[4]

---

[4] *Citizens United v. Federal Election Commission* (2010). The decision did not affect limits on contributions from the corporate treasury to candidates for political office.

Citizens United is and was a conservative lobbying group that is organized as a corporation. In the 1998 Presidential election, the group wanted to air a film critical of Senator Hillary Clinton and to promote the film on broadcast and cable television. *Hillary* was released in theaters and on digital disks, but Citizens United wanted to increase distribution by making it available through video-on-demand on cable television. The Federal Election Commission sued Citizens United on the grounds that its actions violated the McCain–Feingold Act's prohibition on electioneering by corporations and labor unions. An electioneering communication is defined as "any broadcast, cable, or satellite communication" that "refers to a clearly identified candidate for Federal office" and is made within thirty days of a primary or sixty days of a general election. The law makes it a felony for all corporations—including nonprofit advocacy corporations—to engage in such electioneering on pain of criminal sanctions (*Citizens United*, 321).

In the mind of much of the public, the issue at stake in *Citizens United* became defined as whether corporations are entitled to the same rights as natural persons. Populist rage was stoked by the obvious absurdity of the equation of corporations with natural persons. But neither the First Amendment nor the majority opinion mentions "persons." (See also Sepinwall's Chapter 8 in this book.) Nor did the Court's decision in any way depend on the corporation being seen as a person. Rather it turned on the language of the First Amendment. The Free Speech clause does not grant persons or even citizens a right to free speech. It simply bars Congress (and by extension the States) from "abridging the freedom of speech."[5] Indeed, as Justice Stevens admitted for the minority dissenting in *Citizens United*: "Recognizing the weakness of a speaker-based critique of *Austin* [1990],[6] the Court places primary emphasis not on the corporation's right to electioneer, but rather on the listener's interest in hearing what every possible speaker may have to say." (*Citizens United*, 469).

Although Stevens evidently grasped this point, he did nothing to disabuse the public of this error. Instead, he devoted much of his dissent to ridiculing the pretensions of the corporation to personhood. In his ninety-page dissent, part of which he read from the bench to emphasize his displeasure, he implied that the majority opinion depended on the "conceit that corporations must be treated identically to natural persons in the political sphere" even though the majority reached its decision without relying on any such assumption. He complained that "The fact that corporations are different from human beings

---

[5] "Congress shall make no law respecting an establishment of religion, or prohibiting the free exercise thereof; or abridging the freedom of speech, or of the press; or the right of the people peaceably to assemble, and to petition the Government for a redress of grievances."

[6] *Austin v. Michigan Chamber of Commerce* (1990) was overruled by *Citizens United* (2010).

might seem to need no elaboration, except that the majority opinion almost completely elides it" (id., 465).

Stevens faced a twofold task. He had to explain why corporate electioneering was (1) "likely to impair compelling governmental interests," and (2) "why restrictions on that electioneering are less likely to encroach upon First Amendment freedoms" (id., 466). The first claim required that he show that corporate speech menaces our democracy. Stevens contends that corporate electioneering would corrupt our politics and would compel shareholders to fund corporate speech with which they disagreed. The second claim required that he disparage the likely constitutional harms from restricting corporate speech (id., 468). Both claims required that Stevens turn up the volume of his anti-corporate rhetoric.

In order to establish his second claim—that is, to justify his contention that the harm to the Constitution would be minor—Stevens had to distinguish corporations from natural persons. Thus he pointed out that:

- "the speakers in question [corporations] are not real people...." (id., 473);
- [corporations] have no consciences, no beliefs, no feelings, no thoughts, no desires (id., 466);
- [corporations] are not themselves members of "We the People" by whom and for whom our Constitution was established (id.);
- corporate speech, however, is derivative speech, speech by proxy (id., 466); and
- [advocacy by corporations] bears "little or no correlation" to the ideas of natural persons or to any broader notion of the public good (id., 470).

The heart of Stevens' argument is that the restrictions on electioneering did not raise any constitutional concerns because they only impacted artificial persons. The restrictions, he said: "impose only a limited burden on First Amendment freedoms.... because they leave untouched the speech of natural persons" (id., 468).

But this claim is clearly false. Notwithstanding Stevens' denials, natural persons *were* impacted by the law. Of course, corporations are legal fictions, and in themselves they don't merit constitutional protections, but corporations are also a means by which natural persons may exercise their speech. It was left to Justice Scalia to rebut Stevens' claim that what was at stake was merely corporate speech. In his concurrence, Scalia wrote that "activities are not stripped of First Amendment protections simply because they are carried out under the banner of an artificial legal entity.... [T]he individual person's right to speak includes the right to speak in association with other individual persons" (*Citizens United*, 390, Scalia, J., concurring).

Stevens got the causation backward. The corporation has never enjoyed constitutional protection by virtue of its legal personhood or, least of all, because of any supposed resemblance to natural persons. Rather the corporation has for limited purposes been deemed a fictitious person because that is an efficient way of protecting the constitutional (and other) interests of the natural persons comprising it. Thus, corporate personhood was just a red herring. The proper question before the Court was whether McCain–Feingold unconstitutionally trammeled the free speech rights of natural persons who had associated in corporate form.

This point was appreciated from the outset. The courts that invented corporate personhood always firmly anchored the practice in the understanding that the corporation was an association of individuals. As Blair and Pollman (2015)) remind us, the landmark *Santa Clara Railroad* case of 1883 said that a corporation was nothing other than an association of individuals, who "do not, because of such association, lose their rights to protection, and equality of protection. . . . So, therefore, whenever a provision of the constitution or of a law guaranties to persons protection in their property, or affords to them the means for its protection, or prohibits injurious legislation affecting it, the benefits of the provision or law are extended to corporations; not to the name under which different persons are united, but to the individuals composing the union" (id., 1689–91, quoting *Santa Clara*).

As Robert Hessen (1979, 46) has also pointed out, "anyone who proposes to deny or destroy the rights of a corporation is really attacking individual rights." I may have misread Stevens' motives. But even if they were not exactly as I have speculated, *Citizens United* illustrates how the concept of legal personality might be abused. Short of consigning the jurisprudence of corporate personality to oblivion (my own preference), the obvious antidote would be for the courts to pierce the corporate veil whenever the constitutional rights of the members of the corporation may be at stake.

GRAND THEFT CORPORATION

My final example is how the entity theory of the corporation has been used to try to oust shareholders from what some see as their privileged position in the corporation. Many progressive scholars see corporations as potential instruments for great good in society. But they view this potential as underexploited because managers are severely constrained by their duties to shareholders. So if corporations are to address pressing social needs, they must first be liberated from their shareholders. The entity theory of the corporation is seen as one promising tool for effecting this backdoor socialization of the corporation.[7]

A pioneer in this use of the entity theory of the corporation for this purpose is Merrick Dodd (1932). Dodd's essay in his famous debate with Adolph Berle has served as a template for subsequent versions. According to David Millon (1990, 217–18), Dodd "demonstrated how the natural entity idea could provide a theoretical basis for corporate social responsibility." Millon continues:

> Dodd's article presented a solution that depended on an entity theory of the corporation. If management's role was to act solely as agent of the shareholders, failure to promote shareholder interests over other competing interests would violate management's fiduciary responsibility. If, however, management were the agent of a corporate entity distinct from the shareholder aggregation and that entity were obliged to be a "good citizen," then management, acting for the corporation, would enjoy the power to discharge the corporation's citizenship responsibilities, even in situations in which the shareholders might object. Dodd thus concluded that management was trustee for the corporation, not for its shareholders.

Schematically, the key moves in the strategy can be recapitulated as follows:

1. The first step is to drive a wedge between the corporation and its shareholders by attributing to the corporation an identity of its own separate from its shareholders. Thus, for example, Lan and Heracleous (2010, 294–5) argue that "the principal is not the shareholders but, rather, the corporation [in its own right]."

2. Once the corporation is accepted as an entity in its own right, it is a short step to the conclusion that the corporation can have goals or purpose that are unrelated to the interests of the shareholders. Blair and Stout (1999, 300) say: "American law views the corporation as an entity with interests of its own and not just a proxy for shareholder interests."

3. The possibility of conflict between the interests of the shareholders and the corporation, in turn, raises the question of to whom management's loyalties lie. If it is successfully argued that management's fiduciary duties run to *the corporation* rather than its shareholders, then the door is open for management to disregard the interests of shareholders

---

[7] Exponents of versions of the argument that I sketch here include Dodd (1932), Phillips (1994), Blair and Stout (1999), Elhauge (2005), Avi-Yonah (2005), Lan and Heracleous (2010), and Stout (2012a). Avi-Yonah provides a succinct statement of the argument: "The basic argument is that under the real view, which is historically the dominant view of the corporation, CSR [corporate social responsibility] is normatively acceptable even when it does not contribute to the long-run welfare of the shareholders" (Avi-Yonah 2005, 767). It is ironic that the legal historian, Morton Horwitz (1986), has argued that the real entity theory of the corporation was a major factor in *legitimizing* big business in the late nineteenth and early twentieth centuries (Millon 1990).

and/or to "balance" them with other priorities. In Delaware, the directors must act "in the honest belief that the action taken was in the best interests of the company" (*Smith v. Van Gorkom* (1985), 872–3, quoting *Aronson v. Lewis* (1984)). Some scholars have seized on this formulation to suggest that because management's duties are owed to the corporation, they are not owed only to the shareholders.

4. However, without more, it is quickly apparent that if corporate officers and directors are accountable to no one but this spectral entity, then they are accountable only to themselves. Our legal tradition abhors such a vacuum. As Iwai (2013) points out, "any contract between managers and the corporation would necessarily degenerate, at least in part, into managers' contract with themselves" (see also Iwai 1999, 622). This is plainly an untenable state of affairs, so it inevitably gives rise to demands that managers of corporations be made accountable.

5. Now, with shareholders safely out of the way, corporations are up for grabs, and the way is clear for progressives to substitute their own beneficiaries or priorities. As Avi-Yonah (2005, 814–15) says, "under the real entity theory, since the corporation is regarded as a person just like individuals, it is permitted to act philanthropically just like individuals are, and should in fact be praised to the extent it does so."

6. By these steps, property in the corporation has successfully been redistributed from the shareholders to stakeholders or to society. The expropriators have been expropriated.

So far, of course, this logic hasn't carried the day, but there are many days left. It remains one of the arguments of choice for those who would free management from the thrall of the doctrine of shareholder primacy.

Without space for a fuller critique of this argument, I think it is still worth pointing out its main flaws. The premise of this argument is that it is meaningful to conceive of the corporation as an autonomous entity independent of its shareholders—or apparently anyone else. One problem is that this premise is based on a fundamental misunderstanding of the function of entity status in our law. Entity status means that a corporation can sue (and be sued) as a unit, in its own name, instead of having to specify the name of every shareholder, and it can hold legal title to property despite changes in the composition of its shareholders (Hessen 1979, 16). Entity status is not a privilege—for one thing, it makes it easier it easier for the corporation to be sued. It is a labor-saving device (Hessen 1979, 42, citing Maitland). In the common law, only an individual person could be sued. But with the advent of limited liability, that became problematic, since the people who owned the corporation might enjoy limited liability and so could not be sued for the debts of the corporation. To solve this problem, the courts created the fiction of the corporation as a *person*. No doubt the practice of treating corporations as persons spared Congress from having to engage in a wholesale rewrite of the statute books as well. In short, the convention evolved to benefit shareholders and the parties they transact with by reducing transaction costs. It was never intended to expropriate shareholders.

Of course, this objection fails to reckon with the ingenuity of attorneys and law professors. In the hands of progressive legal scholars the concept of the corporate entity has been stretched to the point where any link with its original purpose has broken. No longer is the corporate person simply a convenient fiction. It is a "real entity" (Avi-Yonah 2005). It is capable of having interests of its own, quite apart from—and even at odds with—its shareholders (Blair and Stout 1999). It can have its own "purpose" (Stout 2012b). It is a "principal" in its own right (Lan and Heracleous 2010). Much of this frankly belongs in the realm of what Felix Cohen (1935) called "transcendental nonsense" (see also Hasnas 2010).

Corporations are incapable of conceiving goals or purposes. If it makes any sense to refer to a corporation's purpose at all, it is only as a shorthand for the corporation's shareholders and/or management, depending on the circumstances. But that is not the sense these scholars intend. The best defense that that can be made of this claim is that, on a stakeholder view, the term corporation can be said to comprise or encompass a range of stakeholders, not just shareholders, so that—assuming that the corporate purpose is determined by consensus—the purpose found by a court may not coincide precisely with the interest of any particular stakeholder. In that sense the "purpose" might be deemed to be an emergent property. But that argument fails because it presumes what it is has the burden of proving—namely that the corporation does not owe a fiduciary duty of loyalty exclusively to its shareholders.

It is also hard to know what sense to make of the assertion by Lan and Heracleous (2010) that the corporation is its own principal. By definition, there can be no principal without an agent, and vice versa. So which is which in the case of the corporation? Presumably only a schizophrenic can simultaneously be both principal and agent. But Lan and Heracleous's corporation is apparently a unitary actor. It would make as much (or as little) sense to talk of the corporation owning itself. Plainly, in law, a corporation may own another corporation, but to own itself, without any ultimate natural owners, also falls into the category of transcendental nonsense. It is the equivalent of claiming that an object can be suspended from itself in space.

To see why the claim that the corporation can own itself is absurd, we can use a thought experiment applying elementary principles of contract law. The assets of a corporation have been financed by promoters and shareholders and lenders. The lenders have contracts that typically provide for interest payments and repayment terms. But what consideration do shareholders receive in exchange for financing the corporation? The natural way to answer that question is by inquiring into the mutual understandings of the shareholders and the corporation (that is, its agents or management) when they made their contracts—both express and implicit—with the corporation. It is a safe generalization that the parties understood that the corporation would be managed in the interests of the shareholders. We know that from, among others, Lynn Stout (2012a, 98). She notes that "even though law does not dictate shareholder primacy, as a practical matter today's public companies pay far more attention to shareholder value than American companies did two or three decades ago." If this is right, I think the progressive scholars' attempt to use the concept of entity status to drive a wedge between the corporation and its shareholders fails not only as a matter of law, but as a matter of ethics too, because its effect would be defeat the settled expectations of the parties and to confiscate the property of shareholders.

CONCLUSION: PERILS OF ENTITY THINKING

Lasciate ogni speranza, voi ch'entrate.[8]

In my discussion, I have carefully avoided entering into the debate over the metaphysical or ontological status of the corporation or other collective actors. That way lies madness. Instead, I have tried to show, by means of a *reductio*, that the practice of treating corporations as real entities can lead to absurd results and/or results that violate our intuitions of justice.

I have argued that the anthropomorphization of the corporation is an open invitation to abuses. In the first section, I showed how the US practice of subjecting corporations to criminal as well as civil liability for the wrongful actions of natural persons who act in their name has insulated the actual wrongdoers from the legal responsibility for their acts. The "corporation" has, in effect, come to function as a scapegoat that bears the liability in their place. Rather than cure a supposed "responsibility deficit," the practice of imputing liability to the artificial person of the corporation has reduced accountability. In the second section, I described how the US Supreme Court came within a single vote of curtailing the free speech rights of natural persons by inventing a specious distinction between corporate speech and the speech of individuals and arguing that the McCain–Feingold Act only limited corporate speech. In the last section, I argued that progressive legal scholars have used the real entity theory of the corporation to try to drive a wedge between corporations and their shareholders and so deprive shareholders of their property rights over the corporation. In short, I have shown how, in various contexts, the

---

[8] "Abandon all hope, you who enter here" (from Dante's *Divine Comedy*, canto III).

anthropomorphization of the corporation has been used by insiders to camouflage actual moral and legal responsibility and to use indirection to deprive outsiders of their legal rights and property.

At the root of these abuses lie the concepts of legal personhood and the real entity theory of the corporation. Traditionally, the concept of legal personhood has been applied circumspectly and only in a narrow range of situations. Its use has generally been accompanied by warnings that the concept is a legal fiction and that the corporation is at best a crude proxy for the "real parties in interest," and that when in doubt we should pierce the corporate veil. But, as we have grown more habituated to the usage, we have shed that caution, those signposts have been defaced, the entity idea has cast a spell on many of us, and some people have developed a vested interest in perpetuating confusion about the idea of corporate personhood. So the concept has taken on a life of its own.

Before they go out and commit more metaphorical excesses, fans of the real entity theory of the corporation need to bring their fevers down by dipping into the cool bath of Robert Hessen's classic treatment of the subject. Hessen (1979, 41) writes that "[a] group or association is only a concept... used to classify different types of relationships between individuals. Whether the concept is a marriage, a partnership, a team, a crowd, a choir, a corps de ballet, or a corporation, one fact remains constant; the concept denotes the relationship between individuals and has no referent apart from it." As a consequence, the "rights of any organization or association, including corporations, are the rights it derives from the individuals who create and sustain it" (id.).

REFERENCES

Aronson v. Lewis, 473 A.2d 805 (Del. 1984).

Austin v. Michigan Chamber of Commerce, 494 U.S. 652 (1990) (overruled by *Citizens United*).

Avi-Yonah, Reuven S. (2005). "The Cyclical Transformations of the Corporate Form: A Historical Perspective on Corporate Social Responsibility." *Delaware Journal of Corporate Law* 30: 767.

Blair, Margaret M. and Elizabeth Pollman (2015). "The Derivative Nature of Corporate Constitutional Rights." *William and Mary Law Review* 56: 1673.

Blair, Margaret M. and Lynn A. Stout (1999). "A Team Production Theory of Corporate Law." *University of Virginia Law Review* 85: 247.

Citizens United v. Federal Election Commission, 558 U.S. 310 (2010).

Coffee, John C., Jr. (1981). "No Soul To Damn: No Body To Kick: An Unscandalized Inquiry into the Problem of Corporate Punishment." *Michigan Law Review* 79: 386.

Coffee, John C. Jr. (2009). "The End of Phony Deterrence? SEC v. Bank of America." *New York Law Journal*, September 17: 5.

Cohen, Felix (1935). "Transcendental Nonsense and the Functional Approach." *Columbia Law Review* 35: 809.

Dodd, Merrick (1932). "For Whom Are Corporate Managers Trustees?, *Harvard Law Review* 45: 1145.

Elhauge, Einer (2005). "Sacrificing Corporate Profits in the Public Interest." *New York University Law Review* 80: 733.

Garrett, Brandon L. (2011). "Globalized Corporate Prosecutions." *Virginia Law Review* 97: 1776.

Garrett, Brandon L. (2014). *Too Big to Jail: How Prosecutors Compromise with Corporations.*

Hasnas, John (2010). "Where Is Felix Cohen When We Need Him? Transcendental Nonsense and the Moral Responsibility of Corporations." *Brooklyn Journal of Law and Policy* 19: 55.

Hessen, Robert (1979). *In Defense of the Corporation.*

Horwitz, Morton J. (1986). "Santa Clara Revisited: The Development of Corporate Theory." *West Virginia Law Review* 88: 173.

Iwai, Katsuhito (1999). "Persons, Things and Corporations: The Corporate Personality Controversy and Comparative Corporate Governance." *American Journal of Comparative Law* 47: 583.

Iwai, Katsuhito (2013). "The Foundation for a Unified Theory of Fiduciary Relationships: 'One May Not Make a Contract With Oneself.'" Keynote Presentation to INSEAD–Wharton conference on "The Moral Responsibility of Firms: For or Against?" December 12–13.

Kraakman, Reinier H. (2000). "Vicarious and Corporate Civil Liability." In *Encyclopedia of Law and Economics*, vol. II, ed. Boudewijn Bouckaert and Gerrit De Geest, http://encyclo.findlaw.com/3400book.pdf.

Lan, Luh Luh and Loizos Heracleous (2010). "Rethinking Agency Theory: The View From Law." *Academy of Management Review* 35: 294.

Lee, Ian B. (2006). "Efficiency and Ethics in the Debate about Shareholder Primacy." *Delaware Journal of Corporate Law* 31: 533.

Lewontin, R.C. (2001). "In the Beginning Was the Word." *Science* 291: 1263.

Macaulay, Thomas Babington (1831). "On Moore's Life of Lord Byron." *Edinburgh Review* 53: 544.

Millon, David (1990). "Theories of the Corporation." *Duke Law Journal* 39: 201.

Phillips, Michael J. (1994). "Reappraising the Real Entity Theory of the Corporation." *Florida State University Law Review* 21: 1061.

Protess, Ben and Matthew Goldstein (2014). "Overruled, Judge Still Left a Mark On SEC Agenda." *New York Times*, June 5.

Rakoff, Jed S. (2014). "The Financial Crisis: Why Have No High-Level Executives Been Prosecuted?" *New York Review of Books*, January 9, http://www.nybooks.com/.

Rakoff, Jed S. (2015). "Justice Deferred Is Justice Denied." *New York Review of Books*, February 19, http://www.nybooks.com/.

Rönnegard, David (2013). "How Autonomy Alone Debunks Corporate Moral Agency." *Business and Professional Ethics Journal* 32: 77.

Rothfeld, Michael (2014). "Firms Get Penalized, But Many Workers Don't." *Wall Street Journal*, January 16, http://www.wsj.com/articles/SB10001424052702304419104579324962459771186.

Santa Clara County v. Southern Pacific Railroad, 118 U.S. 394 (1886).

Securities and Exchange Commission v. Bank of America Corp., 653 F. Supp.2d 507 (S.D.N.Y. 2009).

Securities and Exchange Commission v. Citigroup Global Markets Inc., 827 F. Supp.2d 328 (S.D.N.Y. 2011).

Smith v. Van Gorkom, 488 A.2d 858 (Del. 1985).

Sorkin, Andrew Ross (2010). "Punishing Citi, or Its Shareholders?" *New York Times* (Dealbook), August 3, http://dealbook.nytimes.com.

Stout, Lynn A. (2012a). *The Shareholder Value Myth: How Putting Shareholders First Harms Investors, Corporations, and the Public*.

Stout, Lynn A. (2012b). "The Problem of Corporate Purpose." *Issues in Governance Studies* 48: 1, http://view2.fdu.edu/legacy/brkpresstoutdec12.pdf.

Velasquez, Manuel (1983). "Why Corporations Are Not Morally Responsible For Anything They Do." *Business and Professional Ethics Journal* 2: 1.

Velasquez, Manuel (2003). "Debunking Corporate Moral Responsibility." *Business Ethics Quarterly* 13: 531.

Wall Street Journal. Editorial (2015). "The Bank That Won't Buckle: Nomura Goes To Court Over the Fannie Mae Mortgage Fairy Tale," March 8.

Werhane, Patricia H. (1985). *Persons, Rights, and Corporations*.

Werhane, Patricia H. (1989). "Corporate and Individual Moral Responsibility: A Reply to Jan Garrett," *Journal of Business Ethics* 8: 821.

7

On (Not) Attributing Moral Responsibility
to Organizations

David Rönnegard and Manuel Velasquez

We often describe organizations as having features that we ordinarily attribute only to human beings. We may credit them with virtues and vices, for example, which we ordinarily ascribe only to human beings. We may say that an organization is carrying out a plan, that it has beliefs, that it makes decisions, and that it desires or seeks some end. The US Supreme Court rulings in *Citizens United* (2010) and *Hobby Lobby* (2014) are two recent examples of extending to corporate organizations rights normally associated with citizens. In short, we anthropomorphize organizations.

How are we to understand such anthropomorphic attributions of human characteristics to organizations? Some people, including many of those engaged in the academic field of business ethics and philosophy, believe that such attributions are not anthropomorphic, but should be taken literally. In this view—a view that recent Supreme Court decisions seem to have endorsed—organizations are like people, that is, they are persons, and like human persons, they literally have real beliefs, desires, intentions, rights, and obligations.

For most people not engaged in the academic field of business ethics and philosophy, however, the notion that organizations are human-like persons seems counter-intuitive and implausible. Organizations are comprised of individuals who are real people of flesh, blood, and minds, and there is no reason to believe that organizing those individuals into the structured groups we call organizations somehow turns the group into a human-like agent with beliefs, desires, and the like.

In what follows we address one limited aspect of the large question whether attributions of human characteristics to organizations should be taken literally. The question we will address is this: Can organizations[1] be morally responsible

---

[1] The debate that we are engaging with is often referred to as being about "corporate moral agency" or "corporate moral responsibility." However, the term "corporation" can be a source of

for what they do in the same literal sense that human beings can be morally responsible for what they do? We will argue that the answer to this question is that organizations are not capable of being morally responsible for what they do in the same literal sense that human beings are. In what follows we begin by first setting the stage for our arguments, and then we turn to providing six arguments for why attributions of moral responsibility to organizations are anthropomorphic and misguided.

SETTING THE STAGE

Consider several people who are organized by the kinds of roles and relationships that constitute them into an organization, such as a club, a soccer team, a school, an army, a gang, the Mafia, or a business. Suppose that those people, including the organization's leaders, deliberately cooperated and coordinated their actions through their organization with the conscious aim of intentionally injuring other innocent people, and that they did so without the assistance of any parties outside the organization. Then it makes sense to say that: (a) each of those individual human members of the organization who freely and intentionally took part in the infliction of those injuries through their actions or omissions was an agent[2] whose actions or omissions brought about or helped to bring about the injuries; (b) each individual human agent is therefore morally responsible for his or her part in bringing about or helping to bring about those injuries; and (c) each deserves whatever punishment is merited for the part he or she played in the infliction of the injuries. But does it make sense to make two additional claims? Does it make sense to claim in addition that: (1) the organization itself can bear a moral responsibility for the injuries that is separate from, and additional to, the moral responsibility of its individual human members? And does it make sense to say, moreover, that: (2) besides the punishments given to every individual member who deliberately and knowingly participated in the wrongdoing, it is morally justifiable to impose a separate and additional burden of punishment on the organization itself because of the separate and additional responsibility it bears for what was done?

confusion due to the legal connotations of the term. We are here not concerned with the corporation as a legal entity or attributions of legal responsibility, and therefore we choose to speak of the responsibility of *organizations* in order to make clear that we are speaking of moral responsibility.

[2] We use the term "agent" here in its most basic philosophical sense to refer to any entity capable of causing acts or events. "Agent" can also be used to refer to an entity that is capable of causing acts or events and doing so intentionally. And agent is sometimes used in legal terms to refer to one who serves the interests of another in an agent–principal relationship.

Those who take a so-called "individualist" approach to moral responsibility affirm (a), (b), and (c), but deny (1) and (2). The individualist view of moral responsibility, of course, is that individual human beings can be morally responsible for their own actions and also morally responsible for what their organizations do, but organizations themselves are not morally responsible for what they do and so do not merit punishment. In contrast, those who take a collectivist approach to moral responsibility likewise affirm (a), (b), and (c), but, in addition, they assert (1) and (2). The collectivist view, then, is that individual human beings can be morally responsible for their own actions and for what their organizations do, but in addition, organizations themselves can also be morally responsible for what they do and so can merit punishment.

The collectivist claim (1) has an important corollary. It implies that the organization itself is an additional agent that is distinct from the agents that are its members. More specifically, claim (1) implies that when an organization acts, the individuals who are members of the organization were not the only agents acting because in addition to the organization's members another distinct agent was also acting and that distinct agent was the organization itself. To see why the collectivist claim (1) implies that the organization itself is an additional agent that is distinct from the agents that are its members, consider the following. Suppose that when an organization acts, the organization itself is not an additional agent that is distinct from the agents that are its members. In that case, the only agents that were involved in bringing the organization's act about were its individual members. Then the actions of those members and only the actions of those members could have caused or helped to cause the organization's acts (assuming, of course, that they acted without the assistance of any agents external to the organization). This implies that only the individual members of the organization can be morally responsible for the acts of the organization, because only those agents that cause an act or help to bring it about through their actions or omissions can be morally responsible for the act. Thus, if the organization itself is not an additional agent that is distinct from the agents that are its members, then we can attribute to it no additional and separate moral responsibility for any organizational actions. Hence, if organizations themselves can bear a separate and additional moral responsibility for what they do, they must be agents that are distinct from and additional to the agents that are its members.

The logical commitment of the collectivist position to the corollary that organizations are agents that are separate from and additional to the agents that are its members is explicitly stated by many (though not all) collectivists who have thought clearly about what their view implies. Philip Pettit, for example, writes that organizations that impose certain rational constraints on their decisions are morally responsible "social integrates" and "a social integrate is an intentional subject that is distinct from its members—that exists over and beyond its members" (Pettit 2003, 184). In a similar way, but two

decades earlier, Peter French stated that a corporate organization is a "full-fledged moral person," a "non-eliminatable subject" of "equal standing with…
biological human beings," and with a "non-eliminatable agency" (French 1979, 207). "Non-eliminatable" for French means distinct from and not reducible to the corporate organization's members or their agency. There are, of course, many others, besides Pettit and French, who hold the collectivist position (Copp 1984; DeGeorge 1981; Dubbink and Smith 2011; Gibson 1995; Gilbert 2006; Goodpaster 1983; May 1987; Phillips 1992; Seabright and Kurke 1997; Werhane 1985). And there are many who hold the individualist view (Miller and Makela 2005; Searle 1990; Hasnas 2012; Rönnegard 2013, 2015; Velasquez 1983, 2003).

There are several arguments that have convinced individualists, like ourselves, that attributions of moral responsibility to organizations should not be understood in the way that collectivists claim. Because of the restricted space available here, we are only able to provide extremely broad and necessarily un-nuanced summaries of some of the arguments that we believe show that it is wrong to accept claims (1) and (2) above, and so wrong to accept the collectivist view. We devote the rest of this paper to outlining those arguments.

FIRST ARGUMENT

Some individualists hold that the corollary to claim (1)—that is, that an organization is an agent that is distinct from and additional to the agents that are its members—is counter-intuitive, bizarre, and false (Rönnegard 2013; Wall 2000; Velasquez 2003). Intuitively, the organization does not appear to be another agent that exists as a distinct entity alongside the several agents that are its members: the organization is simply the whole of which the members are parts. Once each of its parts have been counted, the whole organization is not an additional entity that must be added to the count of the parts. It would be bizarre, for example, for me to try to distribute a pie that is sliced into quarters among four people and then to try to give a fifth person the additional entity that the whole pie constituted. In exactly the same way, once all of the members of an organization have been counted and each has been removed from, say, a building, there does not remain an additional entity—the organization—still waiting in the building to be counted and removed: the truth is that there simply is no such additional entity. Yet as we showed above, attributing a moral responsibility to an organization that is separate from and additional to the moral responsibility of its members logically implies that the organization is an agent that is distinct from and additional to its members. This implication, then, is not merely counter-intuitive; it is bizarre and false.

It is important to add that the individualist view does not imply that an organization is identical to or "reducible" to its members. Clearly, many things can be truthfully said about organizations that cannot be said about their individual members, and so logic alone (that is, Leibniz' law)[3] tells us that organizations are not identical with their individual members, any more than one side of a coin is identical with the coin itself. However, just as the claim that one side of a coin is not identical with the coin itself does not imply that the side of a coin is an entity that is separate from and additional to the entity that is the coin itself, so also admitting that an organization is not identical with its members does not imply that the organization must be an entity that exists separate from and in addition to the entities that are its members. An organization consists of more than its members, but that "more" is not the existence of an additional entity or entities. To constitute an organization, for example, the members must have certain relationships and roles. But while relationships and roles are attributes of entities, they are not themselves separate entities and so cannot bear any separate measure of moral responsibility.

Moreover, the individualist view also does not imply that only individuals exist and that groups or organizations do not exist. Obviously, the claim that once all the pieces of a pie have been distributed there is no additional entity—the whole pie—still waiting to be distributed, does not imply that whole pies do not exist. Similarly, the claim that once all the members of an organization have been counted there is no additional entity—the organization—still waiting to be counted, does not imply that organizations do not exist. Organizations exist, however, only to the extent that their members exist and that they bear to each other those relationships and roles that constitute them into an organization. In fact, it is because those relationships and roles are necessary if a group is to be an organization, that organizations cannot be reduced to their human members. That is, if its human members are considered to be the "parts" of an organization, then an organization clearly is more than "the sum of its parts."

SECOND ARGUMENT

Claim (1) that an organization can bear a moral responsibility for its actions that is distinct from and additional to the moral responsibility of its members requires that organizations have properties that they in fact do not have, and so this claim is false. To see why claim (1) requires that organizations have

---

[3] A principle of logic attributed to G. W. Leibniz states that if x is identical to y, then x and y must have exactly the same properties; or, equivalently, if x and y do not have exactly the same properties then x is not identical to y.

properties they do not have, consider the following. If an agent bears its own separate and distinct moral responsibility for some action, that agent must have certain psychological or mind-dependent properties (Quinton 1975; Velasquez 2003; Wolf 1985). At the most basic level an agent that is morally responsible for doing something must have knowledge of what it is doing and must do it intentionally. That is, if an agent acted with absolutely no knowledge of what it was doing or if the agent's action was not in any way intentional, then the agent could not be morally responsible for that action. But knowledge and intentions are psychological or mental states that an agent can possess only if it has a psychology or a mind. Groups as such, including organizations, do not possess a psychology or a mind. Therefore attributions to organizations of a moral responsibility that is distinct from and additional to the moral responsibility of its members cannot be true attributions.

It is possible to claim, of course, as several philosophers have claimed, that a thing may have beliefs, intentions, and other mental states even if it has no mind. This is the claim of those who hold functionalist theories of mind; in fact, it is arguable that if one holds that organizations can be morally responsible for what they do, then one must hold a functionalist theory of mind or one that is very similar. A functionalist theory of mind holds that mental states are constituted by the functional role they play in relating an entity's perceptions to its behaviors and its other inner states, much like a hammer is defined by the function it plays in pounding nails, or a heart is defined by its biological function of pumping blood. Since mental states are identified by the functional role they play, mental states can be realized in any entity that replicates the same type of relationships among its perceptions ("inputs"), its behaviors ("outputs"), and its other inner states that characterize humans when they have those mental states. This is similar to how we might call anything a hammer that can serve the same functions a hammer serves regardless of what it is made of, or the way we call any animal's organ a heart when it serves the same biological function a human heart serves. Functionalist views of the mind thus enable the collectivist to say that organizations can have any kind of mental state humans can have. Without a theory of the mind that holds, as functionalism holds, that mental states can be exhibited by non-human entities, the collectivist could not say that organizations exhibit the mental states that moral responsibility requires. For those who doubt that functionalism is a viable theory of the mind, therefore, the view of the collectivist will be equally doubtful.

Consider the view of Pettit, a collectivist who claims that even a mechanical artifact can have beliefs and desires. Suppose a small mechanical toy "robot" is constructed, Pettit suggests, so that it will move around a table and set fallen cylinders upright (Petitt 2007; see also Pettit's contribution in Chapter 1 of this book). When its optical sensor contacts a fallen cylinder, that contact triggers the toy's metal arms to move in such a way that the robot sets the cylinder upright. Such a mechanical toy, he asserts, has a "desire" to set the cylinders upright, has "beliefs" about the state of the cylinders on the table, and satisfies its desire by acting on those beliefs. If such simple "systems" can be said to have desires and beliefs, he concludes, then larger systems, like organizations, can also be said to have desires, beliefs, and other mental states.

Let us stand back from Petitt's claims and ask whether the desires and beliefs that Petitt attributes to the toy are true desires and beliefs, or whether they are desires and beliefs only in a metaphorical sense. Consider the role that real desires and beliefs play in explaining actions. For example, if you ask me why I am looking through the refrigerator, I can explain my action by saying that I desired a drink of lemonade, and I believed there was a pitcher of lemonade in the refrigerator. Real desires and beliefs can play a role in an explanation of an action. The desires and beliefs that Pettit attributes to his artifact, however, can play no similar role in explaining its actions. If I ask why the artifact picked up a fallen cylinder, nothing is explained by saying that it did so because it had a desire to do so, or that it believed a fallen cylinder lay before it. A real explanation of the machine's activities would tell me, instead, how the machine is constructed and how that construction causes it to move toward a fallen cylinder and set it upright. In this real explanation of the artifact's movements, the supposed desires and beliefs of the artifact would play no role. They would play no role because the metaphorical desires and beliefs we attribute to such moving non-human objects are mere re-descriptions of the motions that we already perceive and know about. Because they merely re-describe the activities we see, they cannot explain them. The beliefs or desires Pettit attributes to his toy, then, are not beliefs and desires in any literal sense, but are merely metaphorical ways of re-describing what we see, that is, we describe the behavior of the toy by saying that it is moving or acting "as if" it had certain beliefs and desires. Moreover, literal beliefs and intentions are accompanied by awareness, and mechanical artifacts and organizations have no awareness. Nor can literal beliefs exist in isolation. They require a network of associated background beliefs to give them meaning. The belief that a fallen cylinder lies before me, for example, implies the presence in my mind of other beliefs about what a cylinder is, what it is for something to be fallen, what my position is relative to the cylinder, and so on. Artifacts and organizations do not possess such bundles of background beliefs and so cannot have beliefs in a literal sense.

But not all mental states that we attribute to organizations are metaphorical "as if" descriptions. Some metaphorical "as if" attributions of mental states are "prescriptive attributions" (Velasquez 2003). A prescriptive attribution occurs when we agree or have previously agreed to treat some object as if it had characteristics it does not really have (Searle 1995). We use prescriptive attributions all the time. When two people sit down to play a game of chess, for example, they will treat the chess pieces as if each had certain powers, such as the power to eliminate another piece by moving to the square it occupies. Of course, chess players do not explicitly agree to this every time they play but rely on standing conventions embodied in the rules of chess that stipulate that players are to treat the pieces as if they had these powers. Prescriptive attributions are frequent in legal contexts. California law, for example, prescribes that under certain conditions those actions of a child that damage the property of others, are to be treated as if they were the actions of the parent (California Civil Code, § 1714.1).[4] And the laws of most states in the US, under the doctrine of "vicarious liability," prescribe that under certain conditions, the actions, beliefs, and intentions of employees are to be treated as if they were the actions, beliefs, and intentions of the corporate organization for which they work (Orts 2015, 139–43). What is important to note is that any mental states that are thus prescriptively attributed are not real, for if they were real there would be no need to attribute them prescriptively.

Finally, we need to add that there is a third category of attributions of mental states to organizations that are neither metaphorical "as if" re-descriptions, nor prescriptive "as if" attributions. We sometimes attribute beliefs, desires, intentions, and other mental states to organizations as elliptical ways of saying that all or many of the individual members of the organization or key members have those mental states. We might say of a team of players of American football, for example, that they tried to kick a field goal because they believed they would otherwise lose possession of the ball. Here, the belief that is being attributed is a real belief for it really explains the team's action, something that, we argued, metaphorical descriptions cannot do. But while the belief in this case is a real belief, it is not being attributed to the organization as such. For the belief could explain the team's action only if it was held by most of the team members, or a significant subset of the team members, such as the quarterback who, as leader of the group, determined what the team would do. It is clear that the belief must be held by all, most, or some individual members of the team, since if it were to turn out that no member of the team had the belief, then the belief could no longer explain why the team acted as it did.

We can summarize these points as follows. Moral responsibility can be attributed to agents only if they have certain mental states in the same literal sense that humans have mental states. But the mental states that we sometimes attribute to organizations are either non-literal "as-if" re-descriptions, or non-literal "as-if" prescriptive attributions; or, if they are literal, then they are not being attributed to the organization as such but to all or some of its individual

---

[4] Note that in such cases the parent is not *punished* (for example, imprisoned or fined) for the act of the child, but is merely held liable for the damages that resulted. Instead of being *punished* (imprisoned or forced to pay a fine to the state), the parent must compensate the injured party to make him or her whole.

human members. It follows that organizations as separate entities cannot be morally responsible for any actions its members cause it to perform through their own actions or omissions.

THIRD ARGUMENT

The collectivist claim (1) asserts that organizations can be morally responsible agents. But a morally responsible agent must not only know and intend, it must also be capable of having certain emotions, as well as other capacities that are logically required if one is to be morally responsible for one's actions. Among these are the ability to feel guilt and remorse, to have full control of one's actions, to make one's own decisions based on one's own practical reasoning, to determine which actions are right and which are wrong, to know how to cause actions and events in the world, to be able to cause actions and events in the world, to have the competency of a sane and rational adult, and so on (Alschuler 2009; Moore 2010; Watson 1987; Wolf 1985). Moreover, the presence of each of these abilities implies the presence of additional capabilities. To determine which actions are right and wrong, for example, requires an acquaintance with moral standards, an understanding of what harm, injury, and benefit are, and the capacity to be motivated by moral standards. And to be able to determine whether an action is right or wrong requires the ability to put oneself in the position of those who will be touched by one's actions, the ability to understand how one's actions will affect them, and the ability to empathize with them. To feel guilt and remorse requires that those emotions be triggered within oneself involuntarily in the appropriate circumstances.

Yet organizations do not seem to have the abilities and capabilities that moral responsibility requires. Organizations do not seem to have the capacity to experience emotions at all since they do not have affective faculties. Circumstances that should trigger the involuntary emotions of guilt and remorse do not trigger involuntary feelings of guilt and remorse in organizations. Organizations do not have full control of their actions since all their actions are controlled by their members. Organizations do not seem to make their own decisions since all their decisions are made for them by members of the organization; their decisions are not based on their own reasoning, but on the reasoning and considerations their members employ. Organizations do not know what right and wrong are because they do not themselves have moral standards; because they are not themselves human they cannot put themselves in the position of a human being; nor can they know what humans feel or empathize with humans. Organizations do not know how to cause actions and events because they do not have knowledge at all; they themselves do not cause actions and events in the world since all of their actions must be brought about by their members on their behalf. In short, moral responsibility requires that the agent possess a complex set of interrelated abilities and susceptibilities that are not present in an organization.

FOURTH ARGUMENT

If an agent is morally responsible for some act or event, that agent must have had some part in the activities that determined whether the act or event would or would not take place; that is, the agent must have brought about or helped to bring about that act or event, either through its own actions or by failing to prevent the act when it could have and should have. Organizational actions, however, are always brought about in their entirety by the activities and omissions of the members of the organization and only by those members' activities and omissions. If the members of an organization do not act, there can be no organizational action whatsoever (Velasquez 2003).

It may appear, however, that organizations carry out some actions on their own, namely those actions that can be predicated of organizations, but not of their individual human members. Almost all collectivists stress the fact that there are many actions that are actions of the organization and not of any of its members. Organizations, for example, can be said to "merge," but their individual human members do not "merge." Baseball teams can be said to have "won the game," yet no individual player can be said to have "won the game."

Nevertheless, even those actions of the organization that can be predicated only of the organization and not of its individual members are all brought about entirely by the actions or omissions of the members of the organization. A corporate merger, for example, is brought about by corporate officials signing the appropriate documents, while the victory of a team is brought about by the skillful actions of the team's players. An organization's actions, even those that can be predicated only of the organization and not of its members, are nevertheless the results of the activity of the organization's members. Consequently, an organization cannot itself be morally responsible for an act or event; moral responsibility for the acts of an organization must lodge in the members of the organization whose own acts or omissions determined whether the act or event would occur.

Of course, as suggested above, in our second argument, in legal contexts corporate organizations are routinely held responsible for the acts of their employees under the doctrine of "vicarious liability." We have argued, however, that such attributions of responsibility are prescriptive "as if" attributions. The law instructs us that we are to treat the actions of the members of the corporate organization as if they were the actions of the corporate organization itself, even though we all know that they were really the actions of the organization's members or were actions that the organization's members brought about.

FIFTH ARGUMENT

The collectivist's claim (2) implies that it is morally acceptable to punish innocent individuals who did nothing wrong, and acceptable to punish wrongdoers not just for what they did, but also for the wrongs committed by others. But such punishment is not morally acceptable (Lewis 1948; Hasnas 2012; Rönnegard 2008; Velasquez 1983). Consider that often, when the leaders and members of an organization engage in organizational wrongdoing,[5] some of the other members of the organization will not know what the wrongdoers are doing, others may know but refuse to participate, and yet others may know and try to prevent the wrongdoing. These three latter groups of organizational members are thus innocent of the organizational wrongdoing. Yet the collectivist view that organizations bear a moral responsibility for their wrongful actions that is additional to the moral responsibility of their members and so can be punished for the additional responsibility they bear, implies that after each individual wrongdoer in the organization has been punished for her part in a wrongful organizational act, the organization itself still merits an additional measure of punishment. But such additional punishment, supposedly inflicted on the organization, must necessarily be inflicted on the organization's members if it is to have any effect. When a corporation, for example, is forced to pay fines and "punitive damages" because it is held legally as well as morally responsible for a wrongfully inflicted injury, the money must come from the equity or profits of stockholders, the salaries of managers, or the wages of workers. Similarly, when an organization is disbanded as a punishment for its wrongdoing, it is the individual members who must disband, forfeiting their careers, their source of income, and, perhaps, their pensions.[6] As a result, those who

---

[5] By "organizational wrongdoing" we mean wrongdoing that the members of an organization carry out while acting within their defined organizational roles, that is, wrongdoing in which the defined leaders of the organization, acting within the scope of their authority, command their subordinates to each perform their part in the wrongful activity while also acting within the scope of their role duties.

[6] Arthur Andersen, for example, when convicted of criminal obstruction in an action related to its audits of Enron, was forced to disband because the US Securities and Exchange Commission does not accept audits from convicted felons. Though the Supreme Court later overturned the conviction, the organization's members had by then suffered the injuries of terminated careers, loss of livelihood, and the loss of pensions that relied on Arthur Andersen's revenues. Yet only a few dozen of Arthur Andersen's 85,000 worldwide employees were complicit in the fraudulent audits that led to the firm's conviction.

participated in the wrongdoing and who were already fully punished for their part in the wrongdoing, must now be punished again for what they did not do, that is, for what the organization itself supposedly did. Moreover, those members who were innocent of any wrongdoing (in virtue of their ignorance, or their failure to participate, or their active opposition) and who therefore merit no punishment at all, must now accept punishment for the organizational wrong that another party ("the organization") supposedly carried out. Any punishment inflicted on "the organization" must necessarily be inflicted on one or the other or both of these undeserving groups, and such "collective punishment" is therefore not morally acceptable.[7]

SIXTH ARGUMENT

Lastly, and perhaps most tellingly, the collectivist view requires that organizations have an autonomy that they do not in fact have. Corporate organizations must be autonomous in order to qualify as a *distinct* entity as maintained by claim (1). Virtually all collectivists have tried to argue that corporations and other organizations possess those capabilities of intending and acting that are necessary for moral responsibility. (See, for example, the contributions of Philip Pettit, Michael Bratman, and Peter French in this book.) Hardly anyone, however, tries to argue for the equally necessary capacity of autonomy. They do not because they cannot. As we shall argue, the lack of autonomy also neatly explains why corporations cannot intend or act.

Personal autonomy is also known as "free will," "self-determination," "self-rule," and "self-government."[8] These phrases all draw on the intuition that autonomy involves an agent's ability to hold a vantage point that is distinct from the agent's desires and allows the agent to choose which desire to act upon. Autonomy is thus not merely about the ability to make choices;

---

[7] "Collective punishment" is punishment that is inflicted upon the family of a wrongdoer, or upon those who are friends or acquaintances of the wrongdoer. Collective punishment is widely condemned as unjust because it punishes the innocent for crimes they did not commit. See, for example, the more than one hundred international and national statements produced in support of rule 103, "Collective Punishments," in the study on customary international humanitarian law conducted by the International Committee of the Red Cross (2016).

[8] It is important to keep "personal autonomy" and "moral autonomy" separate. (See essays collected in *Personal Autonomy* 2005.) Personal autonomy is devoid of moral content about how an agent ought to treat others and is exclusively concerned with the capacity for independent choice. In contrast, moral autonomy involves a comprehensive view of moral agency, which includes the ability to choose right from wrong. We employ the condition of personal autonomy (rather than moral autonomy) because it is merely a necessary and not a sufficient condition for moral agency. If corporations cannot meet this necessary condition of moral agency, then they certainly cannot meet the richer sufficient condition.

importantly it is about how choices are made. According to Frankfurt (1971) an autonomous agent must have desires regarding his desires (in order to be able to independently choose intentional actions) which Frankfurt has called "second-order intentionality." For example, I may have a first-order desire to eat meat, but I may also have a second-order desire not to harm animals, and so I form the intention to abstain from eating meat. This ability to have second-order intentionality forms the basis of our autonomy because it enables us to independently choose our intentional actions rather than merely react to our desires. As such, autonomy refers to an agent's ability to be directed by desires that belong to the agent. This is why autonomy is necessary for lodging ownership with an agent for an intentional action. This ownership of actions is the foundation for attributing moral responsibility to an agent. Although most collectivists have ignored the relation between autonomy and moral responsibility, Pettit (2003) has tried to address the issue directly. Pettit explains that a certain type of decision procedure within a purposive organization can result in a decision that no one in the organization desired, and the fact that such decisions are possible implies that organizations possess autonomy. Pettit (2003, 167) starts by saying: "There is a type of organization found in certain collectivities that makes them into subjects in their own right, giving them a way of being minded that is starkly discontinuous with the mentality of their members. This claim in social ontology is strong enough to ground talk of such collectivities as entities that are psychologically autonomous and that constitute institutional persons."

The basis of Pettit's claim that organizations can make decisions that are "starkly discontinuous with the mentality of their members" is called the "Doctrinal Paradox." This is a paradox that can result when a voting procedure involves three or more voters voting on three or more premises (options). Each voter might on the whole be against a proposed motion, yet if one tallies their votes on individual premises the collective result is to approve the motion.

Pettit (2003) asks us to consider a situation where a collective of employees in a factory need to decide if they agree to a pay-sacrifice in order to obtain safety improvements in their workplace. There are three premises to consider with regard to this issue. First, is there a serious danger under the current work conditions? Second, will the suggested measures for improvement be effective? Third, is the loss in pay bearable? The following matrix represents the decision situation assuming that the collective consists of three individuals, A, B, and C:

	Serious danger?	Effective measure?	Bearable loss?	Pay-sacrifice?
A	Yes	No	Yes	No
B	No	Yes	Yes	No
C	Yes	Yes	No	No
	Yes	*Yes*	*Yes*	*?*

The paradox is that a conclusion-centered procedure leads to a unanimous rejection of the motion while a premise-centered procedure leads to a clear acceptance of the motion. Pettit argues that if the organization uses a premise-centered decision procedure this counts as corporate autonomy because the organization may choose a course of action that no member desired.

Organizations that opt for the premise-centered approach are called "social integrates" and, according to Pettit, they deserve metaphysical recognition as intentional and personal subjects. Important for our purpose is that Pettit regards a social integrate as distinct from its members. He does not mean for it to be metaphysically distinct from its members, but rather that it is distinct "in the sense of being a center for the formation of attitudes that are capable of being quite discontinuous from the attitudes of the members" (Pettit 2003, 183). On Pettit's characterization it would be wrong to think that the individuals form their intentions which then become the intentions of the collective. Rather, the group makes its decision on a specific issue in a manner capable of being discontinuous from the attitudes of the members due to the decision procedure. At this procedural level, on his view, an organizational intention can be announced. It is only after the organizational intention is announced that the members form their own intentions to concertedly perform the intended action.

The autonomous nature of the organization for Pettit is displayed by the doctrinal paradox which may result when employing a premise-centered procedure. Does this organizational "choice" that is discontinuous with the attitudes of the individual members actually count as autonomy in any morally relevant sense? We think not.

The organizational intention resulting from a premise-centered procedure is just that: a procedure. There is no sense in which the procedure is aware of its choice. The fact that the procedural choice is discontinuous with member attitudes does not shift any moral responsibility onto the procedure. All the morally relevant choices are made when devising the procedure itself, and when the members choose to abide by the result of the voting procedure.

It is not possible to obtain autonomy (or moral agency) from any decision procedure because after a procedural decision is made it is still up to the individual members (who are moral agents) to realize the decision through autonomous intentional action. Just like a code of conduct cannot be morally responsible, neither can a decision procedure be morally responsible. We attribute responsibility to an agent and not its decision procedure. A decision procedure can at most explain the actions of individual members, but a procedure is not in itself morally responsible for the independent intentional actions of members. The fact that organizations cannot meet the autonomy condition explains why they cannot intend or act. If a corporate organization lacks the autonomy to deliberate and choose its own intention, but must be given the intention by its members, then there is an important sense in which the intention continues to belong to the corporate members. As such organizations miss the mark of claim (1) as they fail to qualify as *distinct* agents from the members. Furthermore, an agent can only have second-order desires regarding first-order desires if it is aware of them, which suggests that the ability to have intentions is also a mental ability. Clearly corporate structures or voting procedures are not consciously aware.

That organizational members are autonomous and free also explains why corporations cannot act. Collectivists often construe the corporation as a principal directing its members to act on its behalf as its agents. However, the construal of the corporation as a principal is heavily contingent on the corporation's ability to have an intention (which is itself contingent on autonomy). Nevertheless, even if we were to hypothetically assume that a corporate structure qualifies as a principal, Feinberg (1968) has shown that moral responsibility is not transferable from the actions of autonomous "free agents" to a principal (instead, merely the liability for the action is transferable).[9] This implies that irrespective of the corporation's status as a principal it can still never be morally responsible for the actions of its free agents.

CONCLUSION

We have argued that attributions of moral responsibility to organizations— including corporate organizations—should not be understood in a literal sense, as the collectivist proposes. Nonetheless, within the field of business ethics the collectivist view is by far the dominant position. Why might this be the case? There are two motivations, we believe, both based on wishful thinking.

The first motivation relates to the belief that attributing moral responsibility only to individuals will sometimes not capture all the blame that must be accounted for. Among many collectivists there appears to be a deep seated desire to hold someone or something morally responsible for untoward business events even when no individual is morally responsible for the event. For example Werhane (1989, 822) frets that if no individuals are morally responsible for an event then we must attribute moral responsibility

---

[9] Feinberg (1968) identifies two different types of vicarious relationships having to do with the degree of discretion that is granted to the agent. In the first type of relationship (type one) the agent merely acts as a delegate who follows the instructions of its principal to the letter. In the second type (type two) the agent has a wide degree of discretion to act, but within some defined boundaries. Feinberg calls such agents "free agents," and they are hired to exercise their professional judgment on behalf of the principal. It is certainly fair to characterize corporate members as "free" in this regard. Because free agents act independently of their principal the *moral* responsibility for their actions is not transferable.

to corporate policies and practices; otherwise the corporation gets off the "moral hook." Likewise Pettit (2007, 194) is concerned that there will be a deficit in the moral "accounting books" if organizations are not ascribed with moral responsibility when its members are not morally responsible for the event in question (see also Sepinwall 2012). Such concerns about a moral responsibility deficit rest on a misconception that someone or something must be *morally* responsible for untoward events.

However, no cosmic injustice is perpetrated if we don't ascribe moral responsibility for harm caused by a corporate organization. It is often the case that unfortunate events occur for which there are only causal but no moral responsibility ascriptions to be made, for example if a storm fells a tree and kills a man. This is clearly a non-intentional event and as such there are only causal but no moral responsibility attributions to be made. Likewise when harm is caused in the course of satisfying corporate goals it may be the case that no one within the organization intended the resulting harm (nor had an obligation to prevent such harm). If that is the case then there is no moral difference between the storm that felled the tree and the corporate organization that brought about the harm; neither is morally responsible.[10]

Many collectivists (for example, French 1979; Werhane 1985; Pettit 2003) maintain that corporate structures, such as corporate policies, can be attributed with moral responsibility in a manner that is separate from the moral responsibility of corporate members and can thus be responsible when no corporate member is responsible. However, this is to confuse the notion of "organizational responsibility" with that of "organizational ethics."[11] The two concepts need to be kept separate. Organizational ethicists may evaluate the ethicality of organizational policies, procedures, or codes based on how various stakeholders are meant to be taken into account for corporate decisions,

---

[10] The feeling that there is a moral difference between the harm caused by the falling tree and the corporate members seems to arise from the *potential* for moral responsibility that an individual or collective of individuals might have within an organization, while the tree can never be attributed with moral responsibility. The fact that the corporation consists of individuals that are moral agents makes it possible that those individuals may be morally responsible for certain events, but it does not in itself add credence to the view that the corporation as distinct from its members can be attributed with moral responsibility.

[11] The issue of *corporate moral agency* also needs to be kept conceptually separate from issues of *collective moral agency*. This distinction is not always made clearly enough and can be a cause of confusion in the debate. On the one hand, corporate moral responsibility requires agency that is logically distinct from the agency of corporate members so that moral responsibility can be attributed to the corporation as a distinct entity even when no member is morally responsible. On the other hand, collective moral responsibility requires that at least someone within the collective is morally responsible. On some interpretations one or more responsible individuals may represent a group such that the entire group is considered morally responsible. Keeping the distinction between corporate moral responsibility and collective moral responsibility in mind is important because with the latter the agency is entirely dependent on the abilities of the members while with the former it is not.

but the notion of moral agency concerns the identification of the proper bearers of moral responsibility for the actual treatment of the stakeholders. Corporate policies may at most be causally responsible[12] for harm, but policies can never be morally responsible because they are enacted by autonomous corporate members. A policy may be unethical, but it cannot be morally responsible because it's not a moral agent.

The second reason why many business ethicists support the collectivist view relates to what the proper object of ethical analysis should be. There is a desire among business ethicists to see the "business organization" as the unit of ethical analysis when querying what it has done and what it ought to do (see, for example, Collier 1998). Ethical theory, as discussed throughout the history of moral philosophy, prescribes behavior applicable to individual moral agents. And moral agents have been traditionally construed as human persons. Business ethicists, regarding business ethics as a field of applied ethics, have thus wanted to apply the body of ethical theories to the behavior of *corporate organizations* in a manner that is analogous to the way they have been applied to the behavior of individual human persons.

The desirability of such a move is easy to understand. Equating the moral status of corporations with that of persons would allow the field to transpose ethical theories to the corporation as a unit of ethical analysis instead of developing new theories that recognize the morally relevant differences between corporate organizations and persons. By prescribing that corporate organizations act along the lines of previous deontological and utilitarian ethical theories allows business ethicists to ascribe moral responsibility to corporations themselves for transgressing such prescriptions.

However, if the collectivist view is not correct, as we argue, then it will be difficult to maintain that moral prescriptions apply to corporate organizations. Such prescriptions would have to be couched in terms of the moral duties of the organization's members. To argue that the member of an organization or a group of its members ought to carry out certain corporate moral duties is by no means a straight forward exercise. One would need to show how and why the organization's members would have individual or collective moral respon-sibilities that are equivalent to the prescribed corporate moral responsibilities. The members of a corporate organization can have moral duties but they cannot have *corporate* moral duties; that would be a category mistake. By implication, we cannot simply regard corporate moral responsibility as a metaphor that is actually meant to refer to the moral responsibility of corpor-ate members.

---

[12] The sense in which the corporation can be causally responsible for a result is when the corporation is conceived as an organization where coordinated human interactions lead to a certain result. Those interactions might be influenced by the corporate structure, such as policies or decision procedures, and as such the structure might have causal influence.

To illustrate this point consider the importance of circumstances and the myriad duties that any particular member of a corporate organization faces. For example, how should a senior director at BP relate to the prescription that "BP has an obligation to clean up the oil spill in the Gulf of Mexico"? Does this obligation apply to the director only if she contributed to the spill (or had a duty to prevent it)? Assuming that the director did contribute, how does that obligation relate to other corporate members having a similar obligation? How does the obligation relate to the director's other work obligations such as furthering shareholder interests or caring for the safety of employees? How does the obligation relate to private duties as a wife, mother, daughter, citizen, and so on? Now multiply these circumstance and duty considerations for one employee by the number of corporate members, and we can see that using corporate moral prescriptions as metaphors do not translate easily into members' moral duties.

The collectivist view is clearly desirable for business ethicists who have worked hard at maintaining the counterintuitive position that corporations possess the same moral abilities as persons. However, most collectivists only focus on establishing the corporation's purported abilities to intend and act. These abilities are certainly necessary for moral responsibility but few would regard them as sufficient. We maintain that collectivists miss the mark in their attempts to establish these necessary abilities for moral responsibility, and they are nowhere close to hitting the tall order of meeting sufficient conditions. This is decidedly inconvenient for business ethicists, but wishful thinking doesn't change the implausibility of the collectivist view of moral responsibility.

REFERENCES

Alschuler, Albert W. (2009). "Two Ways To Think About The Punishment Of Corporations." *American Criminal Law Review* 46: 1359.

Collier, Jane (1998). "Theorising the Ethical Organization." *Business Ethics Quarterly* 8: 621.

Copp, David (1984). "What Collectives Are: Agency, Individualism and Legal Theory." *Dialogue* 23: 249.

DeGeorge, Richard (1981). "Can Corporations Have Moral Responsibilities?" *University of Dayton Law Review* 5: 3.

Dubbink, Wim and Jeffrey Smith (2011). "A Political Account of Corporate Moral Responsibility." *Ethical Theory and Moral Practice.* 14: 223.

Feinberg, Joel (1968). "Collective Responsibility." *Journal of Philosophy* 65: 674.

Frankfurt, Harry G. (1971). "Freedom of the Will and the Concept of a Person." *Journal of Philosophy* 68: 5.

French, Peter A. (1979). "The Corporation as a Moral Person." *American Philosophical Quarterly* 16: 207.

Gibson, Kevin (1995). "Fictitious Persons and Real Responsibilities." *Journal of Business Ethics* 14: 761.

Gilbert, Margaret (2006). "Who's To Blame? Collective Moral Responsibility and Its Implications for Group Members." *Midwest Studies in Philosophy* 30: 94.

Goodpaster, Kenneth (1983). "The Concept of Corporate Responsibility." *Journal of Business Ethics* 2: 1.

Hasnas, John (2012). "Reflections on Corporate Moral Responsibility and the Problem Solving Techniques of Alexander the Great." *Journal of Business Ethics* 107: 183.

International Committee of the Red Cross (2016). "Practice Relating to Rule 103. Collective Punishments." www.icrc.org/customary-ihl/eng/docs/v2_rul_rule103.

Lewis, H.D. (1948). "Collective Responsibility." *Philosophy* 23: 3.

May, Larry (1987). *The Morality of Groups: Collective Responsibility, Group-Based Harm, and Corporate Rights.*

Miller, Seumas and Pekka Makela (2005). "The Collectivist Approach to Collective Moral Responsibility." *Metaphilosophy* 36: 634.

Moore, Michael S. (2010). *Act and Crime: The Philosophy of Action and Its Implications for Criminal Law*, paperback ed.

Orts, Eric W. (2015). *Business Persons: A Legal Theory of the Firm*, rev. paperback ed.

Personal Autonomy: New Essays on Personal Autonomy and its Role in Contemporary Moral Philosophy (2005). Ed. James Stacey Taylor.

Pettit, Philip (2003). "Groups With Minds Of Their Own." In *Socialising Metaphysics: The Nature of Social Reality*, ed.(Frederick S. Schmitt, 167–93.

Pettit, Philip (2007). "Responsibility Incorporated." *Ethics* 117: 171.

Phillips, Michael J. (1992). "Corporate Moral Personhood and Three Conceptions of the Corporation." *Business Ethics Quarterly* 2: 435.

Quinton, Anthony (1975). "Social Objects." *Proceedings of the Aristotelian Society* (new series) 76: 1.

Rönnegard, David (2008). "Collective Responsibility; Collective Punishment." In Robert W. Kolb (ed.), *The Encyclopedia of Business Ethics and Society.*

Rönnegard, David (2013). "How Autonomy Alone Debunks Corporate Moral Agency." *Business and Professional Ethics Journal* 32: 77.

Rönnegard, David (2015). *The Fallacy of Corporate Moral Agency.*

Seabright, Mark A. and Lance B. Kurke (1997). "Organizational Ontology and the Moral Status of the Corporation." *Business Ethics Quarterly* 7: 91.

Searle, John R. (1990). "Collective Intentions and Actions." In *Intentions in Communication*, ed. Philip R. Cohen, Jerry Morgan, and Martha E. Pollack.

Searle, John R. (1995). *The Construction of Social Reality.*

Sepinwall, Amy J. (2012). "Guilty by Proxy: Expanding the Boundaries of Responsibility in the Face of Corporate Crime." *Hastings Law Journal* 63: 101.

Velasquez, Manuel (1983). "Why Corporations Are Not Morally Responsible For Anything They Do." *Business and Professional Ethics Journal* 2: 1.

Velasquez, Manuel (2003). "Debunking Corporate Moral Responsibility." *Business Ethics Quarterly* 13: 531.

Wall, Edmund (2000). "The Problem of Group Agency." *Philosophical Forum* 31: 187.

Watson, Gary (1987). "Responsibility and the Limits of Evil: Variations on a Strawsonian Theme." In *Responsibility, Character, and the Emotions: New Essays in Moral Psychology*, ed. Ferdinand Schoeman.

Werhane, Patricia H. (1985). *Persons, Rights, and Corporations.*
Werhane, Patricia H. (1989). "Corporate and Individual Moral Responsibility: A Reply to Jan Garrett." *Journal of Business Ethics* 8: 821.
Wolf, Susan (1985). "The Legal and Moral Responsibility of Organizations." In *Criminal Justice: NOMOS XXVII*, ed. Ronald Pennock and John W. Chapman.

8

Blame, Emotion, and the Corporation

*Amy J. Sepinwall**

Are corporations moral agents?[1] Does it make sense to hold them responsible for their wrongs? These questions, though hardly new, seem to press upon us with renewed urgency with each new wave of corporate wrongdoing. Thus we have seen very few prosecutions of financial institutions in the wake of the economic meltdown notwithstanding official findings of corporate fraud (Sepinwall 2015a; Garrett 2015). Nor is the apparent corporate impunity restricted to domestic offenses. Corporations have been let off the hook for their alleged participation in international human rights abuses like torture and rape on the ground that they are not the kind of beings contemplated by the relevant statutes and treaties.[2] Paradoxically, and more troubling still, the legal retrenchment that frees corporations from blame and sanction unfolds against an expanding conception of the corporation as the bearer of important legal rights, such as rights to political speech[3] or conscience protections.[4]

Given the stakes in recognizing or denying corporate personhood, one would think that philosophers and legal scholars had long ago settled the question of

* An early version of this chapter was presented at a conference organized by Eric Orts and Craig Smith on The Moral Responsibility of Firms at INSEAD, where it benefited tremendously from the conference participants' feedback. I am especially grateful to Nien-he Hsieh and Eric Orts who each offered extensive written comments, and to Andy Siegel, who remains the best interlocutor a person could have.

[1] By "corporation" I mean to refer to an institutional group—that is, one that can have acts performed in its own name—organized for a business purpose. With that said, the remarks here about corporate capacities for guilt and blame would apply as well to other institutional groups— for example, non-profit organizations, universities, religious institutions, political entities, and so on.

[2] See, for example, *Kiobel v. Royal Dutch Petroleum* (2013) (holding that the Alien Tort Statute does not apply extra-territorially, so Shell could not be sued under it for its alleged complicity in human rights abuses); *Mohamad v. Palestinian Authority* (2012) (holding that the term "individual" in the Torture Victim Protection Act contemplates only natural persons and therefore does not impose liability on organizations).

[3] See *Citizens United v. Federal Election Commission* (2010).

[4] See *Burwell v. Hobby Lobby Stores, Inc.* (2014).

whether or not the corporation is a person. In fact, the debate about corporate personhood continues to rage, as this book attests. This chapter endeavors to enter the fray on the side of those who would deny that the corporation is a person, but it does not entertain the broad question of corporate personhood nor even the only slightly narrower question of corporate moral agency. Instead, the chapter restricts its focus to the idea of blame. In particular, I explore the nature and functions of blame in an effort to show that corporations are not appropriate targets of blame or, as I shall use the term here, *corporations are not blameworthy*. Briefly, I argue that it makes sense to blame only those who can experience guilt, affect is required to experience guilt, corporations have no capacity for affect, and so it makes no sense to blame corporations.

The immediate implication of the argument is that the corporation cannot, and so should not, be blamed. But the account developed here is not in the least intended to function as an apology, and still less a blank check, for corporate wrongdoing. I shall argue instead that the fact that the corporation is not blameworthy does not entail that we may not punish it when it goes wrong. In that sense, my arguments may appear to have a very modest aim. But there is a more far-reaching conclusion to be drawn if it turns out, as I argue it does, that the corporation lacks affect and so cannot be blamed. The affectless corporation, I shall suggest, is ill-suited for membership in our moral community more generally. I conclude by suggesting that the arguments advanced here give us reason to prohibit the corporation from participating in the central institutions and practices of democratic society. Thus the arguments here establishing the corporation's lack of affect may do more than advance our thinking on responses to corporate wrongdoing; they may provide resources for gaining clarity on the role and standing of corporations in society more generally.

EMOTIONS AND MORAL RESPONSIBILITY

I begin by identifying where and why emotions, and their felt correlates, should figure in our thinking about moral responsibility.

Those who defend the notion that corporations can bear moral responsibility—or, equivalently, that they are moral agents—differ in their conceptions of what moral agency requires. Nonetheless, we can for present purposes generalize the relevant criteria. A moral agent, it is held, must be able to act autonomously (that is, act of its own accord, or be the ultimate source of its own actions), form moral judgments, and act in light of those judgments (Arnold 2006; Donaldson 1980; Hess 2014; List and Pettit 2011; Mathiesen 2006; see generally Sepinwall 2016).

Importantly, on both sides of the corporate moral responsibility debate, the ability to form moral judgments is usually if not always construed in purely cognitive terms. Thus the moral agent must be able to form the right kind of beliefs about right and wrong, and she does so by being responsive to moral reasons (Pettit 2007); or the moral agent is one who acts on an intention that originates in her (Velasquez 1983, 3–4).[5] The cognitive emphasis—some might even say bias—here is unsurprising, as the emotions have largely been given short shrift in the literature on moral responsibility more generally. As Maggie Little puts the point, "only trouble, it is thought, can come of [emotions'] intrusion into deliberations.…At best, they are [taken to be] irrelevant distractions, like so many pains and tickles. At worst, they are highly distorting influences" (Little 1995, 117).

Against this view, Little and others have argued persuasively that emotions are necessary for bringing the morally salient features of the world to light. Thus she contends that "there are some truths.… that can be apprehended only from a stance of affective engagement" (id., 118), and she argues that this is especially the case for moral truths. Similarly, Nancy Sherman (1997, 48) hails the "epistemic advantage of emotion," which resides in its "peculiar ability to make vividly present the objects of its evaluative focus." Louis Charland (1998, 72) puts the point succinctly: without emotions, he writes, "reason is blind."[6]

I am doubtful that the corporation has a capacity for emotion in its own right, and elsewhere I have argued that, if it does not, then it should not qualify for moral agency (Sepinwall 2012). I allow here, however, that a corporate capacity for emotion *as a source of moral knowledge* could be sustained by and through the emotional capacities of the corporation's members. I have in mind a strategy that the defender of corporate moral responsibility often uses to support her account. This strategy elides the need for the corporation to possess, *in its own right*, some or all of the capacities necessary for moral agency; instead, the defender of corporate moral responsibility argues that the corporation need only be able to reliably recruit these capacities from its members. I call accounts that adopt this strategy *recruiting* accounts, and I shall have more to say about them below. For now, I note that if we are prepared to accept recruiting accounts when it comes to corporate action (for example, the corporation's members carry out its acts on its behalf, Hess 2014, 249–50) and corporate intentions (for example, Bratman 2014), then we might well have reason to accept the notion that the corporation can rely on its members—especially their emotional capacities—for the formation of the corporation's moral judgments. If the corporation can reliably recruit from its members the moral knowledge that the emotions disclose, and it possesses in its own right or else can recruit from its members whatever other capacities moral agency requires, then, for present

[5] Pettit seeks to defend corporate moral agency, and Velasquez seeks to deny it.
[6] Starkey (2008) argues similarly that emotions are necessary for moral understanding and so for the possession of virtue.

purposes anyway, it will qualify as a moral agent. At this stage of my argument, I assume that these *recruiting conditions* are satisfied.

MORAL AGENCY AND BLAME

The claim that this chapter sets itself against is narrower than the claim that the corporation is a moral agent, though my claim is perhaps no less consequential. That claim is as follows. *Even if the corporation is a moral agent, it is not an appropriate target of blame.* To be an appropriate target of blame, I shall argue, one must have *affect* in addition to the capacities necessary for moral agency, and the corporation cannot feel anything, let alone the feelings central to the practice of blaming. Nor would a recruiting account of corporate moral responsibility save the day here, as it arguably does for at least some of the capacities required for moral agency. For even if we allow that the corporation can recruit its actions and moral judgments from its members and at the same time maintain that those actions and moral judgments nonetheless belong and may be imputed to the corporation, it makes no sense to conceive of feelings as delegable or recruitable in this way. Or so I shall argue.

To that end, I shall seek to make clear the role of feelings in blame, and I will argue that because corporations cannot feel of their own accord, and because no one can do the relevant feeling work for them, they cannot participate in the practice of blaming: They cannot themselves blame and, more pointedly still, they cannot be the targets of others' blame.

Before turning to those arguments it is worth noting that the account advanced here is non-standard to the extent that it assumes a wedge between moral agency and blame. Standardly, once we have ascertained that A is a moral agent, and we learn that A has, without justification, committed some wrong, we take A to be blameworthy for that wrong. Put succinctly, on many accounts of the problem given to date, to say that A is morally responsible for X is just to say that A is blameworthy for X. Yet I believe that there are two senses of "blameworthy," and it will be important here to keep them apart. The first sense, as we have seen, treats "morally responsible" as equivalent to "blameworthy." But we might instead mean by "A is blameworthy for X" that it *makes sense* to blame A for X, where the conditions that make blame sensible include not only those that make A morally responsible for X but also those conditions necessary for blame to perform its paradigmatic functions. More specifically, it will make sense to blame A only if A can experience whatever states blame aims to induce in its targets—paradigmatically, guilt and its attendant feelings, as I shall argue further below. Thus, while a capacity to experience guilt and its affective components might not be necessary for moral responsibility, these capacities are necessary, I shall argue, if blame is to have its intended uptake. It is because corporations lack a capacity for affect that they are not blameworthy on the second way of understanding blameworthiness. Without the capacity for affect, I shall contend, it makes no sense to blame the corporation for wrongdoing.

THE NATURE AND FUNCTION OF BLAME

Blame, as I shall understand it, is a conjunction of a moral judgment that the blamed party has acted wrongly along with an orientation of reproach.[7] The moral judgment is not alone sufficient for blame because one can judge that another has acted wrongly with no condemnation at all, or perhaps even in a spirit of celebration (for example, Wallace 2011, 348). For example, where two individuals intentionally commit a crime together, each of them will know that the other engages in wrongdoing. But the conspirator's judgment of his co-felon's wrong will likely be devoid of censure; if they believe their criminal activity is righteous (perhaps as an act of civil disobedience against a regime deemed unjust) each will likely laud the other's efforts.[8] So blame must consist of something more than a judgment of wrongdoing.[9]

I have identified this additional element as an orientation of reproach, but theorists disagree about just what this orientation must consist in. Some theorists contend that this orientation must be conative (that is, it consists of desires, attitudes, dispositions, and so on), while others contend that it must be constituted by the emotions. I explore each option in turn.

Generally speaking, on conative accounts, to blame is to judge that another has acted wrongly and to be disposed to change one's attitudes or behavior in light of that judgment. For example, George Sher construes blame as a belief–desire pair, where the belief consists of the judgment of wrongdoing, and the desire consists of a wish that the offender have had a commitment to morality that would have caused her to refrain from committing the offense (Sher 2006, 127–8). For Sher, the desire prompts the behavioral and emotional responses that typically accompany blame, but these are not constitutive of blame itself.

---

[7] For an excellent and more comprehensive overview of accounts of blame, see Coates and Tognazzini (2012).

[8] Cf. Coates and Tognazzini (2012) describing a conspirator who admires the deftness of her partner in crime.

[9] The claim that blame must involve more than a moral judgment fits more readily with an externalist rather than internalist account of reasons. On the latter, to arrive at a judgment that X is wrong is already to feel the force of that judgment, to be motivated to refrain from X-ing (Williams 1981, 101–13). If internalism is correct, then it is not clear that the corporation can arrive even at the moral judgment involved in blaming. So much the worse then for accounts defending corporate moral responsibility.

Thomas Scanlon offers a different version of a conative account. According to Scanlon, blame is a conjunction of the judgment that another has acted in a way that impairs her relationship with you, and the disposition to alter your relationship with her as a result (Scanlon 2008, 128–9).

Sher and Scanlon, then, deny that blame need have an emotional component, but other theorists contend that the emotions figure crucially in blame. Peter Strawson (1962, 1993) offers an account of moral responsibility that foregrounds the role of moral emotions.[10] For Strawson, our assignments of moral responsibility are constituted by the *reactive attitudes*—the emotional responses we have to the attitudes and intentions of others as these are displayed in their actions (Strawson 1993, 49, 56–7). When it comes to wrongdoing, the reactive attitudes consist of a perspective-based triad of emotions—guilt, for our own wrongdoing; resentment, for wrongdoing against us; and indignation, for wrongdoing aimed at others (Strawson 1993). Importantly, for Strawson, the reactive attitudes are not simply practical corollaries or emotional side effects of one's theory of responsibility; instead, they are constitutive of moral responsibility. On a Strawsonian account, as Gary Watson notes, "to regard oneself or another as responsible just is the proneness to react to them in these kinds of ways under certain conditions" (Watson 1987, 256–7).[11]

While Strawson wasn't concerned with blame per se, others have extended his account in an effort to argue that blame is centrally about the reactive attitudes. Thus R. Jay Wallace (1994, 52) contends that "to blame someone is to be subject to one of the reactive emotions in terms of which the stance of holding people responsible is essentially defined." In other words, to hold you responsible (or, equivalently for Wallace, to blame you) is to recognize that you have violated a moral obligation and to have that recognition elicit, or at least prime one to experience, resentment as a result (Wallace 1994).

Finally, even among those who insist that the emotions are central for blame, there is a further possible divide. On the one hand, there are those who think that the phenomenological component of the emotions involved in blame is crucial to their experience (for example, paradigmatically, when one blames, one experiences anger, along with angry sensations such as excitement, flushed cheeks, racing heart, and so on).[12] Wallace, for example,

---

[10] Strawson's seminal essay, "Freedom and Resentment," was originally published in 1962 (Strawson 1962). Citations here are to the reprinted version in Strawson (1993).

[11] Other theorists, as we shall see, dispute Strawson's contention that a judgment of responsibility is *constituted* by the reactive attitudes, but they nonetheless agree that the reactive attitudes are the regular products of a judgment of responsibility (see Watson 1987; Sher 2006).

[12] I contend that the felt component of an emotion arises in the *paradigmatic* experience of it, not that the felt component *necessarily* accompanies it. The latter contention is too demanding, as Elisa A. Hurley and Coleen Macnamara ably argue (Hurly and Macnamara 2010). I return to this argument below and will seek to explain why affect can be central to blame even if it is not necessary on each and every occasion when one blames.

contends not only that blame is constituted by the reactive attitudes but also that the reactive attitudes are themselves constituted by their felt sensations. "To count as blaming a person," he writes, "you have to be exercised by what they have done, and to be exercised in the relevant way just is to be subject to one of the reactive sentiments" (Wallace 2011, 358). Similarly, Susan Wolf also identifies the feeling of anger as central to blame (Wolf 2011, 344).

By contrast, others think the phenomenological correlates of blaming emotions mere expendable appendages.[13] For example, Pamela Hieronymi concedes that feelings often accompany blame but she nonetheless contends that blame—especially its moral import—cannot be about these feelings (Hieronymi 2004, 121). Tognazzini does not offer a settled view, but he allows at least for the possibility that feelings need not form part of an emotion (Tognazzini 2013, 1312).

On Behalf of an Emotional Account of Blame

How should one decide between these competing conceptions of blame's components? The challenge is that our actual instances of blame often have more than one, and sometimes all, of the candidate elements. Thus, in many instances, we blame in a state of resentment, desiring that the offender not have been the kind of person who would wrong us, and with an eye to distancing ourselves from her in light of her wrongdoing. Both emotional and conative accounts ring true because both point to elements that often figure centrally in our everyday experiences of blame and blaming.

I do not seek to deny that a desire that the wrongdoer have done otherwise or a disposition to distance oneself from her might be essential elements of blame. My claim instead is that whatever else blame involves, it centrally involves felt emotions. I adopt a three-fold strategy for arguing on behalf of a *felt emotional* account of blame: (1) I describe a hypothetical world in which blame never arises in conjunction with feelings and argue that such a world is implausible; (2) I address and seek to explain away apparent counterexamples; and (3) I describe blame's paradigmatic functions, with a view to foregrounding the ways in which these functions necessarily involve feelings.

1. A World Without Guilt and Anger? To begin, I borrow a thought experiment from Strawson (1993, 53–6). He invites us to consider what it would be like to live in a world where we ceased responding to others' displays of ill will with resentment or indignation, and he contends that this world would be so unfamiliar to us as to require a complete revision in our interpersonal relationships. We could not go on as we are. If such is the case for our

---

[13] See for example Gilbert (2002), Hieronymi (2004).

responsibility practice in general, it is, I shall now suggest, a fortiori true for our blaming practice in particular.

Imagine, then, a world in which blame was always devoid of an emotional response. In such a world, perhaps blame typically carried with it a disposition to distance oneself from the offender, or a wish that the offender had acted otherwise. But blame never involved anger. This fictive world is not perhaps as inconceivable as the one Strawson conjures, and indeed some would undoubtedly find it superior to our own. But they would be led to do so, I believe, because of undue misgivings about the emotions, especially their felt aspects. These theorists cast emotions as unruly (see Hurley 2007, 84), and negative emotions as ugly to boot. They then see our dispassionate counterparts in the imagined world as more enlightened than, and so superior to, those of us who are characterized somehow as "too emotional."[14]

Against this view, notice that some of our most cherished experiences not only require but also revolve around feelings. Romantic love is exemplary here (Hurley 2007). Someone who experienced only the dispositions and attitudes that love prompts, without its felt components, would not, we would rightly hold, really be in love. Indeed, one might even wonder what source these dispositions and attitudes would have, and so whether they could even be present, in one who could not experience the feeling of being in love. Similarly, as Hurley writes, "Think, too, of what grief or remorse, compassion or gratitude, would be like and would mean without feelings. Feelings seem to be somehow *essential* to what emotions are…" (Hurley 2007, 83). Feelings, that is, seem to be constitutive of some of our most positive emotional experiences.

Still, one might think the situation is different for negative emotions. We might be worse off, one might concede, without romantic love or compassion or gratitude, but better off were we to jettison guilt and resentment. Yet the thought that we could be moved by love or compassion, but not guilt and resentment, may be too fanciful even for hypothetical contemplation. For one thing, the ability to experience positive emotions might require that we be able to experience negative emotions. There is the common thought that we know pleasure only in light of its opposite (and vice versa); appreciating the positive emotions might then require experience of the negative emotions. With that said, the truth of the duality of pleasure and pain, if it is a truth, need not be physiological. In other words, it need not be the case that the neurological components that allow us to experience pleasant feelings are not specialized enough to turn us off to painful feelings. Nor is it necessarily an epistemic claim—that is to say, that our brains need pain in order to know pleasure. Instead, the point is, importantly, conceptual: What it is to love someone is, among other things, to feel acute

---

[14] Buddhist psychology is exemplary here, as it characterizes anger as a source of suffering, and a disposition that can and should be overcome (see, for example, Dalai Lama and Cutler, 1998, 50, 260–2).

resentment when they betray you. What it is to sympathize with someone is, among other things, to share their disappointment when they fail and imagine their guilt when they offend. The positive and negative emotions are not then separate experiences, but mutually constitutive. So too, it would follow, for their phenomenological correlates. As such, we cannot pick and choose which emotions we will retain in this (supposedly) ideal world, for the conditions of any of them might be conditions of them all.

At any rate, the prospect of picking and choosing takes us outside the intended thought experiment. The question the thought experiments asks us to consider is not whether we (or some more "evolved" or "enlightened" version of us) would be better off without negative emotions; it is whether we would be ourselves at all—whether we would be recognizable to ourselves—without the feelings of guilt, resentment, and indignation. Even assuming we could have love, compassion, and so on without their negative counterparts, it is doubtful that human relations would remain intelligible to us absent anger and guilt. These are just the ways we mark the unacceptability of others' failures to display the appropriate regard for us, or our own failures to have displayed the appropriate regard for others. Our sense of the worth that we hold qua persons demands that we respond with anger when someone denigrates us, and that we react with guilt when we realize we have denigrated another. A world in which slights and transgressions were met with cool detachment would be a world in which we failed to register these affronts in the right way. Put differently, anger, on this understanding, is not some base, unenlightened reaction that we would be better for having overcome; it is instead the proper response for securing and insisting upon our own standing.[15]

2. Passionless Blame. At this point, someone might object: If blame is inconceivable without felt emotions, how is it that we can sometimes blame with no emotional activation? Thus, George Sher (2006) points out that we rarely experience anger when we blame famous people long dead. And others marshal instances when even the blame we aim at people living in the here and now is experienced dispassionately.[16]

In response to Sher's worry, Wallace has argued that we do not in fact blame historic figures: We judge them blameworthy, but we do not blame them. (Wallace 2011). And Hurley has sought to explain contemporary instances of passionless blame by appeal to the notion of salience: the virtuous person, she

---

[15] It is for something like this reason, I take it, that some have charged that Scanlon's account of blame is unacceptably anemic. See McGreer (2013), Wolf (2011), and Wallace (2011) (accusing Scanlon of having taken the blame out of blame).

[16] Huebner (2011) offers a third category of (purportedly) affectless emotions—namely, those that exist in our unconscious states. Unconscious emotions are, of course, not felt. One can respond, however, that for that very reason unconscious emotions are not the same kinds of things as conscious ones.

contends, "is one who attends to what she ought to in a situation; she will notice just what is most *deserving* of her attention" (Hurley 2007, 89). Since anger is not always the most productive or appropriate response to an offender, Hurley suggests that anger is not normatively required in every instance when one blames.

These responses may go some distance toward answering the objection, but it is not clear to me that either response fully dispels it. Wallace's effort would seem to build emotion into the notion of blame by definition, and so it is possible that it does no more than beg the question. And Hurley's suggestion cannot account for cases where there is no competing emotional demand, and yet we blame without activated feelings.

A better response, I believe, would understand these cases as instances of blame where the anger is latent. In other words, the feeling component is dormant at the time blame is expressed but it is able to be activated if prompted and prodded. Our capacity to sustain an emotion often outlasts our capacity to experience its typical phenomenological correlates. It is in this sense that one can be "emotionally spent." On the other hand, one can feel anger long after the target of one's resentment or indignation has expired. Thus, it is not uncommon for people who had difficult relationships with a loved one to indulge resentment, and sometimes even to get worked up into a state of anger, long after the loved one has died. As such, our common experiences of blame would seem to counter the objection that we can blame even in the absence of felt anger.

Further, the objection is belied not just by anecdotal evidence but by the strictures of logic too, for the objection urges a wholesale rejection of a theory on the basis of its inability to account for what might well be only marginal instances of the phenomenon the theory is meant to elucidate. To see this, consider an argument with the same structure as the objector's: Some think we should keep promises out of respect for the promisee. But we keep promises to dead people, and we have no reason to respect them once dead (alternatively, there is no person left to respect once dead). So our reason for keeping promises cannot be respect for promisees. Even assuming the truth of the second premise, it is not clear why the exceptional case of keeping promises to the dead should impugn the rationale for the much more common case of keeping promises to the living. By the same token, it is not clear why the marginal case of blaming the dead, or coolly blaming the living, should cause us to reject wholesale a rationale for blame that accounts for the most common cases.

Of course, whether cases of dispassionate blame really are marginal is precisely what is at issue. But the foregoing should make clear that we cannot resolve this issue solely by appeal to our own experience, for that experience includes cases of angry and dispassionate blame alike. It is for this reason that the Strawsonian thought experiment is illuminating. It asks us to contemplate not whether we could *ever* blame dispassionately but whether we could *only* blame dispassionately. It is this latter possibility that should strike us as altogether foreign. And an appreciation of blame's paradigmatic functions, which I will now consider, should provide still more support for impassioned blame.

3. *Blame's Teleology.* On the account developed here, I allow that blame may have many functions. For example, blame might permit the wider community to reinforce its condemnation of certain acts (McKenna 2012; Bennett 2012). It might be used to vindicate the victim's sense that she has been wronged (Bennett 2012; cf. Duff 2003). Or it might, as Scanlon (2008) describes, register an impairment of the relationship between the blaming party and the offender. Whatever the other functions of blame might be, I want here to foreground blame's role as *punishment*.[17]

Blame's punitive function has two dimensions. First, to blame someone is to register a demerit in her moral ledger; it is to record her moral failure and lower our appraisal of her character (for example, Zimmerman 1988, 38). This is painful, and so punitive, in two respects. The blamed party should care about being moral, so the fact that her ledger reflects her wrongdoing should already pain her. Further, the experience of being judged by others as having lost some moral credit is an additional source of distress. In short, the blamed party is the subject of a negative moral judgment, which is punitive in its own right, as is the corresponding loss of standing that the blame reflects.

But blame paradigmatically hurts in another way too. Blame expresses anger; warranted blame expresses righteous anger. It can be deeply uncomfortable, sometimes even agonizing, to be the target of anger one knows one deserves. One might think that the agony here comes exclusively from the negative judgment blame conveys, which cannot be gainsaid where it is justified; on this thought, the blamer's anger adds nothing to the unpleasantness of being blamed. But this way of understanding blame underestimates the power of anger, as a moment's contemplation reveals. The blamer does not marshal anger as a didactic or punitive tool. The causal story goes the other way: she expresses blame as a way of releasing the anger she already feels; and it is partly because her anger is raw and real, and not manufactured for purposes of teaching a lesson, that it can have the didactic and punitive force it does. In this way, angry blame makes manifest the pain the offender has caused. It allows the offender to see the effect of his transgression in all its force. The empathic offender—the one who can appreciate the blamer's pain—cannot but help feel pain herself, knowing that she is the source of the anger that she is, through blame, intended to absorb. A similar dynamic obtains for the third party who expresses felt indignation in response to an

---

[17] Coates and Tognazzini (2012, 198) suggest that a speech-act account of blame, such as Elizabeth Beardsley's (1970), might reflect the notion that to blame is to punish. List and Pettit (2011) also adduce the punitive function of blame.

offense of which he was not the victim. It is in this sense, then, that blame functions to make its target feel bad—both about herself and the pain she has caused.[18]

Notice, though, that accounts of blame that overlook its affective component cannot capture blame's full punitive force. This is not to say that these accounts must deny that blame has any punitive dimension. As we have seen, the cognitive component of blame—the judgment of wrongdoing—can be painful in its own right. But the confrontation with the anger of the victim or that of the community brings to light the gravity of the offender's wrong to a further degree still. If the offender cares about others' feelings, angry blame will cause her pain additional to that which a dispassionate judgment of opprobrium can inflict.

Further, a Scanlonian account of blame (Scanlon 2008) will be little better than a cognitive account at capturing the full force of blame's punitive dimensions. For blame on a Scanlonian account might be painful, but it need not be: the offender might already have anticipated the relationship impairment that blame registers; indeed, we might see the offense as itself reflecting the offender's sense that the relationship is less important to her than it once was, such that she can now treat the victim in a way that the relationship, in its prior and better state, would have forbidden. The victim's blame is then not so much what marks the victim's retreat as it is the victim's signaling that she recognizes the retreat that already prompted, or was enacted by, the offender's offense. At any rate, Scanlon does not conceive of the impairment as a kind of punishment; it is instead just the practical consequence of the offender's offense.

It is, then, only with an understanding of blame that foregrounds its affective elements that we can fully track all of the ways in which blame can be seen and properly understood as punishing.

CORPORATIONS AND BLAME

I have shown that a capacity for affect is necessary not only for blaming others but for being a suitable target of blame oneself. I now seek to argue that corporations lack the requisite capacity for affect. As such, they cannot be blameworthy in the robust sense described above. I begin by arguing against accounts of corporate emotion that locate the emotional apparatus within the corporation itself. I then consider two alternative strategies meant to secure a corporate capacity for emotion, including felt emotions, and show also that neither of these alternatives is feasible.

---

[18] R. Jay Wallace also insists on the role of affect in blaming, but his focus is on the centrality of feelings for the blamer, not the target of blame (Wallace 2011, 353, 358).

Corporations and Emotion

Peter French is among the most prominent defenders of corporate moral responsibility, and his account at least nominally incorporates a role for the emotions. In an early formulation of his account, he argues that the corporation can experience regret, where that experience consists of viewing oneself as having done "x (where x is some untoward action) and to feel or wish that one had not done x, or that x had not had certain upshots" (French 1984, 91). And, in a later refinement of the account, he contends that the corporation is sensitive to blame where and because it has a capacity for "responsive adjustment." That is, the corporation can "appreciate that an event for which [its] intentional or unintentional behavior has been causally responsible is untoward or worthy," and it can "intentionally modify [its] ways of behaving to correct the offensive actions or to adopt the behavior that was productive of worthy results" (French 1984, 166). Both formulations revolve, then, around a conative conception of blame—one that goes to the attitudes and dispositions that blame prompts. Both formulations, that is, might advert to an emotion (such as regret), but they conceive of that emotion in purely functionalist terms. Thus the account tells us what the emotion is likely to cause the corporation to do, but not what, or even whether, the corporation will feel. In these ways, French's account does not contemplate, and does not have the resources to sustain, a corporate capacity for affect.

Margaret Gilbert offers an account of collective remorse that, at least at first glance, appears to do better than French's on this score. According to Gilbert, "*A group G feels remorse over an act A* if and only if the members of *G* are jointly committed to feeling remorse as a body" (Gilbert 2000, 135). Yet, while Gilbert's understanding of collective remorse invokes the word "feeling," she does not in fact mean that the group *feels* anything; remorse, for her, is exhausted by the actions and utterances of the individuals who together constitute the group (id., 135, 137–8). Indeed, Gilbert denies that "'feeling-sensations'" are a necessary part of remorse, whether experienced by an individual or a collective, and so she is untroubled by the collective's inability to suffer pangs of remorse (id., 135–6). Gilbert acknowledges that there may be de facto connections between collective remorse, as she understands it, and members' feelings of remorse over what the collective has done, but she insists that her account of collective remorse does not depend upon these connections. Collective remorse makes sense, she argues, even if *no* member of the group *feels* remorse over what the group has done.

Against Gilbert's account, we might note that, even at the intuitive level, something seems amiss here. For example, we wouldn't be assuaged by some purportedly remorseful corporation, no matter how many public mea culpas it issued, if its members were all the while laughing their way to the bank.[19] But suppose that the corporation's members did feel pangs of remorse over some wrongful corporate act. The question Gilbert's account prompts is whether the collective itself can satisfy the conditions for remorse if *it* is incapable of the feeling sensations that, at least typically, accompany remorse.

One way to answer that question is to imagine someone who meets Gilbert's definition of remorse: he displays all of the outward trappings of remorse in all of the appropriate circumstances but lacks any internal states that correspond to the outward displays. Can he be said to experience remorse? It is not clear that he can, for his reaction to a wrongful act would seem to be no different than that of the psychopath. The psychopath is also largely capable of saying the appropriate things and performing restitutionary acts when he recognizes that he has violated a moral rule.[20] But the psychopath is, by definition, remorseless. So it is not clear that Gilbert's account of remorse, pared down as it is, ought to count as remorse at all (cf. Bakan 2004).

More damningly, it is not clear that Gilbert's definition of remorse is even coherent. A condition of the sincerity of remorse—and especially its concili- atory power—seems to be that the person who experiences it *feels bad* about the act prompting the remorse. But if remorse is, paradigmatically, constituted by felt guilt then how could one who could not feel guilt ever be said to be remorseful?

At this point, the defender of corporate emotions might seek to dismiss the line of argument I have pressed as nothing more than chauvinism, privileging as it does the ways humans experience the emotions (Huebner 2011, 112; Gilbert 2002). Guilt may feel a certain way for us, but why think our experi- ence of guilt authoritative for other kinds of beings? If we were to come across a species of alien whose skin turned from green to purple whenever one of them felt guilt, we would think the color change an interesting but inessential feature of guilt. After all, we do not change color when we experience guilt, and yet we think our experience of guilt as robust as is necessary to qualify as having the emotion. Why not then think that guilt's peculiar phenomenology for us is no more central to having the emotion than is the color change for the alien?

The answer, I believe, rests in denying that the felt correlates of guilt (or any other moral reactive attitude) really are peripheral in the way the objection would have it. We know guilt in part through the beliefs and dispositions underpinning it, but we know it also in significant part through the way it

---

[19] See Sepinwall 2015a (commenting on the public outrage emerging from the US Depart- ment of Justice's findings that bank fraud was a major contributor to the financial crisis alongside its failures to prosecute any high-level individual bankers for crimes of fraud).

[20] I purposely avoid referring to these acts as "reconciliatory" (though Gilbert does so) because the possibility of reconciliation without the perpetrator's feeling of remorse is precisely what's at issue.

feels. And that feeling is useful not just for identifying guilt as the emotion it is but also, I have argued, useful for furnishing its regulative and conciliatory functions. The pain of guilt causes us to refrain from performing the guilt-inducing act in the future, and it causes others to recognize that we too have suffered as a result of our wrongdoing, and so perhaps deserve forgiveness. Correspondingly, blame is most keenly expressed when the offender appears not yet to have appreciated her own wrongdoing; we aim to bring about this appreciation through the expression of blame. But we could not achieve this aim—blame would be hopeless—if the target of blame had no feelings. It is true then that our understanding of guilt is conditioned by the human experience of it; and so too is our understanding of blame. To operate with a conception of blame that didn't require feelings in its target would be to operate with a conception of blame wholly foreign to our own.

In short, our survey of French's and Gilbert's accounts reveals that the capacities required for the corporation to be blameworthy cannot be secured on the basis of the corporation's own capacities. That conclusion is just a more specific version of Roger Scruton's claim that a "corporation cannot possess mental states which must be 'felt' or 'experienced' if they are to be possessed at all" (Scruton 1989, 253). I turn now to recruiting accounts, to see if they fare any better.

Corporations Recruiting Members' Emotions

Deborah Tollefsen raises the interesting possibility that a group emotion need not be experienced by the group itself in order for it to count as a collective emotion. Instead, the collective emotion is the emotion "one feels in response to the actions of one's own group" (Tollefsen 2003). In this way, Tollefsen's account preserves the phenomenological dimensions of the reactive attitudes, which French's and Gilbert's accounts eschewed as unnecessary.

Though Tollefsen's account goes a good distance toward making sense of the notion of a collective emotion, it does not establish that collectives (and so corporations) experience the reactive attitudes in the way they should if they are to be blameworthy. On the understanding of blameworthiness that I have defended above, one is not a suitable target of blame simply because one *can* experience the reactive attitudes; when one confronts the moral nature of one's acts, one *ought* to do so, for doing so is part and parcel of the confrontation. Thus, if a group has acted badly then, to qualify for blame, it (or its members, if we are to adopt Tollefsen's account) ought to experience collective guilt. But nothing in Tollefsen's account secures the requisite "ought," for nothing in her account explains how group members will necessarily, or even regularly, come to experience guilt on behalf of their group. Indeed, she argues that, for any given member, the appropriateness of the collective emotion turns on whether that member concludes that the group has failed to satisfy demands to which the *member* believes the group ought to be held. For example, on her account, whether an American ought to experience collective guilt over the lack of universal health care will turn on whether that American believes that the government has an obligation to provide universal health care (Tollefsen 2003, 235). But if the emotion is truly collective, then it ought not to be contingent upon vicissitudes among members' assessments of the group's act. In any event, even if all of the group's members agree that the group has failed in some respect, it is not clear that their shared determination will in fact guarantee their experience of guilt. To the extent that, *ex hypothesi*, it is the collective that is the primary locus of responsibility, its members may well have *less* reason to experience guilt on its behalf. In short, Tollefsen's account of collective emotions makes sense of these emotions at the expense of severing the connection to *collective* attitudes of self-assessment, which at least the punitive aspects of blame require. Nor does it seem likely that one could overcome this difficulty, for emotions cannot be compelled; at any rate, their significance would likely be greatly undercut if they could.[21] Finally, even if the collective's members willingly felt on the corporation's behalf, it is doubtful that their "vicarious" feelings (Tollefsen 2008, 12) would count as legitimate substitutes for the corporation's.[22] If blame aims at making its target feel bad, then those who blame the corporation aim (however misguidedly) to make *it* feel bad. The fact that someone else will feel bad—indeed, even if the group's members are under an obligation, qua members, to feel bad—won't be sufficient to make corporate blame sensible. The corporation will not itself

---

[21] Paul Sheehy presents a possible way around the concern about compelled emotions when he argues that members' emotional responses follow as a matter of course from reflection upon the group's deeds: "To be a true member entails that one just does respond in certain ways in particular contexts. To take pride in *our* achievements and feel shame at *our* failures may just be part of what it is to be a member" (Sheehy 2006). If this claim is empirical, it fails. It is not at all obvious that members of a group experience remorse in response to group transgressions. Indeed, members who protested the group transgression may be more liable to respond to the transgression with indignation than remorse. If, on the other hand, Sheehy thinks the connection between group act and members' emotion is conceptual (what it is to be a group member is to experience remorse where the group transgresses) or normative (what it is to be a group member is to be under an obligation to experience remorse where the group transgresses), then I might well be inclined to agree. But neither the conceptual nor the normative versions of the claim would suffice for establishing collective emotion without some account explaining why members' emotions count as emotions of the collective.

[22] It is not clear to me that Tollefsen's notion of vicarious feelings is coherent (Tollefsen 2008, 12). To use Tollefsen's example, if my husband trips in a fit of clumsiness I might well feel embarrassed "*for* him." But even if we can and perhaps do feel embarrassed for other individuals in the sense Tollefsen has in mind, this tells us nothing about whether we can feel embarrassed for a being that has no and never had any affect at all. If a computer were to flub up in an asinine way, we would not feel embarrassed for it because it would never be subject to embarrassment in its own right. More generally, our capacity to feel for others almost certainly depends on their being able to feel for themselves. Thus we can mirror the emotions of other human beings; we cannot do so for entities that have no feelings of their own.

have absorbed the blamer's anger, and so his blame will not have had its intended uptake.

In short, collectives cannot co-opt members' capacities to experience the reactive attitudes, for experience of them cannot be delegated and, even if it could, we are without an account that would explain why or how members could be counted upon to experience them in all of the instances that the collective should. Recruiting accounts thus cannot secure the corporation's suitability to blame; the most they can do is to signal grounds for holding members themselves responsible.

Strawsonian Accounts of Blaming Corporations

But perhaps we need not decide whether the corporation is a suitable target for blame by appeal to its capacities. For one can take the Strawsonian insights further than I have, eschewing a capacities approach altogether, and focus solely on our blaming practices. Deborah Tollefsen and David Silver are two theorists who have each adopted this strategy. Each notes that we routinely blame corporations, and each argues that, just as our practice of holding individuals morally responsible would be recalcitrant in the face of a finding that we lacked free will, so too our practice of blaming corporations would not falter in the face of a finding that corporations lacked the hallmarks of blameworthiness (including a capacity for affect) (Tollefsen 2003; Silver 2005, 2006). In this way, each believes that we need not fixate on the corporation's capacities, for the meaning and justification for our practice of blaming corporations can be found within the practice itself.

The tactic here is interesting but, I believe, ultimately unsuccessful, for it is unclear that our statements blaming corporations should be taken at face value.[23] When we offer these statements, do we mean to target the corporation in its own right or are we instead invoking the corporation as a placeholder for some set of its members who are the true intended targets of our blame? This ambiguity does not plague Strawson's analysis for, in the case of individuals, the buck must stop with them—there is no part of the individual that is itself a moral agent and could thus qualify as an appropriate target of blame.[24] By contrast, corporations are comprised of members each of whom is a moral agent in his or her own right. We cannot discern, then, from the face of our practices of blaming corporations (to the extent that we do blame

---

[23] The text in this and the next two paragraphs follow closely that in Sepinwall (2012).

[24] I am reminded here of the old-school parenting tactic of asking the child-culprit of some offense, "which hand did it?" and targeting that hand for the ensuing sanction. That the question and resulting punishment are ridiculous supports, I believe, the claim made in the text accompanying this note. (I do not consider the highly interesting though fortunately marginal case of individuals with multiple personality disorder here.)

them) whether we mean that the corporation itself is blameworthy or instead whether we invoke the corporation as a shorthand way of referring to those of its members who bear blame in its stead (cf. Velasquez 1983; see also Rönnegard and Velasquez's Chapter 7 in this book).

Perhaps in recognition of the inadequacy of the existing data, theorists who want to defend corporate responsibility on Strawsonian grounds ask us to consider counterfactual evidence for their position. More specifically, they invite us to contemplate a world in which we relinquish our reactive attitudes toward corporations.

Tollefsen finds the result of the exercise no more conceivable than the result of Strawson's original thought experiment, which invited us to contemplate a world with no reactive attitudes at all: "eliminating our emotional responses to collectives," she writes, "would eliminate the possibility of relationships with collectives and relationships of this sort are a substantial part of human society" (Tollefsen 2003, 230; see also Tollefsen 2008, 11).

But the relevant counterfactual is not one where we abandon our reactive attitudes when it comes to collective action; it is one where we abandon the notion that collectives are the ultimate targets of our reactive attitudes. I do not believe that an abandonment of that kind would yield the impoverishment, let alone practical impossibility, that Strawson envisions in asking us to imagine relinquishing the reactive attitudes in our treatment of individuals. Without the ability to blame corporations themselves, we might well aim our indignation at the corporation's members. If anything, then, the Strawsonian strategy for interrogating our practices of blaming corporations would seem to reveal that corporations need not be the intended targets of our reactive attitudes. As such, we might give up nothing of consequence in declining to blame them.

IMPLICATIONS

At this point, one might think the analysis has gone too far. Even if corporations cannot experience the punitive aspects of blame, one might contend, surely there are still plenty of other good reasons to blame them. Corporate wrongdoing is widespread, and corporate impunity is a real threat.

In response, it is worth noting that there are ways of staving off corporate impunity even if we refrain from blaming corporations. For one thing, civil sanctions might be effective in deterring corporate wrongdoing. Managers have incentives—for example, those built into performance-based pay arrangements—to prevent their corporations from committing crimes and incurring fines as a result. But suppose one is moved by the distinctive expressive power of the criminal law (see Uhlmann 2016). Do the conclusions reached here—in particular, the claim that the corporation is not an appropriate target of blame—take prosecution and punishment off the table?

I do not believe they do. To see why, consider the various rationales for punishment. Deterrence is one, and we have already seen that the corporation's lack of affect need not insulate it from measures—for example, fines—that would discourage corporate malfeasance. The criminal law also has expressive ambitions. In particular, it aims to single out conduct we have reason to deplore (Feinberg 1965) and to vindicate the worth of those whom that conduct wrongs (Hampton 1992). These aims can be achieved whether or not the target of punishment has a capacity for affect. But consider next retributive rationales for punishment. On a positive retributivist account, we punish in order to give the offender his "just deserts" (Moore 1997). This rationale cannot obviously sustain corporate criminal liability since the corporation's lack of affect presumably makes it impervious to pain, and infliction of pain is, on the positive retributivist account, at least among the ends that punishment aims to serve (see Hampton 1984, 235–7). Still, positive retributivism is a minor position, repudiated by many as too primitive or vengeful (see Hampton 1984). Most jurists and criminal law theorists instead embrace negative retributivism,[25] or the view that desert is a necessary condition for just punishment but not punishment's aim (or even one among its aims). For the negative retributivist, desert functions as a side-constraint, restricting the set of defendants legitimately subject to state-sponsored violence—that is, punishment—to those who are blameworthy for some wrong (Dolinko 1991).

In light of the considerations invoked here, one might then think the corporation ineligible for punishment on a negative retributivist account too. After all, (1) if being an appropriate object of blame is a prerequisite for just punishment (as the negative retributivist holds), and (2) if the corporation is not an appropriate object of blame (as I have argued), then it would seem to follow that it would not be just to punish the corporation. Put succinctly, the argument appears to establish that we cannot justify corporate criminal liability on retributivist grounds.

That appearance, though, is deceiving. In fact, the argument turns on an equivocation since the two premises involve different senses in which one is an appropriate object of blame. The negative retributivist contends that one is an appropriate object of blame if and only if one is at fault for the wrong in question, for the negative retributivist seeks to ensure that only the guilty are punished.[26] But there is a second, more global sense in which one is, or is not,

---

[25] Russell Christopher contends, for example, that "[t]he U.S. Supreme Court, state courts, state legislatures, philosophers, and legal scholars alike are increasingly acknowledging retributivism as the dominant theory of punishment" (Christopher 2002, 846–7).

[26] As Kyron Huigens writes: "Fault—also known as desert, culpability, or blameworthiness—is the distinctive feature of the criminal law" (Huigens 2000, 945). Similarly, Douglas Husak

an appropriate object of punishment, which turns not on whether one is guilty for this or that particular act but instead on whether one is the kind of being that can experience guilt in the first place.[27] It is in this sense that the corporation is not an appropriate object of blame.

Now the negative retributivist insists on restricting punishment to the guilty because punishment is painful or burdensome, and so it should be inflicted only on those who deserve it (namely, the guilty). Innocent individuals would be made to suffer unduly were the state to punish them. But if I am right that the corporation has no affect, it cannot be made to suffer at all. So the negative retributivist has no reason internal to her theory to care about corporate punishment.[28]

If I am right that we can justly punish corporations without worrying about whether they are blameworthy in the global sense adduced above, then one might wonder why we cannot also blame corporations even though they are not blameworthy in this global sense. The reason, I believe, is that expressing anger and inducing guilt are far more central to the practice of blaming than they are to the institution of punishment. It matters to us that the anger blame expresses has uptake, that its target can absorb the outrage we release. This chapter has aimed to demonstrate as much by drawing out the role of emotions in blame. By contrast, moral outrage and retributive desire are not central to the institution of punishment. Punishment does not lose its point if its target cannot experience suffering, but blaming becomes no different from a dispassionate pronouncement of wrongdoing if the blamed party cannot absorb the anger constituting or conveyed by blame. In this way, and to paraphrase Susan Wolf, blaming an affectless entity is no more sensible than is shaking one's fist at a volcano (Wolf 1985; but cf. Dempsey 2013).

All of this is to argue that we can secure a role for punishment of corporations even if, as I have argued, the corporation lacks the capacities for affect that blaming requires.[29] But there is a further implication to which the insight

---

contends that "any acceptable justification of punishment presupposes desert, which requires blame or fault in the defendant" (Husak 2010, 162–3).

[27] The more general way to put the point would be to say that one must be a moral agent if one is to be appropriately subject to blame and punishment. Since I am focusing here only on the more limited capacity to experience guilt, I use a narrower formulation in the text accompanying this note.

[28] This isn't to say that the negative retributivist has no reason at all to care about punishing corporations. She might notice that corporate punishments have collateral consequences from which innocent individuals will indeed suffer (for example, employee layoffs in the wake of large corporate fines). But the problem of collateral consequences, to the extent that it is a problem (see Cunningham 2014), arises for those who hold that the corporation is the kind of being that deserves to be punished, and it arises as well any time the corporation is subject to civil fines. Whatever one might say to the negative retributivist to justify corporate sanctions in either of these scenarios would dispel the worry about collateral consequences here too.

[29] Those who nonetheless want some blame with their punishment of corporate wrongs would do well to consider doctrines that allow for the prosecution of punishment of corporate

about affectless corporations gives rise, and which I can only sketch here. Recognizing that the corporation lacks affect should cause us to reevaluate its moral, political and social standing more generally. Lacking any feeling at all, the corporation lacks in particular fellow feeling, which is a prerequisite for citizenship (Rousseau 1758),[30] social cooperation (Smith 1759), and other sociable relations. Thus we have good reason to exclude the corporation from the central institutions and relationships that form human society. We may transact with it, and call upon external incentives to regulate its behavior. We may even bear obligations to refrain from interfering with its welfare. More strongly still, we may also have duties to enhance its welfare when we can. What we do not have are reasons to include it in our thick social relations. Affectless as they are, corporations should thus occupy a narrowly defined space in the structure of human society. Of course, this is just the outcome that Tollefsen feared in contemplating a world in which corporations were no longer the target of our reactive attitudes. As she maintained, "eliminating our emotional responses to [corporations] would eliminate the possibility of relationships with [them]," (Tollefsen 2003, 230). Indeed it would. And, impervious to guilt as the corporation is, as well it should.

REFERENCES

Arnold, Denis G. (2006). "Corporate Moral Agency." *Midwest Studies in Philosophy* 30: 279.
Bakan, Joel (2004). *The Corporation: The Pathological Pursuit of Profit and Power.*
Beardsley, Elizabeth (1970). "Moral Disapproval and Moral Indignation." *Philosophy and Phenomenological Research* 31: 161.
Bennett, Christopher (2012). "The Expressive Function of Blame." In *Blame: Its Nature and Norms*, ed. D. Justin Coates and Neal A. Tognazzini.
Bratman, Michael E. (2014). *Shared Agency: A Planning Theory of Acting Together.*
Burwell v. Hobby Lobby Stores, Inc., 134 S. Ct. 2751 (2014).
Charland, Louis C. (1998). "'Is Mr. Spock Mentally Competent?' Competence to Consent and Emotion." *Philosophy, Psychiatry, & Psychology* 5: 67.
Christopher, Russell L. (2002). "Deterring Retributivism: The Injustice of 'Just' Punishment." *Northwestern University Law Review* 96: 846.
Citizens United v. Federal Election Commission, 585 U.S. 310 (2010).

executives—that is, individuals who *do* have the capacities to absorb blame—for corporate crimes for which these executives need not have been at fault (see Sepinwall 2012, 2015a).

[30] I note also the somewhat inchoate sentiments to this effect in Justice Stevens' dissenting opinion in *Citizens United* (2010). There, Justice Stevens seeks to deny that corporations have rights of political speech by noting, inter alia, that corporations have "no consciences, no beliefs, no feelings, no thoughts, no desires" (*Citizens United* 2010, 466) (Stevens, J., concurring in part and dissenting in part).

Coates, D. Justin and Neal A. Tognazzini (2012). "The Nature and Ethics of Blame." *Philosophy Compass* 7: 197.

Cunningham, Lawrence A. (2014). "Deferred Prosecutions and Corporate Governance: An Integrated Approach to Investigation and Reform." *Florida Law Review* 66: 1.

Dalai Lama and Howard C. Cutler (1998). *The Art of Happiness.*

Dempsey, James (2013). "Corporations and Non-Agential Moral Responsibility." *Journal of Applied Philosophy* 30: 334.

Dolinko, David (1991). "Some Thoughts about Retributivism." *Ethics* 101: 537.

Donaldson, Thomas (1980). "Moral Agency and Corporations." *Philosophy in Context* 10: 54.

Duff, R.A. (2003). "Punishment, Communication and Community." In *Debates in Contemporary Political Philosophy*, ed. Derek Matravers and Jonathan E. Pike.

Feinberg, Joel (1965). "The Expressive Function of Punishment." *Monist* 49: 397.

French, Peter A. (1984). *Collective and Corporate Responsibility.*

Garrett, Brandon L. (2015). "The Corporate Criminal as Scapegoat." *Virginia Law Review* 101: 1789.

Gilbert, Margaret (2000). *Sociality and Responsibility.*

Gilbert, Margaret (2002). "Collective Guilt and Collective Guilt Feelings." *Journal of Ethics* 6: 115.

Hampton, Jean (1984). "The Moral Education Theory of Punishment." *Philosophy and Public Affairs* 13: 208.

Hampton, Jean (1992). "An Expressive Theory of Retribution." In *Retributivism and Its Critics*, ed. Wesley Cragg.

Hess, Kendy (2014). "The Free Will of Corporations (and Other Collectives)." *Philosophical Studies: An International Journal for Philosophy in the Analytic Tradition* 168: 241.

Hieronymi, Pamela (2004). "The Force and Fairness of Blame." *Philosophical Perspectives* 18: 115.

Huebner, Bryce (2011). "Genuinely Collective Emotions." *European Journal of Philosophy of Science* 1: 89.

Huigens, Kyron (2000). "The Dead End of Deterrence, and Beyond." *William and Mary Law Review* 41: 943.

Hurley, Elisa A. (2007). "Working Passions: Emotions and Creative Engagement with Value." *Southern Journal of Philosophy* 45: 79.

Hurley, Elisa A. and Coleen Macnamara (2010). "Beyond Belief: Toward a Theory of the Reactive Attitudes." *Philosophical Papers* 39: 373.

Husak, Douglas (2010). "Strict Liability, Justice and Proportionality." In *The Philosophy of Criminal Law: Selected Essays.*

Kiobel v. Royal Dutch Petroleum, 133 S. Ct. 1659 (2013).

List, Christian and Philip Pettit (2011). *Group Agency: The Possibility, Design and Status of Group Agents.*

Little, Margaret (1995). "Seeing and Caring: The Role of Affect in Feminist Moral Epistemology." *Analytic Feminism* 10: 117.

Mathiesen, Kay (2006). "We're All in This Together: Responsibility of Collective Agents and Their Members." *Midwest Studies in Philosophy* 30: 240.

McGeer, Victoria (2013). "Civilizing Blame." In *Blame: Its Nature and Norms*, ed. D. Justin Coates and Neal A. Tognazzini.

McKenna, Michael (2012). *Conversation and Responsibility*.

Mohamad v. Palestinian Authority, 132 S. Ct. 1702 (2012).

Moore, M.S. (1997). *Placing Blame: A Theory of Criminal Law*.

Pettit, Philip (2007). "Responsibility Incorporated." *Ethics* 117: 171.

Rousseau, Jean-Jacques (1758). *Lettres Morales*. Ed. Cyril Morana (2002).

Scanlon, T.M. (2008). *Moral Dimensions: Permissibility, Meaning, Blame*.

Scruton, Roger (1989). "Corporate Persons." *Aristotelian Society: Supplementary Volume* 63: 239.

Sepinwall, Amy J. (2012). "Guilty by Proxy: Expanding the Boundaries of Responsibility in the Face of Corporate Crime." *Hastings Law Journal* 63: 101.

Sepinwall, Amy J. (2015a). "Crossing the Fault Line in Corporate Criminal Law." *Journal of Corporation Law* 40: 101.

Sepinwall, Amy J. (2016). "Corporate Moral Responsibility." *Philosophy Compass* 11: 3.

Sheehy, Paul (2006). "Holding Them Responsible." *Midwest Studies in Philosophy* 30: 74.

Sher, George (2006). *In Praise of Blame*.

Sherman, Nancy (1997). *Making Necessity of Virtue*.

Silver, David (2005). "A Strawsonian Defense of Corporate Moral Responsibility." *American Philosophical Quarterly* 42: 279.

Silver, David (2006). "Collective Responsibility, Corporate Responsibility and Moral Taint." *Midwest Studies in Philosophy* 30: 269.

Smith, Adam (1759). *The Theory of Moral Sentiments*.

Starkey, Charles (2008). "Emotion and Full Understanding." *Ethical Theory and Moral Practice* 11: 425.

Strawson, Peter F. (1962). "Freedom and Resentment." *Proceedings of the British Academy* 48: 1.

Strawson, Peter F. (1993). "Freedom and Resentment." In *Perspectives on Moral Responsibility*, ed. John Martin Fischer and Mark Ravizza.

Tognazzini, Neal A. (2013). "Blameworthiness and the Affective Account of Blame." *Philosophia* 41: 1299.

Tollefsen, Deborah Perron (2003). "Participant Reactive Attitudes and Collective Responsibility." *Philosophical Explorations* 6: 218.

Tollefsen, Deborah Perron (2008). "Affectivity, Moral Agency, and Corporate-Human Relations." *APA Newsletter on Philosophy and Law* 7: 10.

Uhlmann, David M. (2016). "The Pendulum Swings: Reconsidering Corporate Criminal Prosecution." *U.C. Davis Law Review* 49: 1235.

Velasquez, Manuel (1983). "Why Corporations Are Not Morally Responsible for Anything They Do." *Business & Professional Ethics Journal* 2: 1.

Wallace, R. Jay. (1994). *Responsibility and the Moral Sentiments*.

Wallace, R. Jay. (2011). "Dispassionate Opprobrium: On Blame and the Reactive Sentiments." In *Reasons and Recognition: Essays on the Philosophy of T.M. Scanlon*, ed. R. Jay Wallace, Rahul Kumar, and Samuel Freeman.

Watson, Gary (1987). "Responsibility and the Limits of Evil: Variations on a Strawsonian Theme." In *Responsibility, Character and the Emotions*, ed. Ferdinand Schoeman.

Williams, Bernard (1981). *Moral Luck.*

Wolf, Susan (1985). "The Legal and Moral Responsibility of Organizations." In *Nomos XVII: Criminal Justice*, ed. Ronald Pennock and John W. Chapman.

Wolf, Susan (2011). "Blame, Italian Style." In *Reasons and Recognition: Essays on the Philosophy of T.M. Scanlon*, ed. R. Jay Wallace, Rahul Kumar, and Samuel Freeman.

Zimmerman, Michael (1988). *An Essay on Moral Responsibility.*

Part III

New Directions in Moral Responsibility of Firms

9

The Unrecognized Consensus about Firm Moral Responsibility

Kendy Hess

The current debate about firm moral responsibility began—as much as any philosophical debate ever begins—with Peter French's "The Corporation as a Moral Person" (1979). French argued that firms were "moral persons" with moral obligations and—thus—moral responsibility, the critics responded, and the game was on. Since that time the debate has ebbed and flowed with the focus shifting from the philosophical literature to the business literature and back again. The debate never seems to reach any widely accepted conclusions, but it never really goes away either. It just subsides periodically. There is nonetheless some significant consensus just below the surface—or so I shall argue—and I suspect it's this deeply felt consensus that keeps the debate going.

I begin this chapter by bringing the first significant piece of that unrecognized consensus to the surface: firms shouldn't do things that are morally wrong. In the philosopher's mind this observation—so apparently simple and unobjectionable—immediately vanishes into a haze of metaphysical and meta-ethical complexity, some of which is discussed below. There is nonetheless a meaningful sense in which that claim is usually held to be true. Once we recognize this fact, we can see that we have not really been arguing about *whether* firms have moral obligations or responsibility; we've been arguing about how best to *theorize* their moral obligations and responsibility. Much of the literature then resolves into an empirical debate about *how* firms exercise their moral agency, often conflated with a debate about how best to *conceptualize* that state of affairs. Recognizing this reality and accepting it allows us to reframe the debate in helpful ways.

Once we've reframed the debate, however, two bad habits immediately intervene to block progress. The first is to assume—falsely—that every significant firm commitment (and thus every significant firm action) comes into being because some person or small group of people considered options and chose it. In effect, people seem to assume that there is a "little man inside" who is effectively controlling the firm's behavior, so I will call this "the homunculus theory of firm behavior." This both misrepresents actual practice and leads us sadly astray in our theorizing. The second bad habit is to assume that all moral agency must be just like human moral agency; this unjustifiably hampers our ability to recognize the moral agency of firms.

Setting aside these bad habits lets us move forward to discover another piece of consensus below the surface of the debate: namely, that any adequate account of firm moral agency must incorporate both individualist and holist concerns. I suggest that the apparently opposing positions adopted by "individualists" and "holists" are actually correlates, and that much of the apparent disagreement between the two sides is the result of emphasizing different aspects of the situation rather than real disagreement about the situation itself. I close by briefly outlining an approach that integrates both individualist and holist concerns into a single account, dissolving the apparent conflict and revealing the underlying consensus. All that remains is to live up to the results.

THE FIRST SIGNIFICANT POINT OF CONSENSUS: "FIRMS" HAVE MORAL OBLIGATIONS

It may seem rather odd to suggest that there is a general consensus on this point—that firms have moral obligations—when I've just acknowledged that philosophers and other scholars have been debating the question of firm moral responsibility for the last thirty-five years.[1] Nonetheless, I think this is true, and that much of what appears to be debate about *whether* firms have moral responsibility is really just debate about how best to *talk about* the moral responsibility that firms have.

The biggest stumbling block to recognizing this consensus is the question of what we mean by "the firm" when we say that "the firm has moral obligations" (or responsibility). Scholars on the individualist side of the debate say that we really mean the group of individual people associated with the firm; scholars on the holist side of the debate say that we literally mean "the firm itself" as a distinct entity.[2] There are a number of points at which the two sides can part

---

[1] Moral obligation and moral responsibility are generally taken to go together, as two sides of the same coin, and moral agency is generally assumed to go with them (though that is less generally recognized). The concepts are mutually entailed. One must have moral obligations—an obligation to meet moral standards—before one can be morally responsible for one's success or failure at meeting them, and all and only moral agents can have moral obligations. So the three generally appear together or not at all. (But see Wringe 2010.)

[2] Both individualists and holists focus on the "collective," the group of people that constitute or otherwise make up the firm; whatever else the collective might be, it is a material object (or

ways, here. Among other possibilities, the disagreement may be ontological, metaphysical, meta-ethical, or methodological.

As an *ontological* matter, individualists and holists disagree about whether there is a distinct entity that is "the firm," an entity with a sufficiently robust existence that something is lost if we fail to recognize it. Ontological individualists say there is no such entity as "the firm," that there are only individuals engaging in regularized interactions that create the illusion of a new whole. Ontological holists say there is such an entity, and that refusing to recognize the existence of an entity (the firm) is like refusing to recognize the existence of forests or the solar system.[3]

As a *metaphysical* matter, even granting some kind of existence to "the firm," individualists and holists may disagree about whether it can have certain properties or capacities. For example, metaphysical individualists may recognize the existence of the firm but deny that it can possess intentional states, arguing that only (human) individuals have that capacity. Metaphysical holists may argue that the firm can possess certain properties and capacities, even including intentional states.[4]

As a *meta-ethical* matter, individualists and holists may grant the existence and basic properties and capacities of "the firm" (which at this point can be called a "corporate entity" or "corporate agent").[5] This still leaves room for

---

objects). It is also possible to approach "the firm" as a legal entity, or some other kind of abstract entity—such as a "nexus of contracts" or a "creature of statute" (see, for example, Eisenberg 1998, for introduction and critical discussion). Despite superficial similarities, this would be an unrelated debate. The question of whether the firm (so understood) has moral obligations would have to be resolved on the basis of legal status, legal doctrine, or contract rather than the ontological, metaphysical, and meta-ethical grounds discussed above.

[3] See Quinton (1976) for a classic statement on the individualist side; see Copp (1984) and Phillips (1992) as examples on the holist side.

[4] There may also be disagreements about how best to understand the metaphysical structure of the corporate entity; I set those aside, for now. Regarding firms' possession (or not) of intentional states, see List and Pettit (2011), Tollefsen (2002), Clark (1994) (all in favor); see also Velasquez (2003) (opposed). There are also scholars and approaches that try to identify versions of belief, desire, and intention that are distinctively "collective" without being truly "corporate" (held by a metaphysically distinct entity); see, for example, Gilbert (1994) on beliefs and Helm (2008) on desires or "cares." There is also some very interesting work on "collective but not corporate" versions of the higher level capacities discussed under the "meta-ethical" bullet above. See, for example, Gilbert (2000, 2006), Silver (2002, 2006), and Tollefsen (2006) on collective reactive attitudes; see Schmid (2014) on collective phenomenal consciousness. For the purposes of brevity I will not generally include references to those literatures.

[5] The terms "corporate entity" and "corporate agent" are on the verge of becoming terms of art in this debate. A "corporate" entity or agent is a subset of the broader group of "collective" entities or agents (see Isaacs (2011), List (2014) for two different takes on taxonomy). The term typically designates a highly disciplined, highly structured collective (like the stereotypical modern firm or "corporation"), but makes no reference to legal status or to the domain within which the entity or agent operates. Most business firms will probably qualify as corporate agents, but so too will many governments, colleges and universities, religious orders, NGOs, and branches of the military. It is in this technical sense that I use the phrase "corporate agent" in this chapter.

disagreement about whether this corporate agent has the more sophisticated capacities necessary for moral agency: higher order reasoning, reactive attitudes, and free will, among others.[6]

Finally, as a *methodological* matter, individualists and holists may simply set aside all of the preceding issues. Scholars taking the methodological route argue that we ought to approach "the firm" *as if* it were simply a collection of individuals or, from the other side, *as if* it were an entity and an agent in its own right, regardless of the ontological and metaphysical "facts" of the matter.

In presenting all this, my point is not that the debate is complicated (though it is). My point is that much of the debate between individualists and holists about whether firms have moral obligations is actually a debate over the initial claim that there *is* "a firm," or that it can bear moral obligations. It is *not* a debate about ethics, about whether there are moral obligations in play. Unfortunately, the debate has often been treated as if it *is* a debate about ethics, and framing it this way has had the unfortunate effect of suggesting that professional ethicists disagree about whether business behavior is subject to ethical norms. Nothing could be further from the truth. If we bracket all the metaphysical and methodological disagreements, two significant points of agreement emerge.

First, to my knowledge, everybody involved in the debate agrees that the individual members of firms have moral obligations—that their actions should meet moral standards. This may seem obvious, but it's worth stating the matter clearly. The members of firms are human persons, and as such they are moral agents subject to all the same moral obligations as everyone else. Nothing about "going to work" or becoming a member of a firm somehow absolves us of traditional obligations to consider consequences, respect rights, fulfill duties, develop virtues, and so on. Regardless of both the myth and (sadly) the fact of much of contemporary practice, business is not a morality-free zone. There is no "dirty hands" exemption for business.[7] The moral

---

[6] See, for example, Velasquez (1983), Haney (2004), Miller (2007), and Rönnegard (2015) arguing against the possibility of firms possessing such "higher order" capacities; see Rovane (1998) and Hess (2010) arguing in favor. For more specific capacities, see, for example, Björnsson and Hess (2016) on the possibility of truly corporate reactive attitudes; McKenna (2006) and Haji (2006) against corporate free will; and Hess (2014b) for corporate free will. A related matter may be whether firms have the capacities necessary to qualify as moral subjects (or patients), or even as persons. See, for example, Ranken (1987) and Miller (2006) arguing that such corporate agents would qualify as persons (though the claim is generally presented as a *reductio*); see also Manning (1984) and Hess (2013) arguing that such corporate agents would not qualify as persons.

[7] The idea of a "dirty hands" exemption goes back to Sartre's play by the same name, though Walzer (1973) is the contemporary source and Benn (1983) gives it its fullest development. The original problem of dirty hands arises in a political context, when an action is "exactly the right thing to do in utilitarian terms and yet leave[s] the [person] who does it guilty of a moral wrong" (Walzer 1973, 161). The problem is especially sticky in a political context because, arguably, it is the politician's *job* to do the thing that leaves her hands dirty, to sully herself for the common

obligations of members are very complex, as members take on new obligations in virtue of their membership: obligations to colleagues and customers, stakeholders and sometimes shareholders, professional organizations, and all the rest. Members frequently have to choose among conflicting obligations on the basis of inadequate information, and often there are no particularly attractive options. Nonetheless, the additional moral obligations that follow from membership are exactly that: *additional*. They do not somehow exempt members from the basic moral obligations that all moral agents have (whatever those obligations may be). If it's wrong for me to lie, cheat, or steal in my personal life, then it is wrong for me to lie, cheat, or steal in my professional life; the fact that I'm being paid to do it at work doesn't change that. My actions should meet moral standards regardless of the role I occupy.[8]

Second, I suspect that everybody involved in the debate likewise agrees that the "actions of firms" should also meet moral standards. To see this, again, just bracket all the philosophical complexity outlined above and treat references to "firm actions" as equivalent to "the members acting collectively." The reasoning goes as follows:

(1) Events in the world can be meaningfully ascribed to firms (the members of firms acting collectively).

(2) Some of those events are bad.[9]

(3) Generally speaking, *pro tanto*, firms (the members of firms acting collectively) shouldn't do those bad things.

The first and second claims are uncontroversial. Bearing in mind the equivalency just established, there is no question that firms do things (that coordinated member activity brings about new states of affairs). Firms (their members acting collectively) manufacture products and provide services, hire and fire employees, perform research, and so on. There is likewise no question that some of those events are bad, that sometimes the actions of firms (the

---

good. So, in a sense, the political actor enjoys a kind of "exemption" from ordinary moral constraints, though Walzer is clear that she remains tainted nonetheless. The problem has generally been considered unique to the political context, because only in that context can the actor truly be both bound and authorized to pursue "the common good" at such cost. (The actual standard is more complex and demanding in both Walzer and Benn.) Neither "business" as an arena nor the general business person can claim to be so bound and authorized.

[8] "The role I occupy" will of course have some bearing on the moral standards I have to meet; it will likely add a great many moral obligations to the load I already carry. My point here is simply that occupying that role—whatever it is—does not magically exempt me from my non-role-based moral obligations. Again, as noted above, role-based obligations are *additive*. We cannot "contract out of" morality.

[9] This language is as neutral as I could manage while still maintaining the simplicity of the claim. The same logic applies regardless of the chosen normative framework: the "event" can be a state of affairs, an action, or even the creation of a vicious trait, and the "bad-making qualities" could be unnecessary pain, violation of rights, or failures of love or excellence.

coordinated activities of the members) bring about new states of affairs in which people are injured or oppressed, communities are undermined or destroyed, ecosystems are fouled or broken, and so on.[10]

The third claim follows easily, perhaps even necessarily. I am not suggesting that firms (the members acting collectively) should *never* do anything that might be considered "bad"—that they should *never* cause any harm, disadvantage any person or community, or impact any ecosystem. That would be silly (and impossible); human agents are not held to such a standard, which makes it doubly implausible to suggest that this would be the appropriate standard for firms. Instead, I am suggesting that there are standards that govern these matters, establishing when it is appropriate for firms (the members acting collectively) to harm, disadvantage, or impact others, and when it is not appropriate and they should refrain. To make the implicit point explicit: existing moral standards govern these matters. Firm (collective members) actions are governed by the same moral standards as individual actions, or something closely related to them.[11] To suggest otherwise—to deny that the sustained, structured, collective behavior of groups is subject to moral standards—is to engage in a kind of moral laundering in which an impermissible action becomes permissible simply because it's been passed through enough people. It suggests that while I'm not allowed to kill a person by myself, it's somehow okay to kill that person as long enough people contribute to the killing. That just can't be right.

If I'm right that we agree about that, then...we agree that firms (their members acting collectively) have moral obligations, and thus moral responsibility. This is a somewhat fragile consensus, and one that is likely to dissolve almost immediately into real disagreements about whether the language is appropriate, whether it's appropriate to talk about "the firm" acting or having

---

[10] Note, again, that this could as easily include a disrespectful or vicious corporate action or trait as a harmful outcome. I set aside for now the many situations in which these new states of affairs (or actions or traits) are good, despite the fact that it's remarkably difficult to separate praiseworthiness and blameworthiness. If firms can do bad things, shouldn't do bad things, and can be blamed for doing bad things, then it would seem to follow that firms can do good things, ought to do good things, and can be praised for doing good things. And there's an unfortunate tendency for all of us to forget the many, many good things that firms do. Still, it is more controversial to say that firms *ought* to do good things than to say that they *ought not* do bad things, so I will set that claim aside.

[11] I make this claim only with respect to the actions of so-called "corporate agents" (see footnote 5 above). Less structured collectives that do not qualify as moral agents in their own rights may well be governed by a different set of moral standards. Further, I think it is an interesting question whether firms are governed by *precisely* the same moral standards as human individuals rather than by "something closely related." On a utilitarian or Kantian approach to morality, they would be; on an Aristotelian approach, I suspect the standards would be different (though related). See Hess (2015) for a brief treatment of the former claim, but see Altman (2007) for an explicit rejection of the claim that corporations could be Kantian moral agents; see also my "A Matter of Corporate Character" (unpublished) regarding the latter.

obligations, and so on. The question of the relationship between the members and the firm they constitute becomes especially fraught when moral responsibility is at stake: if the firm is morally responsible, are the members excused? That seems unfortunate, but if the members are not excused, then in what sense is the firm responsible?[12] These latter questions have serious practical implications for everyday business practice, and for legal judgments about liability. I don't mean to suggest that these disagreements are somehow insignificant. Yet I think it would be a shame to lose track of what seems to be a basic consensus: that whatever language we use, and however fuzzy the implications may be around the edges, we generally agree that moral standards govern business practice at *both* the individual and firm (collective) level.[13]

Before moving on to discuss how recognizing this consensus reframes the debate, however, I should mention the enormously influential work of Milton Friedman. Friedman is often cited for the proposition that there are no moral obligations in business, either for the members *or* for the firms, usually with reference to his famous article in the *New York Times Magazine*: "The Social Responsibility of Business Is to Increase Its Profits" (Friedman 1970).[14] Two quick points about this claim: First, Friedman is talking about *social* responsibility, not moral responsibility. As is clear from his discussion, he is opposed to businesses and business people taking on what he considered a governmental ("social") role, not to businesses and business people abiding by basic moral standards. Second, as far as moral standards go, Friedman explicitly acknowledges that business practice *is* governed by moral standards. Business people are to "stay within the rules of the game" and practice "without deception or fraud" in addition to their further (moral) obligations to their stockholders.[15] He never addresses the question of whether firms themselves (or the collective actions of their members) might likewise be subject to these moral standards, but having recognized that the individual members are

---

[12] See Miller (2006), Narveson (2002), and Ranken (1987) (suggesting that recognizing corporate moral responsibility exempts the members); but see Goodpaster (1987) (rejecting this claim).

[13] There are scholars who argue against this claim, or at least appear to do so. Rönnegard (2015) is an excellent example. Rönnegard argues at length that "the market" is "a zone of moral exception" because of the overriding value of its function as an efficient allocator of resources—a function it cannot fulfil if the actors within it are motivated by concerns other than price point (id., 192–9). Rönnegard nonetheless softens this claim in a number of places, acknowledging that the lack of "perfect" competition, laws, and regulations opens up a space for legitimate moral intrusion. Moreover, his objections to "moral" actions in a market context seem to focus on things like charity and philanthropy; he leaves room for the moral obligations of respect, kindness, and generosity. Thus I would suggest that even in this case it's not a claim that moral obligations do not apply at all, but an argument that countervailing concerns blunt the force of the moral obligations that do apply. If that is the case, then the market is no different from every other area of human life, where moral obligations have to be balanced against other concerns.

[14] Scholars also often cite Friedman (2002, especially ch. 8).   [15] Id., 133.

subject to those standards in their business practices it is—again—a bit awkward to suggest that they may do things collectively that they may not do individually. There is no suggestion that the business arena is a morality-free zone, at any level.

Once we acknowledge the general consensus—which even Friedman shares to some extent—that business practice is governed by moral standards, we can reframe some of the supporting debates. Instead of arguing about *whether* firms have moral obligations and moral responsibility, we can shift to a discussion of how best to *account* for the fact that they do. When we do that, two things happen.

First, some debates about *whether* firms are morally responsible resolve themselves into debates about *how* firms exercise their moral agency. (Or, to restate that in individualistic terms, it resolves into an empirical debate about *how* the activities of individual members are coordinated such that their collective actions will comply with moral norms.) Recasting the debate in this way, from a debate about moral responsibility to (essentially) a debate about moral agency reveals that much of what appears to be a philosophical debate is actually empirical. Different theorists have put forward different accounts of how firms go about exercising their moral agency, some (for example) focusing on shared intentions, under a variety of different names,[16] while others focus on the presence of certain organizational structures and practices.[17] Debating the merits of these different accounts in terms of firm moral responsibility suggests that it's the possibility of moral responsibility that is at stake. It suggests that these accounts pick out something that must be present before firms can have moral obligations or be morally responsible. For example, presenting firm moral agency exclusively in terms of shared intentions suggests that, if shared intentions are absent, the firm is not morally responsible for the action that nonetheless took place. Similarly, presenting firm moral agency exclusively in terms of specific structures (like French's formal "corporate internal decision structures") or mechanisms (like List and Pettit's preference aggregations) suggests that, if these structures or mechanisms were not utilized, then the firm is not morally responsible for the action that nonetheless took place. But this is implausible, to say the least, and in many cases I doubt that the theorists necessarily intended this result. Firms (their members collectively) *act*, and they are morally responsible for those actions. Firms are blameworthy when their actions fail to meet moral standards, regardless of the mechanism involved or not involved in the particular action.[18] If firms *can* act in the absence of shared intentions, corporate internal

---

[16] See, for example, Bratman (1987, 1999), Gilbert (1989, 2000), and Miller (2001).

[17] See, for example, French (1984) and List and Pettit (2011).

[18] The firm "action" in this case must still qualify as an "action"—a behavior arising from the agent's own "actional springs" (to use a lovely phrase from Haji 2006). This is the same standard

decision structures, preference aggregation, and so on—and the empirical evidence suggests that they can—then they remain morally responsible for those actions regardless of the specific mechanism by which they acted. Reframing the debate in terms of firm moral agency, as I just did, reveals these allegedly competing accounts as correlates: each describes one mechanism by which a firm could go about exercising its moral agency (coordinating the collective behavior of its members). There is no reason to prefer one over another for all cases, no reason to expect an actual firm to utilize only one approach, and certainly no reason to suggest that only one such mechanism results in firm action that should meet moral standards, while other mechanisms are somehow exempt.

Second, some debates resolve into competing conceptual schemata. Again, the question is not *whether* corporations act morally or immorally but how best to *capture* the phenomenon. The debates between competing schemata can (and should) be resolved on traditional grounds of accuracy, predictive and explanatory power, and simplicity. I close this chapter with an account that is particularly promising along these lines, but turn first to two habits of thought that prevent the debate from moving in this direction.

TWO BAD HABITS

Reframing the debate in this way doesn't resolve all the disagreements, of course, but there is still a further point of consensus to be discovered. The previous consensus was masked by the general habit of framing the debate about *how* firms exercise their moral agency in terms of *whether* firms have moral agency (that is, obligation and responsibility). The further consensus is masked by a general reluctance to recognize firms *as* moral agents—to resist the reframing I described above. Two particular habits of thought and discourse mark this reluctance and bar progress.

First, the literature on firm moral obligation is overwhelmingly focused on explicit decision-making, usually at the executive level. In our examples and assumptions, every significant corporate commitment seems to come from a single person or small group of persons considering options and then explicitly choosing the commitment to adopt. Commitments and actions that are not the result of this kind of process are treated as errors or aberrations when they are mentioned at all. I call this "the homunculus theory of firm behavior": this idea that every firm contains a little man (or small council) who

---

that applies to human behaviors, in which not all movements are "actions," and there is a rich literature discussing the intricacies in the case of human agents that can be used to guide debates about whether a specific corporate behavior qualifies.

knowingly and intentionally makes every decision that significantly shapes firm behavior. It treats the firm as a kind of inert puppet whose only significant impetus for action comes from "the little man inside" who's pushing its buttons and pulling its strings. I'm not aware of anyone in the debate who actually argues for this claim, but the literature is generally silent on alternative mechanisms for firm action; the myopic focus on intentional executive decision-making implies that such accounts are sufficient, and they are not.

In this vision, firms reliably "do what they're told" by some governor or governing council, and any executive (or lawyer) can tell you that's simply not the case. Most executives (and their lawyers) wish desperately that it were so simple and easy to guide firm actions in the desired direction! Instead, both the processes of adopting new commitments and the implementation of existing commitments are distributed across the firm, and the larger the firm, the more radically distributed these processes will be, and the less subject to executive control (or even awareness). This does not mean that these processes are random. Firms have a number of mechanisms in place to guide the behavior of the individual members and to shape the general form that their collective actions will yield. Nonetheless, these mechanisms do not *control* the members, and their choices will often yield commitments and actions that were not explicitly considered or chosen—or anticipated—by anyone, least of all the members who participated in the process. These commitments nonetheless shape firm actions, often settling in and becoming part of the guiding mechanisms themselves (bound up in assumptions about what is typical, expected, tolerated, and rewarded, sometimes even codified after the fact into "standard practices"). These "unchosen" commitments thus end up guiding the actions of the firm (the collective actions of members across the firm) in ways that then *become* reliable and predictable. While no individual member may have chosen these commitments, "the firm" effectively has.[19]

Theories that approach firm commitments and actions as if they are unfailingly chosen by explicit decision-making are thus unsatisfactory. For one thing, they fail to account for what actually happened, focusing almost entirely on isolated executive decisions and ignoring relevant contextual factors and other players. In addition to being inaccurate, taken together these theories encourage executive scapegoating—the practice of blaming the executives for every single thing a firm does *as if they had explicitly chosen it*[20]—and perhaps a kind of megalomania, encouraging executives to

---

[19] See Hess (2014a, 2014b) and Björnsson and Hess (2016) for more detailed discussion and examples.

[20] This is not to say that executives have no responsibility for unchosen, unwanted corporate actions that happen on their watch. Nonetheless, most theories of moral responsibility (and most reactive attitudes) recognize a difference between *choosing* to do something wrong and *failing to prevent someone else* from doing something wrong. Moreover, the solutions are significantly different, as noted above.

believe that they actually have this kind of power and control. Neither is particularly healthy or helpful. For much the same reason, such theories fail to predict what will happen next and—most importantly—often fail to direct our attention to where it is most needed.[21] They suggest that if we could just reform the executives we could automatically thereby reform the entire firm, and perhaps all of contemporary business practice. The truth of the matter is vastly more complicated. If our theories are to be relevant to actual business practice, then they need to be adapted to recognize the radically distributed nature of actual business practice. This is a point the holists have been making for some time (although perhaps not as effectively as possible). I return to the question of the relationship between individualist and holist accounts below.

The second habit of thought that interferes with reframing the debate in terms of firm moral agency is the habit of assuming that all moral agency must be like human moral agency in every respect. The traditional approach to most questions about moral agency is to begin with the paradigm of the human moral agent and apply pressure to it: what does it take to become this kind of thing or to act in this way? Beginning with a human paradigm, this approach has, of course, yielded distinctively human answers. For example, the great moral philosophers of the past have concluded that moral agency requires leisure and education (Aristotle), love of the good (Aquinas), sophisticated sentiments (Hume), and respect for the law (Kant), among other things.[22] Contemporary scholarship generally adopts the same approach with the same results. This would not be a failing if philosophers acknowledged that their answers are only relevant to questions about the human practice of moral agency, but they rarely do. Their conclusions, drawn from a human paradigm, are treated as if they speak to issues of moral agency per se rather than being limited to human practices of moral agency, and the entire discourse continues subject to this unacknowledged constraint. Thus, for example, philosophers tend to argue that a human being who lacks consciousness or empathy would be incapable of moral agency, and they then conclude that "moral agency" requires consciousness or empathy. The first claim is plausible, but the second is a non sequitur. The truth of the first would establish only that

---

[21] Goodpaster (2007) is an excellent example of the alternative approach, one that attends to a broad array of inputs into corporate action. See especially ch. 5 ("Orienting Corporate Conscience"), ch. 6 ("Institutionalizing Corporate Conscience"), and ch. 7 ("Sustaining Corporate Conscience"). Note that while Goodpaster likewise focuses on executive action, he also acknowledges the need to shape extra-executive structures and practices—a point he also makes in Goodpaster (1987). By insisting on the significance of non-executive factors, I am not suggesting that executives are *not* in a uniquely powerful position when it comes to shaping firm behavior; I'm simply joining Goodpaster in denying that they are the *only* significant contributors from within the firm.

[22] See, for example, Aristotle's *Nicomachean Ethics* (bks. 1–3) and *Politics* (bk. 1), Aquinas's *Summa Theologica* (questions 1, 4, and especially 94), Hume's *Treatise of Human Nature* (bks. 2 and 3), and Kant's *Prolegomena* (especially parts 1 and 2).

such a human being would not be a moral agent; it does not establish that *no* entity that lacks consciousness or empathy can be a moral agent. Proceeding in this manner has led us to develop theories of a distinctively *human* morality, one attuned to the wants, needs, and capacities of humans and blind in principle to the wants, needs, and capacities of the non-human world. This effectively ensures that only human beings fit comfortably within our theories (and not even all human beings).

This long-standing practice makes it exceptionally difficult, if not impossible, to recognize non-humans as moral agents.[23] In such cases it is precisely the paradigm of the human moral agent that is being challenged, so starting from that paradigm spikes the challenge before it can even be launched. If we begin our inquiry into the possibility of non-human moral agents in this way, we convert the question from "can this non-human thing be a moral agent" to "can this non-human thing—this firm—be a *human* moral agent?" And of course, when you put it that way, the answer is "no." But that wasn't really the question we were asking in the first place. We need a way to explore the possibility of non-human moral agents that isn't biased against a positive answer. There may be other ways to do this, but my own method (discussed briefly below) is to adopt a functionalist approach, defining moral agency in terms of activities and behaviors rather than in terms of identity. On this account, a candidate qualifies as a moral agent if and only if it is able to act appropriately on the basis of morally relevant information, because it is morally relevant information. It then becomes an empirical matter to determine which entities can perform these functions, and I have argued at length that most firms will qualify (for example, Hess 2010, 2013, 2014a).

THE SECOND POINT OF CONSENSUS: THE INDIVIDUALISTS AND THE HOLISTS ARE RIGHT

I've suggested that there is a hidden consensus underlying the debate about firm moral responsibility: there is a widely shared but generally unacknowledged agreement that firms have moral obligations (in addition to the underlying consensus that the members have moral obligations). The consensus becomes apparent when we translate this contentious claim (stated in holist terms) into its individualist equivalent: that the collective actions of firm members ought to meet moral standards. Recasting the debate to acknowledge

---

[23] It has also made it quite difficult to recognize non-human entities as moral subjects (or patients) entitled to moral concern. We've made somewhat more progress here, of course, most notably with respect to non-human animals and environmental entities like ecosystems. See Hess (2015) for a brief survey.

this consensus reveals that much of what appeared to be debate about whether firms have moral responsibilities is actually debate about how best to conceptualize this state of affairs, and particularly about how firms go about meeting (or failing to meet) those standards—how they exercise their agency. Attachment to "the homunculus theory of firm behavior" and "humanized" assumptions about moral agency (discussed above) have hindered efforts to recast the debate in this way, but there is another bad habit that has caused more needless confusion than all the rest put together and has masked yet another significant point of consensus.

I've already suggested that much of the debate over firm moral responsibility is really a debate over how best to conceptualize that moral responsibility. The debate divides participants into "individualists" and "holists," and that very division then suggests that the two positions are somehow fundamentally opposed—that they are alternatives, or mutually exclusive possibilities. Our habit of thinking of them in this way has hidden the fact that, to the contrary, individualism and holism supplement each other. Each picks out crucial pieces of the mechanisms by which firms exercise their moral agency, and any account that cannot accommodate both sets of insights will be incomplete.[24] I suggest that not only is this true, but that there is general consensus on this point. The consensus is masked by the labels that we've developed (and abused), so I'd like to explore those labels a little further.

The debate is typically cast as a binary, between individualists and holists, when there are in fact four conceptual possibilities: atomism, individualism, holism, and dualism. Two of these positions are so unpopular that I had to make up names for them, which is precisely my point. "Atomism" and "dualism" are the crazy/rabid versions of individualism and holism—the strawmen that we make up when we exaggerate our opponents' positions.

"Atomism" is an exaggerated version of individualism, with adherents insisting that there is nothing more to firm activity than individuals acting in splendid isolation. These individuals are incapable of creating anything effective but immaterial—like a firm hierarchy, policy, or culture—and their behavior is thus not shaped in any way by such illusions. They are also utterly unaffected by ephemeral things like relationships or social bonds, and completely non-reliant on inputs or practical support from other members. The only miracle is that they manage to coordinate their behaviors so effectively without ever dealing with each other in any meaningful way.

"Dualism," however, is an exaggerated version of holism. Its adherents claim that there is a ghostly, disembodied entity that is *"THE FIRM"* (cue spooky music). This thing floats malevolently in a Cartesian ether while its

---

[24] See Orts (2015, 6–7, 177–8) urging a similar point.

members work mindlessly but tirelessly to achieve its mysterious ends, subordinate to its purposes and unable to affect them.

Obviously (I hope), both positions are ridiculous, and I am reasonably confident that nobody is actually proposing either one. I suspect these are nonetheless familiar images, if somewhat exaggerated: these are the bogeymen lurking in the background of the debate, and most of us have at least felt that we were being accused of one or the other. With these positions now properly labeled and removed from the logical space of the debate, though, we can return to the remaining options of individualism and holism and ask what is left over. What is the individualist position, which isn't atomism but remains distinct from holism? What is the holist position, which isn't dualism but remains distinct from individualism? With the distorting exaggerations removed, I suggest that we're now in a position to see that everybody actually engaged in the debate occupies the sliding mix in the middle between individualism and holism. The difference between the two is more a matter of emphasis than anything else, with the real debate revolving around the question of what is *important* rather than what is *true*.

Recast in this way, we see individualists insisting that we need to pay attention to the choices of individuals, to their motivations, intentions, and values—that these things drive firm behavior and shape firm priorities, and they are relevant to questions of moral responsibility. The holists insist that we need to pay attention to extra-individual aspects of the firm, to the hierarchies and policies and culture which form the context within which the individuals make their choices—that these things drive firm behavior and shape firm priorities, and they are relevant to questions of moral responsibility. But once I've put the matter that way . . . who denies *either* of those claims? To my knowledge, almost everybody agrees that we need to recognize the significant roles played by individuals in their individuality, and that we need recognize the roles played by extra-individual or organizational factors such as hierarchy, structure, incentives, culture, and the rest. Actual individualists don't deny the significance of extra-individual factors, and actual holists don't deny the significance of individual actions. Now, individualists and holists will surely disagree on what, precisely, that significance *is*. I don't mean to suggest that the underlying consensus is complete, or that the remaining disagreements are unimportant. But again, this recasting reveals that we all occupy a central position between atomism and dualism that recognizes some kind of role for *both* individualist and holist concerns. What is needed (especially for business practice) is an approach to firm moral agency that comfortably captures both.

Most of the existing accounts of firm moral agency carry a commitment to a specific mechanism for agency, and that has made it difficult to separate the question of moral agency (and thus, moral obligation and responsibility) from the question of how that agency was exercised. My own account avoids this difficulty, and it makes room for both individualist and holist mechanisms.[25] On my functionalist approach to moral agency, a candidate qualifies as a moral agent if and only if it is able to act appropriately on the basis of morally relevant information, because it is morally relevant information. As I have argued at some length elsewhere (for example, Hess 2010, 2013, 2014a), firms can do this. This is a holist approach—or at the very least, I typically present it in holist language—but much of it is susceptible to the same "individualist" translations as provided in the first section above. I will not rehearse the arguments here, but briefly, on my account, we need three things: (1) "a candidate" that (2) qualifies as "an agent" that can (3) "act appropriately."

First, "the firm" qualifies as "a candidate." Whether we want to insist that there really is "a firm" as a distinct metaphysical entity (my own preference) or whether we want to insist that such talk is just shorthand for "the members unified in certain ways," this entity is sufficiently robust that we can speak of it in meaningful ways. Note that describing the firm as "the members unified in certain ways" leaves the form of unification open: the members may be unified by individual characteristics such as shared intentions or collective ends, or they may be unified by holist factors like institutional structure and policy. (I will present the remainder of this discussion in holist terms, because it is simpler and matches my own preferences, but all claims can be translated into individualist—if not atomist—terminology.[26])

Second, the firm qualifies as an agent: it has its own intentional states, and these intentional states guide its actions. Briefly: every firm has certain commitments about fact and value that guide its behavior. These commitments qualify as (literal) beliefs and desires on standard accounts.[27] Moreover, these beliefs and desires form a logically integrated whole, what Carol Rovane (1998) calls a "rational point of view," which is the very hallmark of an agent. These beliefs and desires—and the rational point of view that they constitute—belong to the firm; they are not the beliefs or desires of the members, of whatever rank. When member behavior is guided by the firm's rational point of view, the resulting action is firm action. As the firm is capable of action on the basis of its own intentional states, it qualifies as an agent. Note

---

[25] David Copp (2006, 2007), who relies heavily on arguments from examples, is also generally silent about specific mechanisms and may fit into this category (though he expresses commitments about congruence between member intentional states and corporate intentional states that push him towards a Gilbert-style "shared intentions" approach). Goodpaster (1983, 1987) is likewise non-committal about mechanisms, though his focus on explicit executive decision-making (as discussed in more detail above, in connection with "the homunculus theory") implies a commitment to something like French's institutional structures.

[26] See Hess (2014b) for examples of this kind of translation, regarding corporate beliefs and desires.

[27] "Standard" accounts include interpretationism, dispositionalism, and representationalism. See Tollefsen (2002) regarding interpretationism; see Copp (2006, 2007) and List and Pettit (2011) as (effectively) dispositionalists; and see Hess (2014a) regarding all three.

again that this account is silent regarding the process by which these crucial "firm commitments" arise. Some may arise as a result of shared intentions, others as the result of formal preference aggregation, others by less explicit means such as the radically distributed decision-making mentioned above, and others by still further processes. My account leaves room for all these possibilities, and as a result many of the disagreements between individualism and holism lose their traction.

Third, the firm can "act appropriately on the basis of morally relevant information *because* it is morally relevant information." Having recognized the possibility of firm beliefs and desires about non-moral matters, there is no reason to think the firm cannot likewise develop beliefs and desires about moral matters via the same mechanisms. These moral commitments, when present, will guide its actions and reactions in the same way that beliefs and desires about profit and development guide its actions and reactions. This account is intentionally neutral between competing normative theories, so "morally relevant information" can be cashed out in terms of pain and pleasure, rights and duties, virtues and vices, or any other contender. The "appropriate" action will likewise vary with the normative theory, of course. The only further requirement is that the candidate be capable of responding to morally relevant information *because* it is morally relevant information: it cannot be mere coincidence that the agent acts in ways that maximize pleasure and minimize pain, conform to universalizable principles, and so on. As long as a candidate can act appropriately on the basis of morally relevant information and would not have acted as it did in the absence of said information, it meets this final requirement.

We can use this approach to counter essentially empirical claims that shared intentions, established procedures, or the like are necessary for corporate moral agency, such that collectives that lack them do not qualify. Once a collective—whether a firm or some other kind of collective, like a government, a college, or a religious order—qualifies as a corporate agent on this account, it is irrelevant whether it relies on shared intentions, established procedures, or some other process or processes to achieve the result. We can use a similar approach to counter claims that phenomenal consciousness, emotion, and empathy are necessary for moral agency.[28] As long as it can act morally, in the sense outlined above, it is a moral agent, and again: it seems unquestionable that most firms *can* act morally in some agreed sense. Whether they *do* act morally, amorally, or immorally is a separate matter, and a different kind of problem. Once we've identified the qualifying entities as moral agents, we (and they) can begin the process of recognizing them as moral agents and holding them morally accountable for their actions.

---

[28] See Rovane (1998) and Hess (2010) regarding the irrelevance of a phenomenal point of view to accompany the rational point of view; see Rönnegard (2015) as (effectively) to the contrary. See also Björnsson and Hess (2016) and Hess (unpublished) for further discussion.

CONCLUSION

In emphasizing the agreements among philosophers and business ethicists, I don't mean to make light of our differences. There are real disagreements with real implications, and these are worth resolving. Interest in the intersection of business, firms, membership, ethics, and morality has been on the rise, and it promises to be fascinating time to be a scholar working in the field. This is doubly true because—again—there are real world implications that follow from how we answer these questions.

For precisely that reason I would like to close with an appeal: we don't have to resolve any of those disagreements before we can work together on real and pressing problems. I've suggested that almost everyone involved in the debate actually agrees about *three* things:

(1) The members of firms have standard moral obligations that are not somehow invalidated by the fact that they have joined a firm or engaged in business activity.

(2) Firm actions (the collective actions of firm members) should likewise meet moral standards.

(3) Our accounts of firm moral action (the morally significant collective actions of firm members) need to incorporate both individualist and holist aspects.

We certainly shouldn't let patently false assumptions about firm function (like the homunculus theory of firm behavior), or even more sophisticated ideas about human moral agency, interfere with efforts to pursue our scholarship in ways that acknowledge and build on these shared beliefs. "Business" writ large has become one of the most powerful institutions on Earth, and it is crucial that we avoid any appearance of condoning the idea that business is some kind of morality-free endeavor. Ethics matter, as much or more in business as in any other domain. We cannot afford to let our real and meaningful disagreements about philosophical approaches create the appearance that we—the experts—are not sure about that basic point.

REFERENCES

Altman, Matthew C. (2007). "The Decomposition of the Corporate Body: What Kant Cannot Contribute to Business Ethics." *Journal of Business Ethics* 74: 253.

Aquinas, Thomas (1948). *Summa Theologica: Complete English Edition*, trans. Fathers of the English Dominican Province.

Aristotle (1999). *Nicomachean Ethics*, trans. and ed. Terence Irwin, 2nd ed.

Beck, Lewis W. (1988). *Kant: Selections*.

Benn, Stanley I. (1983). "Private and Public Morality: Clean Living and Dirty Hands." In *Public and Private in Social Life*, ed. Stanley I. Benn and Gerald F. Gaus.

Björnsson, Gunnar and Kendy Hess (2016). "Corporate Crocodile Tears? The Reactive Attitudes of Corporate Agents." *Philosophy and Phenomenological Research* (forthcoming), early version paper available at http://onlinelibrary.wiley.com/doi/10.1111/phpr.12260/pdf.

Bratman, Michael E. (1987). *Intentions, Plans, and Practical Reason*.

Bratman, Michael E. (1999). *Faces of Intention*.

Clark, Austen (1994). "Beliefs and Desires Incorporated." *Journal of Philosophy* 91: 404.

Copp, David (1984). "What Collectives Are: Agency, Individualism and Legal Theory." *Dialogue* 23: 249.

Copp, David (2006). "On the Agency of Certain Collective Entities: An Argument from 'Normative Autonomy.'" *Midwest Studies in Philosophy* 30: 194.

Copp, David (2007). "The Collective Moral Autonomy Thesis." *Journal of Social Philosophy* 38: 369.

Eisenberg, Melvin A. (1998). "The Conception that the Corporation Is a Nexus of Contracts, and the Dual Nature of the Firm." *Journal of Corporate Law* 24: 819.

French, Peter A. (1979). "The Corporation as a Moral Person." *American Philosophical Quarterly* 16: 207.

French, Peter A. (1984). *Collective and Corporate Responsibility*.

Friedman, Milton (1970). "The Social Responsibility of Business Is to Increase its Profits." *The New York Times Magazine*, September 13.

Friedman, Milton (2002). *Capitalism and Freedom* (fortieth anniversary ed.).

Gilbert, Margaret (1989). *On Social Facts*.

Gilbert, Margaret (1994). "Remarks on Collective Belief." In *Socializing Epistemology: The Social Dimensions of Knowledge*, ed. Frederick F. Schmitt.

Gilbert, Margaret (2000). *Sociality and Responsibility: New Essays in Plural Subject Theory*.

Gilbert, Margaret (2006). "Who's to Blame? Collective Moral Responsibility and Its Implications for Group Members." *Midwest Studies in Philosophy* 30: 94.

Goodpaster, Kenneth E. (1983). "The Concept of Corporate Responsibility." *Journal of Business Ethics* 2: 1.

Goodpaster, Kenneth E. (1987). "The Principle of Moral Projection: A Reply to Professor Ranken." *Journal of Business Ethics* 6: 329.

Goodpaster, Kenneth E. (2007). *Conscience and Corporate Culture*.

Haji, Ishtiyaque (2006). "On the Ultimate Responsibility of Collectives." *Midwest Studies in Philosophy* 30: 292.

Haney, Mitchell. R. (2004). "Corporate Loss of Innocence for the Sake of Accountability." *Journal of Social Philosophy* 35: 391.

Helm, Bennett (2008). "Plural Agents." *Noûs* 42: 17.

Hess, Kendy M. (2010). "The Modern Corporation as Moral Agent: The Capacity for 'Thought' and a 'First-Person Perspective.'" *Southwest Philosophy Review* 26: 61.

Hess, Kendy M. (2013). "'If You Tickle Us...': How Corporations Can Be Moral Agents Without Being Persons." *Journal of Value Inquiry* 47: 319.

Hess, Kendy M. (2014a). "Because They Can: The Basis for the Moral Obligations of (Certain) Collectives." *Midwest Studies in Philosophy* 38: 203.

Hess, Kendy M. (2014b). "The Free Will of Corporations (and Other Collectives)." *Philosophical Studies* 168: 241.

Hess, Kendy M. (2015). "Dehumanizing Morality." In *Beastly Morality: Animals as Moral Agents*, ed. Jonathan Crane.

Hess, Kendy M. "Does the Machine Need a Ghost? The Role of Phenomenal Consciousness in Kantian Moral Agency." (unpublished working paper).

Hume, David (1975). *A Treatise of Human Nature*, ed. L. A. Selby-Bigge and P.H. Nidditch, rev. 2nd ed.

Isaacs, Tracy (2011). *Moral Responsibility in Collective Contexts*.

List, Christian (2014). "Three Kinds of Collective Attitudes." *Erkenntnis* 79: 1601.

List, Christian and Philip Pettit (2011). *Group Agency: The Possibility, Design, and Status of Corporate Agents*.

Manning, Rita C. (1984). "Corporate Responsibility and Corporate Personhood." *Journal of Business Ethics* 3: 77.

McKenna, Michael (2006). "Collective Responsibility and an Agent Meaning Theory." *Midwest Studies in Philosophy* 30: 16.

Miller, Seumas (2001). *Social Action: A Teleological Account*.

Miller, Seumas (2006). "Collective Moral Responsibility: An Individualist Account." *Midwest Studies in Philosophy* 30: 176.

Miller, Seumas (2007). "Against the Collective Moral Autonomy Thesis." *Journal of Social Philosophy* 38: 389.

Narveson, Jan (2002). "Collective Responsibility." *Journal of Ethics* 6: 180.

Orts, Eric W. (2015). *Business Persons: A Legal Theory of the Firm*, rev. paperback ed.

Phillips, Michael J. (1992). "Corporate Moral Personhood and Three Conceptions of the Corporation." *Business Ethics Quarterly* 2: 435.

Quinton, Anthony (1976). "Social Objects." *Proceedings of the Aristotelian Society* 76: 1.

Ranken, Nani L. (1987). "Corporations as Persons: Objections to Goodpaster's 'Principle of Moral Projection.'" *Journal of Business Ethics* 6: 633.

Rönnegard, David (2012). "How Autonomy Alone Debunks Corporate Moral Agency." *Business and Professional Ethics Journal* 32: 77.

Rönnegard, David (2015). *The Fallacy of Corporate Moral Agency*.

Rovane, Carol A. (1998). *The Bounds of Agency: An Essay in Revisionary Metaphysics*.

Silver, David (2002). "Collective Responsibility and the Ownership of Actions." *Public Affairs Quarterly* 16: 287.

Silver, David (2006). "Collective Responsibility, Corporate Responsibility and Moral Taint." *Midwest Studies in Philosophy* 30: 269.

Schmid, Hans B. (2014). "Plural Self-Awareness." *Phenomenology and the Cognitive Sciences* 13: 7.

Tollefsen, Deborah (2002). "Organizations as True Believers." *Journal of Social Philosophy* 33: 395.

Tollefsen, Deborah (2006). "The Rationality of Collective Guilt." *Midwest Studies in Philosophy* 30: 222.

Velasquez, Manuel G. (1983). "Why Corporations are Not Morally Responsible for Anything They Do." *Business and Professional Ethics Journal* 2: 1.

Velasquez, Manuel (2003). "Debunking Corporate Moral Agency." *Business Ethics Quarterly* 13: 531.

Walzer, Michael (1973). "Political Action: The Problem of Dirty Hands." *Philosophy and Public Affairs* 2: 160.

Wringe, Bill (2010). "Global Obligations and the Agency Objection." *Ratio* 23: 217.

10

Corporate Moral Agency, Positive Duties, and Purpose

Nien-hê Hsieh

In business scholarship, a long-standing question concerns what standards should apply to the activities of for-profit business firms beyond what is legally required. While the question has particular resonance for business firms operating in countries with fragile public institutions or few regulations, it also arises in countries with relatively established institutions. Consider, for example, the current debate in the United States concerning lobbying and political activity on the part of business firms. Even though legally permissible, there is debate as to whether business firms ought to refrain from such activity. As in this case, much of the debate about the standards for business firms concerns constraints or negative duties—that is, activities from which business firms ought to refrain.

At the same time, a growing portion of the debate asks whether business firms also have positive duties—in particular, duties to engage in activities that benefit parties beyond routine commercial transactions, such as donating medicines to those unable to afford them.[1] Variously referred to as corporate philanthropy, corporate social responsibility (CSR),[2] or corporate social initiatives, what these activities have in common is that they involve conferring benefits to parties that are unlikely to receive them otherwise through the course of normal commercial activity. This may be because the parties lack the financial means or bargaining power to attain these benefits or because these are the sorts of benefits normally

---

[1] For example, it has been argued that pharmaceutical companies ought to donate medications to persons suffering from HIV/AIDS in developing economies who lack access to them. See, for example, Dunfee (2006) and Hsieh (2005).

[2] "CSR" is used to refer to a variety of business policies, standards, and activities, ranging from policies to refrain from certain harmful actions to activities that aim to benefit parties directly. For purposes of this chapter, the term is used in reference to activities that benefit parties beyond routine commercial transactions. For a comprehensive treatment of the topic, see Crane et al. (2008). For a discussion of CSR in relation to multinational business enterprises see Hsieh and Wettstein (2015).

secured outside the commercial realm. These beneficial activities on the part of business firms are sometimes justified on grounds that they ultimately result in greater profits for the firm—for example, through improved reputation and goodwill.[3] The debate is whether there are duties to pursue these activities even if there is no clear case to be made in terms of profitability.

This chapter explores the role that corporate moral agency plays in making the case for such positive duties.[4] Specifically, the chapter examines a series of accounts for such duties that explicitly assume, or for which there is good reason to assume, that business firms are moral agents in their own right. What emerges from this examination is that by assuming business firms are moral agents, these accounts are able to sidestep debates about the purpose of the for-profit business firm. The idea is roughly expressed as follows. A common objection to attributing positive duties to business firms is that such duties are inconsistent with the primary profit-seeking objective of business because they require expending resources for ends other than making profits.[5] Most theories of morality, however, acknowledge positive duties that apply to all moral agents, such as a duty of beneficence, which require moral agents to benefit others even if doing so comes at some cost to their personal projects (Smith 2011). If business firms are moral agents in their own right, then there may be a duty to benefit members of society even if doing so comes at a financial cost to the firm. Given the contentious debate about the purpose of for-profit business firms, there is something appealing about accounts that ground positive duties on the part of business firms without having to engage this debate. By examining the role of corporate moral agency in accounts that attribute positive duties to business firms, a key aim of this chapter is to further our understanding about how best to theorize about moral standards that require business firms to engage in activities to benefit parties who would not receive those benefits through routine commercial activity.

A second aim of this chapter is to further our understanding about the case for corporate moral agency. As noted above, in debates about the standards that ought to apply to business activity, the focus has been largely on constraints or activities from which business firms ought to refrain. It is perhaps not surprising then that in the literature on corporate moral agency, when the discussion concerns assigning responsibility, the focus is largely on assigning responsibility for past wrongdoing.[6] As Amy Sepinwall points out in Chapter 8 in this book,

---

[3] For an overview of the research on the claim that such activities improve corporate financial performance, see Margolis and Walsh (2003).

[4] In this chapter, "corporate moral agency" refers to moral agency on the part of collective or group agents, and is not restricted to organizations with a specific legal form.

[5] A classic statement of this objection is found in Friedman (1962, 1970).

[6] Christian List and Philip Pettit consider both positive and negative actions on the part of agents as central to what it means to hold an agent responsible. They write, "holding responsible in our sense implies that, if what was done is something bad, then the agent is a candidate for

for example, one of the motivations for recognizing corporate moral agency is a concern that the injury inflicted by corporate activities may be greater than the sum of the individual contributions of members of the corporation (see also Philip Pettit's similar argument in Chapter 1). John Hasnas goes further and argues that the only practical significance in recognizing corporate moral agency is that "in the world with corporate moral agency, corporations are liable to punishment, specifically criminal punishment, as collective entities" (Hasnas 2012, 188). By examining whether or not positive duties ought to be attributed to business firms—a question that is not simply about assigning responsibility for past wrongdoing, but rather about forward-looking duties—this chapter aims to further our understanding of what, if anything, is distinctive about corporate, as opposed to individual, moral agency.

The chapter is organized as follows. The first section outlines an argument advanced by Thomas Dunfee (2006) that assigns pharmaceutical companies a duty, on grounds of rescue, to donate medications to patients suffering from HIV/AIDS in sub-Saharan Africa. The second section discusses the case for attributing positive duties to business firms on grounds of beneficence as put forward by Jeffery Smith (2012). The third section concerns a class of arguments that assign business firms a duty, on grounds of justice, to engage in extra-commercial activities that benefit members of society (Caney 2013; Dubbink and Van Liedekerke 2014; Hsieh 2004, 2009; O'Neill 2001; Scherer and Palazzo 2007, 2011; Scherer et al. 2006; Scherer et al. 2013; Wettstein 2009). What emerges from this discussion is that by assuming business firms are moral agents, these accounts are able to sidestep long-standing debates about the purpose of the for-profit business firm. The fourth section takes up the question of whether there is an account of corporate moral agency that is consistent with these accounts. The section then explores whether there is a way to maintain the attractive features of these accounts without having to assume that business firms are moral agents. The challenge, I conclude, is to provide an account of the purpose of the for-profit business firm that is not simply about the pursuit of profit.

RESCUE

There are many situations in which business firms are especially well placed to help alleviate suffering given their competencies and resources. Natural disasters are a case in point. In the wake of the of the tsunami that struck northeast Japan on March 11, 2011, for example, Japanese automakers

---

blame; if it is something good, then the agent is a candidate for approval and praise" (List and Pettit 2011, 154). Their analysis emphasizes the performance of past actions rather than the forward-looking nature of positive duties.

provided vehicles to government officials and trucks to deliver food and water to those in need (Singal et al. 2014). In situations such as these, where there is great suffering and business firms are uniquely well placed to help alleviate that suffering, Thomas Dunfee (2006) argues there is a moral duty to expend the resources of business firms to address that suffering.

Focusing on the spread of HIV/AIDS in sub-Saharan Africa, Dunfee asserts that global pharmaceutical companies have a moral duty to aid the victims of the catastrophe. He articulates this duty in what he terms the "Statement of Minimal Moral Obligation (SMMO)." According to Dunfee's SMMO:

> Firms possessing a unique human catastrophe rescue competency have a moral obligation to devote substantial resources toward best efforts to aid the victims of the catastrophe. Unless financial exigency justifies a lower level of investment, they should devote, *at a minimum*, the largest sum of (1) their most recent investments in social initiatives, (2) their five year average of investment in social initiatives, (3) their industry's average investment in social investments, or (4) the average investment in social initiatives by firms in their home nation. They may devote a portion of those resources to concurrent social initiatives only if there is an equally compelling rationale for such an investment.   (Dunfee 2006, 186, original emphasis)

Dunfee's account provides one way to counter the common objection, raised above, that positive duties to aid others are inconsistent with the profit-seeking requirement of business. To begin, the duty applies to firms with a "unique human catastrophe rescue competency," which suggests that the duty applies to business firms that already have the capability. The duty does not require new investments or a diversion from existing lines of business. In addition, because of the stringent requirements both for something to qualify as a "catastrophe" and for a corporation to qualify as having a "unique human catastrophe rescue competency," Dunfee argues that the SMMO applies "relatively rarely" and "to only a small set of firms" (Dunfee 2006, 200). These limits in the applicability of the SMMO suggest that firms need not incur significant losses in carrying out the duty. Moreover, these limits mean that the SMMO does not require business firms to change from being profit-seeking enterprises engaging in commercial activity. The duty applies within the course of engaging in such activity. Nonetheless, Dunfee is clear there are situations in which there is a moral duty for managers to direct the firm's resources toward the alleviation of human suffering independently of any clear financial return.

A key element of Dunfee's defense of the SMMO is an appeal to the principle of rescue. He cites T. M. Scanlon's version of the principle: "(I)f you are presented with a situation in which you can prevent something very bad from happening, or alleviate someone's dire plight, by making only a slight (or even moderate) sacrifice, then it would be wrong not to do so"

(Scanlon 1998, 224). Appeal to the rescue principle is in part what helps to make Dunfee's account attractive in the ways described above. The principle of rescue does not require individuals to forgo their personal pursuits. The point is that when confronted with a situation of rescue they have a duty to engage in rescue, but there is no duty that they go out and seek such situations. Furthermore, the conditions under which rescue is required are limited. In this respect, appeal to the principle of rescue is what helps to provide a response to the sorts of objections raised against assigning positive duties to business firms.

Dunfee's account, however, leaves open the question of to whom it is that the principle of rescue applies. On one interpretation, the rescue principle applies to the firm's executives in their capacity as moral agents. On this interpretation, given their ability to direct the firm's resources, executives are in a position to be able to prevent a great deal of suffering at little or moderate sacrifice, and as such, the duty of rescue would apply to them. There are two difficulties, however, with this interpretation. The first is that Dunfee locates the ability to provide assistance in the firm's capacities and resources, and not the executive's ability to direct those capacities and resources. The duty of rescue, as understood here, applies to the agent with the ability to engage in rescue, which is the firm, and not the individual executive. The second related difficulty with this interpretation concerns the ownership of the firm's resources. Even if one does not adhere to a view that shareholders are exclusively the owners of a corporate firm and its resources, it still remains the case that the resources being deployed by the firm's executive are not her own resources. She does not incur the cost of engaging in rescue, and so the question arises whether she is permitted to use resources with which she has been entrusted.

On another interpretation, the rescue principle applies to the business firm itself. This interpretation avoids the two difficulties outlined above in that both the capacity and resources for rescue belong to the business firm. One way to make the case that the duty of rescue applies to the business firm itself is to recognize the business firm as a moral agent in its own right.

BENEFICENCE

The application of the duty of rescue to the activities of business firms is limited in what it requires of business firms and their managers. Indeed, that is part of the appeal of an account that looks to the principle of rescue to ground positive duties on the part of business firms. In practice, business firms engage in activities that benefit parties to whom no duty of rescue is owed. In some cases, the nature of the need may not be extreme or severe. In others, it may not be alleviated through immediate action. Consider, for example, students who have dropped out of school participating in a job-training program with a firm. Their need may be great, but their situation is not one that can be alleviated by a one-time intervention. Collectively, these activities are often referred to as "corporate social responsibility" or "CSR."

Jeffery Smith identifies features of CSR that give rise to two challenges in making sense of the practice. The first is what he terms "the challenge of obligation" (Smith 2012, 62). The challenge of obligation is to reconcile the idea that CSR is a responsibility, which suggests a duty or obligation, and the idea that CSR is voluntary and allows for a great deal of discretion on the part of business managers. The second challenge is as follows. CSR activities are intended to benefit parties beyond what they receive through the course of normal commercial transactions. The activities embody the idea of a responsibility. At the same time, there is the view that CSR activities can and should be used to further the strategic aims of business firms. The challenge that arises is whether there is a coherent understanding of responsibility that allows for strategic considerations to enter into a company's decision to pursue CSR activities. Smith terms this "the challenge of integration" (id.).

Building on Norman Bowie's Kantian account of business ethics (Bowie 1999), Smith argues that the solution to these two challenges lies in acknowledging a duty of beneficence on the part of business firms (Smith 2012, 63). In Kantian terms, the duty of beneficence is a *duty of virtue* as opposed to a *duty of right*. Duties of right are "duties that govern individuals' particular actions so that a basic level of justice can be ensured," and "they can be legitimately enforced by the state in order to establish the background conditions for civil society" (id., 64). In contrast, duties of virtue are not meant to constrain individual actions. Rather, they "identify *ends* that our rational planning must take into account when we decide what kind of life to lead" (id.). A duty of beneficence involves "making others' happiness one's [own] end" (id., 65 quoting Kant [1798] 1991, 247). The duty also is an *imperfect duty*. Imperfect duties accord agents "latitude in how the duties are satisfied in any particular circumstances" (Smith 2012, 66). In the case of the duty of beneficence, what is obligatory is that the agent takes the well-being of others as her own end. The concern for the well-being of others "cannot be given up or forgotten" (id., 67). There is discretion in the agent's judgment of how best to promote that end in the light of particular circumstances and her other ends. Given this conception of a duty of beneficence, acknowledging such a duty on the part of business firms and their executives provides a way to address the challenge of obligation. CSR is a responsibility in the sense that the well-being of others parties outside the firm cannot be ignored, but there is discretion in how their well-being is to be promoted.

Another feature of duties of virtue is that they are not "intended by Kant to necessarily stand in opposition to the pursuit of one's own interest" (Smith

2012, 67). In cases when an agent's interests and pursuits are integrated with the lives of those around her, there is no necessary conflict or separation between the agent's pursuit of her own interests and others' happiness. "The crucial Kantian idea," Smith writes, "is that duties like beneficence are not simply duties to maximize desirable states of affairs; they are duties that prescribe what should be taken into account when one aims to autonomously live one's own, particular life, while simultaneously acknowledging the ways in which one's life may happen to be interconnected with the lives of others" (id., 68). If a duty of beneficence applies to business firms, this feature means there is no inherent conflict in pursuing CSR activities that advance the strategic aims of the business firm. In this manner, acknowledging a duty of beneficence on the part of business firms addresses the challenge of integration.

Although Smith is not explicit about whether the duty of beneficence applies to a business firm as a moral agent in its own right or to its individual members, the most plausible interpretation of his account, it seems, is to take the firm as the moral agent. To see why, it will help to turn briefly to another account that argues business firms ought to take into account the well-being of other parties on grounds of beneficence, but by attributing the duty to equity owners rather than to the firm itself.[7]

Samuel Manswell (2013) takes up the question of whether it is permissible for managers to pursue directly the well-being of parties other than share-holders within the framework of shareholder primacy as articulated famously by Milton Friedman (1962, 1970). On standard interpretations of shareholder primacy, the well-being of non-shareholders ought to matter only indirectly. Their well-being ought to be taken into account only insofar as doing so furthers shareholder interests. Manswell argues that although there are con-sequentialist justifications for shareholder primacy, a broadly deontological interpretation is closer to what underlies the account of shareholder primacy put forward by Friedman (Manswell 2013, 584). Under such an interpretation, a duty of beneficence applies to shareholders in their capacity as moral agents (id., 590). In turn, this allows for the managers to take as the proper ends of the firm's activities both shareholder and non-shareholder interests, and share-holders have a duty to hold managers accountable for the impact of business activity on non-shareholders (id., 597–8). CSR activities that are directly aimed to promote the well-being of parties other than shareholders need not be in conflict with the view that the proper aim of the business firm is to maximize profits or shareholder returns because managers must consider not only the interests of shareholders, but also their duties.

---

[7] The account is meant to apply to a broad range of business enterprises, including, but not limited to, corporations with shareholders. I thank Eric Orts for emphasizing this point. For background, see Orts (2015).

One issue that Manswell raises is the question of how managers are to carry out the duty of beneficence on the part of shareholders given the specific ends of each shareholder and the latitude afforded to each shareholder by the duty of beneficence in how to take into account the well-being of others (Manswell 2013, 590). Manswell's proposed solution is for companies to adopt codes or policies that make explicit the way in which the well-being and interests of non-shareholders are taken into account. The difficulty that arises with such a solution is that it seems to reverse the order of deliberation and action with regard to the duty of beneficence. As noted above, the underlying idea is that individual agents are the ones who must take into account the well-being of others and make judgments about how to promote their well-being in the light of the particular circumstances and each agent's specific ends. Indeed, share-holders may judge that the best way to carry out the duty of beneficence is outside of the firm altogether. In the light of these considerations about discretion and judgment, there is reason to hold that the most plausible interpretation of the application of Kant's account of beneficence to business activities is to take the business firm itself as the relevant moral agent, and not its individual members.

JUSTICE

Many activities on the part of business firms are undertaken in response to conditions in society that reflect perceived deficiencies in underlying social and political institutions. For example, business firms may help provide schooling for children in communities where they operate because the education system is lacking in resources. Business firms may pay workers more than what is legally required because the minimum wage in a particular place is seen as inadequate for meeting basic needs. In some cases, business firms are called upon to help stop human rights abuses on the part of governments. Institutions that fail to meet the basic needs of citizens or that violate certain basic rights are often characterized as unjust. Given these kinds of problems, another approach to argue for positive duties on the part of business firms involves reference to a duty to bring about institutions that qualify as just. This section examines the role played by corporate moral agency in this line of argument.

To set the framework for this line of argument, it will help to begin with an account put forward by Onora O'Neill (2001). O'Neill focuses on the case of multinational business enterprises operating in countries with institutions that fail to meet the basic needs of citizens or respect their rights. O'Neill distin-guishes between *primary agents of justice*, which have "capacities to determine how principles of justice are to be institutionalised within a certain domain," and *secondary agents of justice*, which are "thought to contribute to justice

mainly by meeting the demands of primary agents, most evidently by conforming to any legal requirements they establish" (O'Neill 2001, 189). Under ideal
conditions—that is, when states are able to bring about and maintain justice—
multinational business enterprises are best understood as secondary agents of
justice. However, under non-ideal conditions in which states are weak and lack
the means to bring about justice, according to O'Neill, "any simple division
between primary and secondary agents of justice blurs." She continues that
"justice has to be built by a diversity of agents and agencies," and multinational
business enterprises, according to O'Neill, are among those agents (id., 190).

As Simon Caney points out, a difficulty with O'Neill's account is that she
does not explain why multinational business enterprises have a moral duty to
take on some of the functions associated with primary agents of justice (Caney
2013, 142). He concludes that the strongest claim that can be made is "when
an agent (such as a government) is either unable to or unwilling to protect the
entitlements of those to whom it has a responsibility to protect (their citizens
and the citizens of other states), then other agents who have the capacity to
protect those entitlements have a *pro tanto* reason to do so" (id.). According to
Caney, multinational business enterprises "*can* serve as primary agents when
others have failed to perform their role and when they can play a valuable role
without imposing unfair costs on themselves or others" (id.).

One response is to argue that business firms are public or quasi-public
entities that have some of the responsibilities associated with governments.
For example, Christopher McMahon argues that the authority of business
executives is best secured "if corporate executives possess the status of public
officials exercising a subordinate form of cooperation-facilitating authority in an
integrated structure of such authority that is oriented toward the promotion
of the public good and under ultimate governmental control" (McMahon
2013, 110).[8] David Ciepley argues that although for-profit business corporations
are not public institutions, they also are not purely private institutions because
the authority of managers follows directly from being granted a charter that has
been approved by the legislature. On his view, business corporations are best

---

[8] The argument briefly is as follows. McMahon argues that senior executives of large
corporations exercise "subordinating authority," meaning that they stand in relationships with
other economic actors that involve "the issuing of directives to people who are normally
prepared to comply with them" (McMahon 2013, 2). While these actors who defer to the
judgment of senior executives concerning "the way their contributions will find expression in
corporate actions" can include creditors or suppliers, McMahon takes the paradigmatic case to
be that of employees (id., 3). The legitimacy of such authority normally would be grounded in a
promissory obligation on the part of employees to comply with managerial directives in
exchange for pay. McMahon argues, however, that reasonable employees will be able to conclude
that such an obligation is overridden by competing moral considerations, such as concern for the
pollution likely to result from a business plan to which they are directed to contribute. Because
this group of employees can be of significant size, he concludes that the legitimacy of managerial
authority cannot be grounded reliably in the promissory obligations of employees (id., 67–8).

understood as "franchises" of government (Ciepley 2013, 152). "The corporation has always been a public institution serving a genuinely public purpose," writes Florian Wettstein, and "its engagement in facilitating the provision of public goods and policies because of its unique and superior competences seems a matter of course rather than a gimmick" (Wettstein 2009, 336).

A second approach can be found in the work of Andreas Scherer and Guido Palazzo (Scherer and Palazzo 2007, 2011; Scherer et al. 2006; Scherer et al. 2013). As summarized by Wim Dubbink and Luc Van Liedekerke (2014), this approach follows from a "republican model" of the economy. "This model," they write, "holds that society must be able to rely on the 'self-organizing socially responsible activity in other subsystems (i.e., the market), whenever no other rule is available'" (Ulrich 2000, cited in Scherer et al. 2006, 515–16). Under the republican model, commercial agents are both private agents (*bourgeois*) and public agents (*citoyen*). They can never be purely private agents, so if institutions fail or institutional gaps appear, then commercial agents must take up activities associated with public institutions in order to fill the "governance gap." On this account, although business firms are not meant to replace governments, they are to engage in such activities as providing "supplementary governmental functions" (Scherer et al. 2006, 515) as well as serving as "guarantors of rights" (id., 517). As Dubbink and Van Liedekerke (2014, 531) point out, the latter especially "is quite close to a state-like role."[9]

Both of these approaches ground positive duties on the part of business firms by categorizing them as public or quasi-public entities. The problem with doing so, however, is that the sphere of economic activity is commonly understood to be distinct from the public or political sphere. As Waheed Hussain writes, "commonsense morality recognizes that there is...also a *personal sphere* in which we are allowed to pursue any goals, plans and projects we choose" (Hussain 2012, 323). "Implicit in our commonsense view," according to Hussain, "is the idea that the corporation is a *private association*" (id., 326). This is not to say that economic agents ought to be free to do anything they want. The view that the economic sphere is distinct from public or political spheres does not deny that economic activity ought to be constrained by law or regulation. Nor does it deny that basic moral principles apply to economic agents in their capacity as moral agents. Rather, the thought is that insofar as there is a sphere in which individuals ought to be free to pursue goals that are distinct from those of public institutions, then economic activity falls within that sphere.[10]

[9] Assigning human rights obligations to business firms is another approach that often involves a view of business firms as having a public or quasi-public role. For a brief overview of developments in the area of business and human rights from a normative theoretical perspective, see Cragg et al. (2012).
[10] The language of distinct "spheres" of human activity to which different distributive principles apply draws from Walzer (1983).

In the light of this sort of objection, Dubbink and Van Liedekerke argue for a moral (as opposed to political) duty to further justice.[11] Acknowledging that Kant himself did not attribute a duty to further justice as a duty to all moral agents, Dubbink and Van Liedekerke follow a suggestion by Paul Guyer (2000) that Kant must have held the duty applied to all moral agents but failed to make this view explicit (Dubbink and Van Liedekerke 2014, 535). They advance their argument by building on Kant's contract theory on the constitution of the state. Kant held that "human beings are already moral creatures in the 'state of nature'" and that "the duty to attain moral autonomy implies the commandment to leave the state of nature and submit to public authority (i.e., the state)" and enter into the "civil condition" (id., 536). Dubbink and Van Liedekerke extend Kant's account by arguing that the duty to leave the state of nature and to submit to public authority implies a duty to further justice. The idea roughly is that if the public authority is unjust, then simply submitting to it fails to fulfill the duty to leave the state of nature and enter the civil condition. One only fulfills the commandment to leave the state of nature when one enters a justly constituted state. In turn, the commandment to leave the state of nature implies a duty to further justice in an imperfect world.

As understood here, the duty to further justice falls short of a duty to take on the responsibilities associated with primary agents of justice as initially presented by O'Neill (2001). In this respect, the account differs from those that assign to business firms a public or quasi-public role. The point is that business firms are not public or quasi-public entities with the same sorts of duties attributed to government entities. At the same time, the duty to further justice involves more than the duties associated with secondary agents of justice, which are simply to follow the laws established by primary agents of justice. A duty to further justice requires that moral agents work to help establish just institutional arrangements, for example by addressing the underlying circumstances that hinder societies from achieving just institutions, such as extreme poverty and depravation, or working actively to increase the capacity of state institutions.

Dubbink and Van Liedekerke (2014, 528–9) are explicit in their assumption that business firms are moral agents, and as such, that the duty to further justice applies to them. In this manner, even though the duty to further justice does not demand as much of business firms as if they were primary agents of justice, Dubbink and Van Liedekerke's account provides a way to ground positive duties on the part of business firms while also avoiding the objection

---

[11] The argument is developed further in Dubbink and Smith (2011), Dubbink and van de Ven (2012), and Dubbink (2015). This line of argument is also leveled against Hsieh (2004) in which the claim is made that there are conditions under which multinational corporations are well positioned to take up the role of states in providing aid to other countries to help establish just institutions.

that economic activity is to be understood as a sphere that is distinct from the public or political spheres. In this manner, acknowledging business firms as moral agents in their own right helps to underwrite a third argument for positive duties on the part of business firms.

CORPORATE MORAL AGENCY OR CORPORATE PURPOSE?

Underlying the debate about the standards that ought to apply to business firms is the long-standing question of the purpose of for-profit business firms. If business firms are private associations formed to pursue whatever ends their members specify, or if the proper ends of business firms are to pursue profits, then the standards that ought to apply to their activities beyond what is required by the law are usually understood to be fairly minimal. They may involve, for example, requirements not to engage in fraud, not to cause harm, and not to engage in coercion.[12] For those who object to such minimal standards, part of the challenge has been to articulate a plausible conception of the purpose of for-profit business firms that permits activities and the use of firm resources for ends other than the pursuit of profit. Although many such accounts have been advanced, the question of purpose remains a long-standing area of debate.[13]

One way to understand the appeal of the arguments given in the previous sections of this chapter is that they are able to avoid the question about purpose. In the case of the accounts grounded in rescue and beneficence, the accounts take as a starting point widely recognized moral duties that apply to all moral agents and that require moral agents to benefit others even if doing so comes at some cost to their personal projects. By extending these duties to business firms, the claim is that even if business firms have as their purpose the maximization of profit, there are conditions under which it would be wrong not to engage in activities to the benefit of other parties as these conditions apply to all moral agents.

The argument from justice goes further. On this account, although business firms do not have a duty to take on the responsibilities of primary agents of justice, they do have a duty to help bring about just institutions, which

---

[12] Again, consider, for example, the well-known statement of the responsibilities of business as stated by Friedman (1962, 1970).

[13] These accounts include stakeholder theory (Freeman et al. 2010) and theories of corporate citizenship (Crane et al. 2008; Post 2002), as well as accounts that draw on traditions in political philosophy, such as social contract theory (Donaldson 1982) and deliberative democracy (Scherer and Palazzo 2007, 2011).

involves more than simply following the law as required of secondary agents of justice. This duty is potentially more demanding than what is required of rescue and beneficence, and the argument aims to establish this case without assuming any public or quasi-public role on the part of business firms.

The assumption that business firms are moral agents in their own right helps to underwrite arguments for more demanding standards of business firms without having to engage the long-standing question of their underlying purpose.

The question then arises whether there is an account of corporate moral agency that is consistent with the above accounts. Kendy Hess (2014a) advances one such account.[14] Hess argues that collective agents, which include business firms, "have forward-looking obligations to act in ways that avoid harm, respect rights, pursue excellences unique to their kind, or even bring the world closer to perfection for exactly the same reasons that human beings have them: because they can" (Hess 2014a, 203–4). According to Hess, the capacities that are said to ground such moral obligations on the part of individual moral agents are capacities also displayed by collective agents, such as business firms.

Consider, for example, the capacity for belief, which is central to intentionality. On one account of belief, a belief requires an internal representation and a disposition to act on the basis of that representation (id., 212). Following Fred Dretske (1988), Hess defines a representation as "(1) an information-bearing state (2) internal to a system (3) that the system synthesizes from information gathered from the world" (Hess 2014a, 212). To be clear, a representation is not a direct reflection of the external world, but an interpretation based on reports, which are direct reflections of the external world. It is not a mental state. In the context of a business firm, we can understand its individual members as providing direct reflections of the external world— through their actions, statements, or reports—which are then synthesized at the firm level into a single information-bearing state (id., 213). The firm can be said to have a disposition to act on that belief if we can predict and account for the collective actions of its members in terms of that belief—that is, the actions are those one would typically expect given that belief (id., 211). Hess argues that other capacities required by various accounts of moral agency (for example, attitudes of care or respect, reactions of shame or guilt) for individual agents can also be attributed to collective agents, such as business firms. Hess concludes that we can "understand and justify claims of *collective* agency, morality, and obligation in exactly the same terms that we use to understand and justify claims of *individual* agency, morality, and obligations" (id., 204).

Hess's account provides a way to justify the view that business firms are moral agents in their own right, and does so in a relatively straightforward

---

[14] Hess develops other aspects of her broader account in Hess (2010, 2013, 2014b).

manner. On Hess's account, the duties that apply to individual moral agents also apply to collective agents, such as business firms, because they both share the relevant capacities that ground moral obligations. Following Hess's account, duties of rescue, beneficence, and justice apply to business firms as they would to individual moral agents. In turn, the case for positive duties on the part of business firms can be made without having to engage debates about the purpose of the for-profit business firm.

At the same time, Hess's account stands apart from much of the scholarship on corporate moral agency. As noted at the outset, when discussing the responsibility of collective agents, the focus tends to be on negative duties, often with an emphasis on determining accountability for past actions associated with the collective agent. Hess's account of corporate moral agency, in contrast, encompasses forward-looking obligations that include not only negative duties, but positive duties as well. Furthermore, Hess argues that existing theories of moral agency and obligation that apply to individual agents extend to collective agents, such as business firms.[15] In the literature on corporate moral agency, however, some accounts do not recognize collectives as agents in their own right (for example, Gilbert 1989; Miller 2006), and accounts that do recognize collectives as agents in their own right have focused on developing new ways to understand agency and responsibility that are specific to collectives or groups (for example, French 1984; List and Pettit 2011). "Corporate moral agency" on these accounts is best understood as a "corporate" version of moral agency rather than an extension or application of moral agency from the individual context to the context of collectives or groups.

One question for these accounts is whether "corporate" versions of moral agency ground positive duties of the sort considered in this chapter, such as rescue, beneficence, or justice, and if not, what is it about "corporate" versions of moral agency that grounds negative duties, but not positive duties, on the part of collective agents, such as business firms. As noted at the outset of this chapter, in debates about the standards that ought to apply to the activities of business firms, the focus has tended to be on negative duties. By focusing attention on positive duties in the business context by way of moral duties that are widely recognized in the individual context, one aim of this chapter is to broaden the debate about corporate moral agency and to invite greater discussion about what is meant by moral agency on the part of collective agents such as business firms, and what follows for their responsibilities by recognizing them as moral agents in their own right.

---

[15] Patricia Werhane (1985, 2007) characterizes business firms as "secondary moral agents." They are moral agents in their own right, in the sense that their responsibilities cannot be ascribed to their individual members, but because they depend upon individual human action, they are considered secondary with claims that are inferior to those of natural persons. Werhane's account includes positive responsibilities among the responsibilities of business firms.

A second question is whether focusing on the moral agency of business firms represents the most promising approach to theorizing about positive duties on the part of business firms. This question is distinct from the issue of whether business firms are moral agents in their own right. Rather, the question concerns the grounding of positive duties on the part of business firms in ordinary morality as it relates to individuals. On the one hand, as discussed above, by focusing on positive duties that all moral agents are said to have independently of their personal projects and the context in which they operate, the accounts surveyed in this chapter are able to avoid engaging directly the debates about the purpose of the for-profit business firm. Business firms, on these accounts, have positive duties to benefit parties who might not receive them through routine commercial activity even if shareholder primacy is correct, for example, in the context of for-profit corporations. On the other hand, it seems that what motivates the debate about assigning positive duties to business firms is in part an objection to shareholder primacy (or the primacy of other equity ownership interests). What gives rise to the case for positive duties in the first place is the thought that the activities of business firms ought to be directed toward furthering ends in addition to profit. Indeed, by arguing for positive duties that apply to all business firms, there is a sense in which even the accounts surveyed in this chapter say something about the ends that business activity ought to pursue. In theorizing about the proper ends of business firms, the question is whether ordinary morality provides the most appropriate starting point.

As discussed above, there is much to be said for an account that does not ground positive duties on the part of business firms by attributing to them a public or quasi-public role in society. Business firms are widely held to be distinct from public agencies in terms of their purpose and what is required of them. At the same time, it need not follow that the standards they ought to follow are to be derived exclusively from the realm of ordinary morality as it applies to natural persons. This is not to deny that considerations of ordinary morality ought to apply to the activities of business firms or the decisions of their managers. In fact, it may be said that more needs to be done to meet the basic requirements of ordinary morality in many cases in business.[16] Rather, the point is that with respect to theorizing about positive duties and the ends that business firms ought to pursue, we ought to look beyond the realm of individual morality. One thought, for example, is to look to the social functions that business firms perform as a basis for an account of the purpose of for-profit business firms.[17] Although it is beyond the scope of this chapter to

---

[16] Elsewhere I argue that even minimal moral standards can be more demanding than often is held to be the case (Hsieh 2013a), and may even require the establishment of just institutions, for example, on grounds to avoid causing harm (Hsieh 2009).

[17] I sketch the outlines of one such attempt in Hsieh (2013b) and Hsieh (2015).

provide such an account, it is hoped this chapter has made the case that for those concerned with the positive duties of business firms, directly engaging the question of the purpose of for-profit business firms is a project that cannot be avoided.

REFERENCES

Bowie, Norman (1999). *Business Ethics: A Kantian Perspective.*

Caney, Simon (2013). "Agents of Global Justice." In *Reading Onora O'Neill*, ed. David Archand, Monique Deveaux, Neil Manson, and Daniel Weinstock.

Ciepley, David (2013). "Beyond Public and Private: Toward a Political Theory of the Corporation." *American Political Science Review* 107: 139.

Cragg, Wesley, Denis Arnold, and Peter Muchilinski (2012). "Human Rights and Business." *Business Ethics Quarterly* 22: 1.

Crane, Andrew, Dirk Matten, and Jeremy Moon (2008). *Corporations and Citizenship.*

Crane, Andrew, Abagail McWilliams, Dirk Matten, Jeremy Moon, and Donald Siegel (eds) (2008). *The Oxford Handbook of Corporate Social Responsibility.*

Donaldson, Thomas (1982). *Corporations and Morality.*

Dretske, Fred (1988). *Explaining Behavior: Reasons in a World of Causes.*

Dubbink, Wim (2015). "A Moral Grounding of the Duty to Further Justice in Commercial Life." *Ethical Theory and Moral Practice* 18: 27.

Dubbink, Wim and Jeffrey Smith (2011). "A Political Account of the Corporation as a Morally Responsible Actor." *Ethical Theory and Moral Practice* 14: 223.

Dubbink, Wim and Bert van de Ven (2012). "On the Duties of Commission in Commercial Life." *Ethical Theory and Moral Practice* 15: 221.

Dubbink, Wim and Luc Van Liedekerke (2014). "Grounding Positive Duties in Commercial Life." *Journal of Business Ethics* 120: 527.

Dunfee, Thomas W. (2006). "Do Firms with Unique Competencies for Rescuing Victims of Human Catastrophes Have Special Obligations? Corporate Responsibility and the AIDS Catastrophe in Sub-Saharan Africa." *Business Ethics Quarterly* 16: 185.

Freeman, R. Edward, Jared Harrison, Andrew Wicks, Bidhan Parmar, and Simone De Colle (2010). *Stakeholder Theory: The State of the Art.*

French, Peter A. (1984). *Collective and Corporate Responsibility.*

Friedman, Milton (1962). *Capitalism and Freedom.*

Friedman, Milton (1970). "The Social Responsibility of Business Is to Increase its Profits." *The New York Times Magazine*, September 13, 1970.

Gilbert, Margaret (1989). *On Social Facts.*

Guyer, Paul (2000). "Kantian Foundations for Liberalism." In *Kant on Freedom, Law, and Happiness*, ed. Paul Guyer.

Hasnas, John (2012). "Reflections on Corporate Moral Responsibility and the Problem Solving Technique of Alexander the Great." *Journal of Business Ethics* 107: 183.

Hess, Kendy (2010). "The Modern Corporation as Moral Agent." *Southwest Philosophy Review* 26: 61.

Hess, Kendy M. (2013). "'If You Tickle Us...': How Corporations Can Be Moral Agents Without Being Persons." *Journal of Value Inquiry* 47: 319.

Hess, Kendy (2014a). "Because They Can: The Basis for the Moral Obligations of (Certain) Collectives." *Midwest Studies in Philosophy* 38: 203.

Hess, Kendy M. (2014b). "The Free Will of Corporations (and Other Collectives)." *Philosophical Studies* 168: 241.

Hsieh, Nien-hê (2004). "The Obligations of Transnational Corporations: Rawlsian Justice and the Duty of Assistance." *Business Ethics Quarterly* 14: 643.

Hsieh, Nien-hê (2005). "Property Rights in Crisis: Managers and Rescue." In *Ethics and the Pharmaceutical Industry in the 21st Century*, ed. Michael Santoro and Thomas Gorrie.

Hsieh, Nien-hê (2009). "Does Global Business Have a Responsibility To Promote Just Institutions?" *Business Ethics Quarterly* 19: 251.

Hsieh, Nien-hê (2013a). "Multinational Enterprises and Incomplete Institutions: The Demandingness of Minimum Moral Standards." In *Business Ethics*, ed. Michael Boylan, 2nd ed.

Hsieh, Nien-hê (2013b). "Multinational Corporations, Global Justice and Corporate Responsibility: A Question of Purpose." *Notizie di Politeia* 29: 129.

Hsieh, Nien-hê (2015). "Managerial Responsibility and the Purpose of Business: Doing One's Job Well." In *Ethical Innovation in Business and the Economy: Studies in Transatlantic Business Ethics*, ed. Georges Enderle and Patrick E. Murphy.

Hsieh, Nien-hê and Florian Wettstein (2015). "Corporate Social Responsibility and Multinational Enterprises." In *The Routledge Handbook of Global Ethics*, ed. Darrel Moellendorf and Heather Widdows.

Hussain, Waheed (2012). "Corporations, Profit Maximization, and the Personal Sphere." *Economics and Philosophy* 28: 311.

Kant, Immanuel [1798] (1991). *Metaphysics of Morals*, trans. Mary Gregor.

List, Christian and Philip Pettit (2011). *Group Agency: The Possibility, Design, and Status of Corporate Agents*.

Manswell, Samuel (2013). "Shareholder Theory and Kant's 'Duty of Beneficence.'" *Journal of Business Ethics* 117: 583.

Margolis, Joshua and James Walsh (2003). "Misery Loves Companies: Rethinking Social Initiatives by Business." *Administrative Science Quarterly* 48: 268.

McMahon, Christopher (2013). *Public Capitalism*.

Miller, Seumas (2006). "Collective Moral Responsibility: An Individualist Account." *Midwest Studies in Philosophy* 30: 176.

O'Neill, Onora (2001). "Agents of Justice." In *Global Justice*, ed. Thomas Pogge.

Orts, Eric W. (2015). *Business Persons: A Legal Theory of the Firm*, rev. paperback ed.

Post, James (2002). "Global Corporate Citizenship: Principles to Live and Work By." *Business Ethics Quarterly* 12: 143.

Scanlon, T.M. (1998). *What We Owe to Each Other*.

Scherer, Andreas, Dorothee Baumann-Pauly, and Anselm Schneider (2013). "Democratizing Corporate Governance: Compensating for the Democratic Deficit of Corporate Political Activity and Corporate Citizenship." *Business & Society* 52: 473.

Scherer, Andreas and Guido Palazzo (2007). "Toward a Political Conception of Corporate Responsibility: Business and Society Seen from a Habermasian Perspective." *Academy of Management Review* 32: 1096.

Scherer, Andreas and Guido Palazzo (2011). "New Political Role of Business in a Globalized World A Review and Research Agenda." *Journal of Management Studies* 48: 899.

Scherer, Andreas, Guido Palazzo, and Dorothee Baumann (2006). "Global Rules and Private Actors: Toward a New Role of the Transnational Corporation in Global Governance." *Business Ethics Quarterly* 16: 505.

Singal, Manisha, Richard Wokutch, Uaniv Poria, and Michelle Hong (2014). "Ethical Decision-making in Extreme Operating Environments: Kew Garden Principles and Strategic CSR in Three Service Industry Cases." *Business and Professional Ethics Journal* 33: 211.

Smith, Jeffery (2012). "Corporate Duties of Virtue: Making (Kantian) Sense of Corporate Social Responsibility." In *Kantian Business Ethics: Critical Perspectives*, ed. Denis Arnold and Jared Harris.

Smith, Michael (2011). "Deontological Moral Obligations and Non-Welfarist Agent-Relative Values." *Ratio* (new series) 24: 341.

Ulrich, Peter (2000). "Integrative Economic Ethics: Towards a Conception of Socio-Economic Rationality." In *Contemporary Economic Ethics and Business Ethics*, ed. Peter Koslowski.

Walzer, Michael (1983). *Spheres of Justice*.

Werhane, Patricia (1985). *Persons, Rights and Corporations*.

Werhane, Patricia (2007). "Corporate Social Responsibility/Corporate Moral Responsibility: Is There a Difference and the Difference it Makes." In *The Debate over Corporate Social Responsibility*, ed. Steve May, George Cheney, and Juliet Roper.

Wettstein, Florian (2009). *Multinational Corporations and Global Justice: Human Rights Obligations of a Quasi-Governmental Institution*.

Conclusion

The Moral Responsibility of Firms:
Past, Present, and Future

Eric W. Orts

ENVIRONMENTAL FRAUD AT VOLKSWAGEN

In 2009, my family bought a new Volkswagen Jetta diesel relying on high scores this model received for its environmental characteristics. I don't recall the rating service we used, but the top-rated passenger car along this dimension was the Toyota Prius, and the VW Jetta came in a close second. We preferred the performance and "pick up" in driving the Jetta. In 2015, however, we learned along with millions of other owners of VW automobiles one reason for the difference in performance: VW had lied. Our Jetta did not deserve the high ratings it received for its environmental characteristics because VW had intentionally installed software designed to fool routine government testing. A "defeat device" programmed the engine to run with lower emissions when tested, but then shifted during normal driving conditions to spew into the atmosphere twenty to forty times more harmful nitrogen oxide than permitted under the relevant environmental regulations in the United States and Europe (Davenport and Ewing 2015; Hakim 2016b).[1] Another corporate fraud scandal was born: prosecutors unleashed, product recalls ordered, and class action lawsuits filed. As this book goes to press, the story of VW's large-scale environmental fraud has only begun, but it serves to illustrate the practical relevance of the central question addressed in this book of the moral responsibility of firms—or not.

---

[1] VW has admitted to fraud in the United States, but has claimed that its practices regarding the emissions software devices were legal in Europe (Hakim 2016a).

Volkswagen has admitted to its deception, and everyone can agree that what it has done was morally wrong. I feel cheated, as do millions of other consumers, as do governments around the world. The key question, though, is *who* exactly committed this wrong? A letter sent to consumers by Michael Horn, President and CEO of VW America (a subsidiary of the larger German parent), illustrates how easy it is to be imprecise and ambiguous about moral responsibility in firms. He writes to offer a "personal and profound apology" and admits that "Volkswagen has violated your trust." He expresses heartfelt empathy: "I understand and fully appreciate your anger and frustration." He owns the problem and makes a promise: "I would like you to know that we take full responsibility and are cooperating with all responsible agencies. I can also assure you that we are committed to making this right for you—and taking steps to prevent something like this from ever happening again" (Horn 2015).

Notice, though, how easily some of these sentences oscillate between the personal and the institutional. Mr. Horn offers a "personal" apology, but as the CEO of VW's US subsidiary, he likely has no direct knowledge of the fraud perpetrated by engineers and other executives at VW. So his "personal" apology is not really personal: it's institutional. He is apologizing as a senior executive of VW who has the job of dealing with American consumers defrauded by his company. As is ubiquitous in business, he speaks as an authorized legal agent of his big firm (see Orts 2015, 53–62). VW, one of the largest automobile companies in the world, employs hundreds of thousands of people. Most probably, only a relatively small number of people were directly responsible for the skullduggery of creating the deceptive software and installing it in millions of VW cars.[2] Most probably also, only a relatively small number more actually knew about or suspected the mass deception. Mr. Horn's ability to offer a "personal and profound apology" to consumers like me, then, makes a few rather large assumptions. First, his apology assumes that some portion of blame for the wrong can affix to the very large and complex firm called "Volkswagen," as well as the individual people who actually perpetrated or knew about the deception. Second, Mr. Horn assumes that he has authority to speak on behalf of the firm in a manner allowing him to apologize to consumers for the wrong in some meaningful sense.

Notice also that Mr. Horn moves immediately from offering a personal apology to admitting that "Volkswagen has violated your trust." But what does this statement mean in the context of this scandal? Again, there are specific employees and executives who were morally responsible for designing and installing the "defeat devices," and there are probably more who either ordered

---

[2] As of this writing, an internal investigation at VW reported that only nine people have been suspended who are suspected of the participating in the fraud (Ewing 2015). Additional questions concern when and how many executives learned of the problem and may have failed to disclose it (Ewing 2016).

this to be done or knew about and condoned these actions. Moreover, the owners of Volkswagen at the time of the deceptive activity (which occurred approximately from 2009 to 2015) have likely profited from the fraudulent activity. Executive and employee bonuses may well have been paid for hitting performance targets in sales and profits that might not have been reached without the environmental fraud. (On the idea of environmental fraud and the role of citizens in the private enforcement of environmental laws more generally, see Orts 1995, 1324; Thompson 2000.) VW owners who likely profited from the fraud embrace a complex category that describes the capital structure of the modern firm, including not only shareholders, but also bondholders, other creditors, and the company itself in the form of retained earnings. (On the complexity of corporate ownership, see Orts 2015, 71–105).[3]

According to the individualist accounts of moral responsibility offered by many scholars, including several authors of chapters in this book, to say "Volkswagen has violated your trust" is only shorthand for saying "specific participants within the company structure of Volkswagen have violated your trust." Following this line of reasoning, one may conclude that Mr. Horn's statement here is not sensible or coherent. It is not the company as a whole or Mr. Horn in particular who has violated customers' trust but rather the specific people who are employees, executives, and owners of the company who committed the wrong, condoned it, and profited from it. To put the problem more starkly, to accept the personification of Volkswagen as the relevant "entity" that is responsible for the wrong enables agents, such as Mr. Horn, to point to the formal and abstract representation of "the firm" as the source of the wrong rather than to hold particular individual people responsible. Instead, and more precisely, Mr. Horn might have been encouraged instead to say: "Some employees and executives within Volkswagen have violated your trust, and they and some owners of the company have profited from this violation." Then, when Mr. Horn says that "we are committed to making this right for you," he might instead have been encouraged to say: "We promise to find out who within our firm is responsible for this wrongful behavior, and we will cooperate with government authorities in prosecuting them and otherwise bringing them to justice. In addition, we will require any of the firm's owners, executives, and employees who have profited from this wrongful behavior to disgorge their ill-gotten gains—with an appropriate share paid to you as a defrauded customer to compensate you for the harm wrongfully done." In other words, for Mr. Horn to attribute blame vaguely to VW as a formal and abstract firm and to promise consumers that the "royal

---

[3] VW's somewhat unusual corporate structure involving a significant "co-determination" role for labor unions on its supervisory board as well as a large ownership interest by the government of Lower Saxony may have contributed to laxity in oversight. (Van der Heyden 2015). But the overall problem is generic.

we" of VW will "make this right" allows him to avoid saying anything very specific about the business participants within the firm who are immediately and directly responsible. On this view, Mr. Horn's "personal and profound apology" rings hollow.

OUR CONTRIBUTORS' PERSPECTIVES

Chapters in this book by John Hasnas, Ian Maitland, David Rönnegard and Manuel Velasquez, and Amy Sepinwall track this theme—providing various arguments for what might be called the individualist theory of moral responsibility in firms.

Hasnas argues that recognizing moral responsibility for firms qua firms creates a "responsibility deficit" by which individual wrongdoers can escape accountability for their actions. He is particularly concerned that this avoidance of individual responsibility occurs through punishing "innocent" business participants (including employees, shareholders, and perhaps others who suffer from penalties imposed on a firm as a whole) rather than focusing on the specific individuals who have done or condoned the wrong. (See Chapter 5.)

Maitland reinforces this argument. He maintains that a philosophically careless "anthropomorphization" of firms allows a "responsibility deficit" of great magnitude, often amounting to abuse that enables the equivalent of a real-life game of "grand theft corporation." (See Chapter 6.) He references Judge Jed Rakoff's recent opinions taking US prosecutors to task for allowing large corporate settlements of criminal charges in situations in which no individual person is convicted or held personally responsible. (See also Rakoff 2014, 2015).

In a similar vein, Rönnegard and Velasquez advance a set of arguments making the individualist case against attribution of moral responsibility to organizations, including business firms. They argue that collective organizations such as firms cannot correctly be said to bear moral responsibility for the following reasons.

(1) Firms are not "agents" (in the philosophical sense) that can be conceived as meaningfully separate from the individual people that compose them.

(2) Firms do not have the capacities of knowledge and intention required for moral responsibility.

(3) Firms do not have capacity to feel emotions needed for moral responsibility.

(4) Firms cannot "act" in the world themselves and depend instead on the direct involvement of real individual people.

(5) Attributing moral responsibility to firms often has the unacceptable consequence of "punishing" innocent individuals (rehearsing arguments also made by Hasnas and Maitland).

(6) Firms do not have the "autonomy" required to attribute moral responsibility.

(See Chapter 7.)

Sepinwall elaborates on the argument that corporations and other business firms lack emotions. They are, in her words, "affectless." In particular, firms cannot experience "guilt," and it therefore makes no sense to "blame" them for wrongdoing. Doing so is also ineffective. (See Chapter 8.)

These chapters make a strong case for an individualist approach to moral responsibility in firms. They build on previous contributions that these and other authors have made to advance the argument that attributing moral responsibility to firms is philosophically mistaken. (See Hasnas 2010; Maitland 1994; Rönnegard 2013, 2015; Sepinwall 2012, 2015a; Velasquez 1983, 2003. See also Lewis 1948; Miller and Makela 2005). As noted by the philosopher Roger Scruton, these arguments follow in a long historical tradition. Centuries ago, Samuel von Pufendorf argued that a corporation is a *"persona moralis composita,"* and Wilhelm von Humboldt maintained that such a composite person "should be regarded as nothing more than the union of its members at a given time." (See Scruton 1989, 245–6).

Other scholars, who are also represented in the chapters of this book, challenge this individualist theory. They would say that Mr. Horn's attributions of moral responsibility to Volkswagen as a corporation can be justified. The individual actions that caused the fraud affecting millions of vehicles and consumers occurred within the formal legal structure of a corporation, and the organized authority of this structure of the firm is an indissoluble part of the moral wrong that has been committed. VW as an organization is morally responsible because it acts as a rational organization with cognitive attributes and organizationally shared intentions. On this general view, it is impossible to imagine how a fraud on such a massive scale could occur without the assistance—even if a widespread, often innocent, and unknowing assistance— of the thousands of employees and executives who built the offending cars and sold them. The entire enterprise of committing fraud on a massive scale would not have been possible without the complex capital structure that provided the financing to commit the wrong and the internal economic incentives that encouraged and condoned it.[4] It therefore makes sense to say that "VW has violated your trust" and to recognize senior executive agents such as Mr. Horn

---

[4] It has been noted, for example, that the beginning of the environmental fraud in the United States corresponded with a strong commitment and drive of VW's CEO to overtake Toyota as the world's largest automobile company (Ewing 2015).

as having the legal and moral authority to make a public, if not a "personal," apology on behalf of VW as a firm. It makes sense also for consumers like me to feel wronged by the firm itself and to demand a compensatory response.

Versions of this argument for what might be called an organizational or collectivist theory of moral responsibility find support in the chapters collected here by Philip Pettit, Michael Bratman, and Peter French, as well as Waheed Hussain and Joakim Sandberg.

Pettit argues that firms such as business corporations are "conversable agents" that act in the world according to set purposes and objectives. They "speak" as agents in their interactions with other agents in the world through authorized representatives. Business firms organized and operating in this manner therefore have the capacity to hold beliefs, express intentions, and make promises. In this sense, they have "minds of their own." They are "fit to be held responsible" in moral terms when their authorized actions do not meet their expressions of collective purpose, belief, and intention. (See Chapter 1.)

Bratman supports the argument for the collective moral responsibility of firms at least to the extent that his elaboration of a "shared intention" of a group through a sufficient institution of "self-governance" satisfies one important criterion needed for moral responsibility. (He leaves open whether other criteria exist that may or may not be required to attribute moral responsibility to business firms.) Bratman specifies some factors involved in the formation of group intentions, including "shared deliberations" and "shared policies of procedure." His analysis suggests that "shared intentions" created collectively at the firm level may allow for moral responsibility to be attributed correctly to firms qua firms. (See Chapter 2.)

French supplements well-known previous arguments that he has made in favor of finding *how* the moral responsibility of firms can be based on a "functionalist or structuralist account of corporate intentionality and respon-sibility at the time of an action or event" with new reflections about *when* the moral responsibility of a firm for particular actions or consequences may end. He illustrates what he describes as the "diachronic" dimension of the problem by considering the case of energy firm BP and its responsibility for the massive oil spill in the Gulf of Mexico in 2010. Following a study of the more general philosophical problem by Andrew Khoury (2013), French asserts that even though BP bears moral responsibility as a firm at the time of the oil spill (namely, synchronic responsibility), the firm's responsibility dissipates and even disappears over time (namely, diachronic responsibility). This reduction and eventual vanishing of responsibility occurs when BP goes through various changes in its identity through corporate reorganizations, changes of leader-ship, and measures expressing atonement taken to address the wrong, such as admitting responsibility, paying damages, and other acts of contrition or compensation. (See Chapter 3.)

Hussain and Sandberg support arguments for the moral responsibility of firms by taking what they call a "functional normative" approach to the problem. They adopt a constructivist pragmatism and note that business firms such as corporations are legal structures. The plasticity of law allows Hussain and Sandberg to appeal to a larger value of social welfare or what is best for society overall. In their words, "there is no one right way to treat an organization or group as a collective agent." Therefore the moral responsibility of firms translates into a pragmatic moral and legal question rather than a "pre-institutional" moral one. The moral responsibility of firms should be found, in other words, when it serves the broader social good to do so. (See Chapter 4.)

These chapters that generally support an organizational or collectivist view of the moral responsibility of firms also build on other major contributions to the literature by these authors, as well as others. (See, for example, Bratman 2007, 2014; List and Pettit 2011; Pettit 2007, 2008; French 1979, 1995, 1996. See also Arnold 2006; Donaldson 1982, 18–35.)

Is it possible to square the circle of this debate between individualists and collectivists? Two of the contributions in the book provide possible options going forward into the future that seem compatible with both individualist and collectivist accounts of moral responsibility in firms. I will suggest one other possible future direction as well, drawing on a legal perspective.

Kendy Hess suggests that a close philosophical analysis of competing positions reveals "an unrecognized consensus" uniting the individualists and collectivists (whom she also calls "holists"). She points out that much of the debate revolves around ontological, metaphysical, meta-ethical, and methodological questions about the nature of firms. Nobody denies, though, that ethics matter in business. In Hess's words, the "debate over the initial claim that there *is* 'a firm,' or that it can bear moral obligations…. is *not* a debate about ethics, about whether there are moral obligations in play" (original emphasis). Everyone agrees, including everyone writing chapters in this book, that "business behavior is subject to ethical norms" in general. Despite the fact that some contemporary observations may suggest the contrary, "business is not a morality-free zone." Hess encourages a "reframing" that allows for progress to be made on examining many practical ethical dilemmas in a manner that "brackets" the individualist-versus-collectivist debate. Ethical answers may correlate, in other words, to specific practical questions in business ethics (and perhaps law too) whether or not one's background view of the grounding of moral responsibility relies on seeing "firms as collections of people" or "firms qua firms." (See Chapter 9.)

For example, if one accepts the argument that insider trading is wrong (see, for example, Lee 2002; Scheppele 1993; Strudler and Orts 1999), then one can also likely agree that steps should be taken within firms—or by individuals acting within the structure of firms—to prevent insider trading from happening. All can agree to sanction violations of insider trading without agreeing on the moral meta-analysis. If the premise that insider trading is wrong is accepted, in other words, then everyone can agree that individuals in firms should prevent insider trading and that individuals who commit insider trading should be punished, even though individualists and collectivists may diverge on whether a firm qua firm can either commit insider trading or be rightly punished for it. (On the problem of corporations themselves committing insider trading, see Loewenstein and Wang 2005.)

Nien-hê Hsieh encourages forward thinking in another direction that both individualists and collectivists may support. He urges a focus on the "positive duties" that firms qua firms or people acting collectively in firms may owe. Much of the long debate about the proper seat of the moral responsibility of firms focuses on ethics as a negative constraint: what one *should not* do. Hsieh calls for attention to positive moral duties: what one *should* do, particularly in cases of urgent human need. He builds on work that he and others have done, for example, in applying an ethical "duty to rescue" to firms (Dunfee 2006; Hsieh 2004, 2006). He extends this view to include positive duties or virtues of "beneficence," drawing on the work of Bowie (1999) and Smith (2012), as well as positive duties to act in the world following principles of "justice," drawing on the work of various theorists including O'Neill (2001), Caney (2013), and Dubbink and Van Liedekerke (2014). Examining these "positive" duties and virtues can fit within both individualist and collectivist theories of the ethical responsibility of firms. (See Chapter 10.)

A LEGAL PERSPECTIVE ON MORAL RESPONSIBILITY IN FIRMS

Finally, I would like to suggest that a closer legal analysis of the nature of business firms may lead to some other agreements among individualists and collectivists going forward. In a book called *Business Persons*, I've argued that the law plays a very large role in the construction and recognition of what we call business firms (Orts 2015). Firms come in many varieties and in different legal forms: corporations, partnerships, limited liability companies, and other complex combinations (such as corporate parent-subsidiary structures and franchises). And firms range widely in terms of size: from sole proprietors to massive multinational enterprises such as VW and BP. In addition, firms may adopt different objectives and value orientations. There is no natural law requiring "shareholder value maximization" or the pursuit of profits over all other values. To be sure, profit-making describes a primary objective of most if not all business firms, but this does not mean that it is the *only* objective. As the American Law Institute recognizes, a business corporation has the "primary" objective of profit and economic gain, but it is "obliged, to the same extent as a natural person, to act within the boundaries set by law," and it may "take into account ethical considerations that are reasonably regarded as appropriate to the responsible conduct of business." Many firms "devote a reasonable amount of resources to public welfare, humanitarian, educational, and philanthropic purposes," a practice which many statutes sanction and many ethical traditions encourage. (American Law Institute 1994, sect. 2.01).

The normative orientations of family-owned enterprises, which are ubiquitous on the world stage (Landes 2006; Morck and Steier 2007), often imbue particular religious or other moral values into a firm's culture and operations. The recent high-profile US Supreme Court case of *Burwell v. Hobby Lobby Stores, Inc.* (2014), which recognized a right of some family-owned firms to resist legal obligations on religious grounds, illustrates this phenomenon. (See also Orts 2016; Sepinwall 2015b, 2015c.) Statutes establishing benefit corporations, community interest companies, and other "hybrid social enterprises" expand the choice of legal forms to include social or environmental ends as an explicit supplement to profit-making (see Orts 2015, 206–22).

An appreciation of the descriptive and normative complexity of different business firms means that attributions of ethical responsibility require digging into the organizational details of specific firms. Others have previously noticed the need to adjust ethical theory to the legal variations in the types and sizes of business firms, as well as differences in national and cultural contexts (for example, Donaldson 1982, 1989). With respect to the ethical responsibility of firms, a legal analysis drills down into the organizational structure of a specific business to understand who has legal authority for particular decisions and who has rights and benefits of ownership. This legal analysis can provide an understanding of particular firms that may help to ground agreements unifying both individualists and collectivists on particular attributions of moral responsibility.

Consider again, for example, the case of VW and its environmental fraud on consumers. Important questions to ask when attributing ethical responsibility including understanding and, through a proper investigation, finding out *who actually made the decisions and engaged in the actions* to design the "defeat devices" that were installed on millions of cars and *who knew about these decisions and actions*. Another important question is *who profited from these decisions and actions*. For example, employees who met productivity targets at least in part by means of the fraudulent behavior arguably had "ill-gotten gains" (cf. Katz 1996). The executives who met internal incentives for profit-making by accelerating sales of falsely promoted vehicles are in the same boat. Morally speaking, the ill-gotten profits should be returned from those who gained to those who were defrauded (or forfeited to the government in recognition of its role to protect the environment). Moreover, the ill-gotten gains from the fraud should be reversed whether or not a particular employee knew about the fraud, because the profits themselves have been "tainted" by the wrongful activity.[5] Some owners may also have profited from the wrongful behavior. If the economic gains from the fraud were large enough, then the stock price of VW would likely have been affected favorably as a reflection of a greater perceived economic value of the company.[6] If a shareholder sold his or her shares just prior to a market correction following the exposure of the environmental cheating, then a portion of this realized gain is also arguably wrongfully obtained. We may have pragmatic reasons to limit the legal scope of moral responsibility in the context of complex corporate ownership structures, but this is a different matter than a straightforward tracing of moral responsibility to the individuals who are responsible for the fraud, knew about it, and profited from it.

Figure 1 provides a stylized example to illustrate how thinking about a firm's *business participants* in a wrongful action can shed light on how we think about the attributions of moral responsibility to different individual participants and firms qua firms. (For an account of the different business participants in firms and how they are related to each other, see Orts 2015.)

Imagine a firm (perhaps a stylized version of VW) that is making only ethical and legal profits through time T_1. The firm then begins committing massive fraud of some kind at T_1, and at T_2 a wider group of people within the firm becomes aware of the fraud, but it is not discovered and reported to the public until T_3. Revelation of the fraud causes a significant decline in the value of the firm in expectation of the legal and market consequences, which include large legal damages and penalties, as well as reputational harm. T_4 and T_5 indicate times after which the crisis has occurred and begun to fade, as the company stabilizes. The firm may take corrective actions of various kinds at T_4

---

[5] I thank my colleagues Nico Cornell and Sarah Light for alerting me to the idea of morally "tainted" profits which they formulate in an article on "Wrongful Benefit and Arctic Drilling" (Cornell and Light (forthcoming 2017)). This idea relates to what some philosophers call a "remedial" or "rectificatory" obligation to return benefits gained from wrongful behavior to those who were wrongfully harmed (Butt 2007). Additional support for the intuition that wrongful gain from fraud should be transferred back to those defrauded may refer to moral and legal conceptions of "corrective justice" (see, for example, Coleman 1992; Weinrib 1992).

[6] I omit here a discussion of the large empirical assumption regarding the reliability of stock prices as a measure of the intrinsic economic value of firms and the extent to which stock values may be attributable to general market conditions as well as a specific company's economic value. The accurate measurement of economic value in specific time windows—such as VW's environmental fraud and its discovery—is fraught with similar complications. For example, if a fraud occurs in a company that had the consequence of returning ill-gotten gains to the company, but a different external economic shock occurs at the same time which had greater overall effect, then the stock price value would not provide a correct measure of the damage caused by the fraud. One might instead use other accounting measures of the fraudulent gain such as tracking profits-per-vehicle illegally sold in terms of sales and earnings.

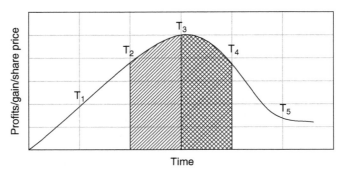

Figure 1. Time and liability in firms

and pay any legally required damages or fines at T_5.[7] The firm may also make efforts to recover its organizational reputation by adopting internal reforms and reaching out to "make things right" with its customers.[8]

It is interesting to note in this example, as moral individualists emphasize, that there are many business participants who may profit from the fraud and yet elude any legal responsibility. In theory at least, those who actually perpetrate the fraud should be brought to justice—including by the criminal law. (In practice, this often doesn't happen for various reasons, as Garrett (2014) has recently documented, and as Craig Smith notes in his introductory chapter in this book with respect to the legal aftermath of the financial crisis of 2008 in the United States.) Many people working within VW who knew about or condoned the fraud may be difficult to prosecute under the criminal law, given high standards of proof (usually "beyond a reasonable doubt") and state of mind requirements (usually actual intent or at least "recklessness"). Also most employees within firms are immunized from being sued individually by outraged consumers or the government. Internal legal principles of firm organization usually protect individual employees. A general shield of "limited liability" covers executives, managers, and employees by operation of agency law principles, indemnification provisions, and insurance (Orts 2015, 146–51; Thompson 1994). A manager or employee who may have known about or suspected fraud will usually escape any legal responsibility, even though we may think that some moral responsibility should attach to this behavior of

---

[7] As of this writing, VW had hired Kenneth Feinberg, a legal expert who had previously advised compensation for victims of BP's oil spoil and the 9/11 terrorist attacks, for advice (Ivory 2015).

[8] For an examination of possible public relations strategies that VW might adopt, including one proposal for VW to relocate its headquarters to Detroit and adopt hip-hop advertising, and another to crowdsource remedies for environmental damages to consumers, see National Public Radio (2015).

"looking the other way," especially when the manager or employee may benefit from the fraud through increases in compensation by hitting sales targets or other goals that the fraud enabled. Recent "clawback" provisions for executives who commit major frauds may have begun to address this problem to some extent. (See Cherry and Wong 2009; Fried and Shilon 2011.) So far, though, these provisions are rather blunt instruments and usually rely for enforcement on the firm itself, which in turn is represented by its top executives.

As moral individualists emphasize, there is a concern that punishing a firm heavily at the institutional level of the firm itself may visit unjust consequences on business participants who are completely innocent of wrongdoing. A common example given is the criminal indictment of Arthur Anderson for the involvement of some of its partners in the massive Enron fraud and the ensuing bankruptcy of Arthur Anderson and loss of thousands of employees' jobs. (See the chapters in this book by John Hasnas and Ian Maitland; see also Brickey 2003.)[9] By the same token, though, the organizational structures of firms may serve to protect complicit individuals. This legal reality provides a pragmatic argument for visiting moral responsibility somewhere—namely, at the level of the firm as a whole—in some circumstances. Otherwise, as Pettit argues in his chapter, a moral deficit would open in the other direction.

The case of VW illustrates also that legal realities track different moral theories in different parts of the world. Germany, for example, does not recognize corporate criminal liability at the level of the firm (Khanna 1996, 1490). Elsewhere in Europe, France and the Netherlands have amended their laws to allow corporate criminal liability at the firm level (id.). In the United States, corporate criminal liability at the firm level has allowed for financial cases to be settled for very large amounts of money without any individual admitting culpability, which has sparked strong criticism (for example, Garrett 2014). In response to criticism, the US Department of Justice revised its prosecutorial guidelines to focus on the role of individuals in corporate crimes. The new guidelines state a "foundational principle" as follows:

> Prosecutors should focus on wrongdoing by individuals from the very beginning of any investigation of corporate misconduct. By focusing on building cases against individual wrongdoers, we accomplish multiple goals. First, we increase our ability to identify the full extent of corporate misconduct. Because a corporation only acts through individuals, investigating the conduct of individuals is the most efficient and effective way to determine the facts and the extent of any corporate misconduct. Second, a focus on individuals increases the likelihood that those with knowledge of the corporate misconduct will be identified and

---

[9] Brickey's account provides important context for an assessment of the Arthur Andersen's "fall from grace," including the fact that the firm had previous serious problems with regulators and prosecutors in major cases and failed to make internal governance changes as a result.

provide information about the individuals involved, at any level of an organization. Third, we maximize the likelihood that the final resolution will include charges against culpable individuals and not just the corporation. (US Department of Justice 2015, 9–28.010)

It is likely that these standards will increase pressure substantially for prosecutors to focus on individual liability for business participants in the future.

Looking deeply into the "black box" of the firm to see the legal complexity of its internal organization proves both individualists and collectivists to be right. Although attributions of moral responsibility to individuals may be ideal, organizational complexities of legal structure and authority make the case for fixing moral responsibility at the firm level, if only for pragmatic reasons. This legal perspective finds support in the moral pragmatism recommended by Hussain and Sandberg. (See also Dewey 1926.) This pragmatic argument does not fully "square" the competing views, but it provides grounds for individualists to agree in practice to a compromise legally that may allow "the firm" to be designated to carry moral responsibility as a proxy in cases when organizational complexities prevent a practical tracing of moral responsibility to all complicit individuals. Both individualists and collectivists may also support legal reforms that attempt to track moral responsibility more closely to hold specific individuals accountable when acting within and on behalf of their firms. One recent intriguing suggestion, for example, would fix greater legal responsibility for organizational wrongdoing on the top executives based on a theory analogous to the traditional view that the captain of a ship bears moral responsibility for negligence by inferior officers regardless of the captain's own knowledge and behavior (see Sepinwall 2012, 2014).

Consider now another category of business participants who may use the legal structures of firms to escape legal responsibility for ill-gotten gains: its owners. Again referring to the stylized facts represented in Figure 1, imagine that the firm is a corporation, and shareholders who hold an ownership interest at T_1 and T_2 then sell their shares at T_3. On the assumption that the fraud was massive enough and secret enough (that is, no traders had knowledge of the fraud ahead of its actual disclosure or at least did not trade in sufficient quantities to correct the stock price), then the shareholder who sold at T_3 made profits that were at least partly composed of ill-gotten gains from the fraud. The well-established principle of limited liability for shareholders in corporate law, however, would prevent anyone from legally recovering these ill-gotten gains. Note also that for longer term shareholders who hold their shares through T_3 and continue to hold their ownership interests through T_4 and T_5, there is no injustice because the stock price would readjust to account for the negative value of the fraud.

A recognition of this legal structure of responsibility—or, more precisely, the legal "shielding" of responsibility—sheds light on the debate between moral individualists and collectivists. On one hand, a moral individualist may respond with an argument for a reform of the corporate law to allow legal responsibility to better follow moral responsibility (that is, to enable recovery of ill-gotten windfalls to either employees or owners).[10] One might even go so far as to argue for a repeal of limited liability for business corporations and other organizational entities on moral grounds. (For such an argument on economic grounds regarding tort liability, see Hansmann and Kraakman 1991.) At least, some especially compelling moral arguments may make the case for disregarding the corporate entity or "piercing the corporate veil" stronger in certain situations (Bainbridge 2001; Orts 2015, 156–68). On the other hand, moral collectivists may point to these limitations on legal liability as good reason to attribute moral responsibility *somewhere*, and a likely target is the firm itself.

The legal structure of business enterprise supplies a rationale for the moral collectivists' argument in this context. It is true that all of the capital and property committed to a business firm such as a corporation is owned, at least in the final analysis, by a specified set of individual people.[11] The capital structure of modern enterprise consists of an often complex amalgamation of equity and debt ownership interests (Orts 2015, 71–99). In addition, and in part allowing for this complexity of ownership, business firms such as corporations are given the legal authority to "own themselves." A corporation, for example, may purchase real estate or capital equipment in its own name. It keeps separate books and records that delineate the assets of "the firm" as separate from the personal assets of the firm's owners. This "asset partitioning" describes an essential feature of the historical development of business enterprise (Hansmann and Kraakman 2000; Hansmann, Kraakman, and Squire 2006). The corporation, as well as other legal forms of business, has the ability to "retain earnings" rather than to distribute them as profits, and its managers may decide with broad authority to reinvest earnings in the ongoing operations of the firm, including salary raises, or new research and development projects (Orts 2015, 99–104). The legal fact that retained earnings are allocated initially to the structural capital and property of the firm supports the view that some degree of collective responsibility may correctly attach to the firm itself. For moral individualists, the capital and property of the firm is indeed "owned" by specific people (namely, the equity and debt holders of claims on profits of the firm over time). To fix financial responsibility on the

---

[10] One of my MBA students, Christopher Dahan, accurately points out that taxes on increased earnings paid by a fraud-committing firm to the government should also arguably be recovered by the firm in order to prevent a windfall from accruing to the government. At least in cases of bankruptcy, there is a case to be made that "ill-gotten taxes" should be made available to compensate victims of a large fraud or major accident rather than retained by the government.

[11] There is a possible exception regarding government-owned firms or public-public hybrid structures which I leave outside of consideration here (see Orts 2015, 194–200).

firm in some circumstances on these owners, then, describes a convenience of legal administration that violates no moral boundaries even on an individualist account.

Again to refer to the example of VW's massive environmental fraud, some of the ill-gotten gains are arguably present as "retained earnings" within the complex ownership structure of the firm. Even if some of the ill-gotten profits may somehow trace to other uses or allocations, the fact that the firm served as a nexus of ownership for these distributions of ill-gotten gains would justify using the firm's capital itself as a target for compensation. By the same token, it seems also true that some owners, as well as executives and employees, may unethically profit from the fraud if they "cash out" their winnings between T_1 and T_3. To the extent that these ill-gotten gains are not legally recoverable (perhaps for practical reasons of difficulty of "following the money" in complex cases), there is a "moral deficit" of accountability for wrongful actions that calls for legal redress.

This legal analysis of moral responsibility in firms presented here is by no means complete. It may, however, serve to shed light on some issues that will continue to be debated into the future. Continuing discussion of moral responsibility in firms may help to inform and drive legal reform along the lines envisioned by John Dewey (1926) in his examination of the "personhood" of corporations and, by extension, other business entities. For Dewey, legal forms and conceptions reflect larger scale political, ethical, religious, and economic debates. In this sense, Waheed Hussain and Joakim Sandberg's chapter here also points in a promising future direction. Perhaps moral as well as legal conceptions of moral responsibility in firms should follow a methodology of pragmatism. Alternatively, other moral theories of the responsibility of firms advocated by various authors in the chapters of this book will, to the extent that they are politically and jurisprudentially persuasive, influence how the law of responsibility of firms progresses. In this sense, the debate between individualists and collectivists regarding the moral responsibility of firms—and the search for common ground between them—will no doubt continue.

REFERENCES

American Law Institute (1994). *Principles of Corporate Governance: Analysis and Recommendations.*

Arnold, Denis G. (2006). "Corporate Moral Agency." *Midwest Studies in Philosophy* 30: 279.

Bainbridge, Stephen M. (2001). "Abolishing Veil Piercing." *Journal of Corporation Law,* 26: 479.

Bowie, Norman (1999). *Business Ethics: A Kantian Perspective.*

Bratman, Michael E. (2007). *Structures of Agency: Essays.*

Bratman, Michael E. (2014). *Shared Agency: A Planning Theory of Acting Together.*

Brickey, Kathleen F. (2003). "Andersen's Fall from Grace." *Washington University Law Quarterly* 81: 917.

Burwell v. Hobby Lobby Stores, Inc., 134 S. Ct. 2751 (2014).

Butt, Daniel (2007). "On Benefitting from Injustice." *Canadian Journal of Philosophy* 37: 129.

Caney, Simon (2013). "Agents of Global Justice." In *Reading Onora O'Neill,* ed. David Archand, Monique Deveaux, Neil Manson, and Daniel Weinstock.

Cherry, Miriam A. and Jarrod Wong (2009). "Clawbacks: Prospective Contract Measures in an Era of Excessive Executive Compensation and Ponzi Schemes." *Minnesota Law Review* 94: 368.

Coleman, Jules L. (1992). "The Mixed Conception of Corrective Justice." *Iowa Law Review* 77: 427.

Cornell, Nicholas and Sarah E. Light (2017). "Wrongful Benefit and Arctic Drilling" *U.C. Davis Law Review* 50: xx (forthcoming).

Davenport, Coral and Jack Ewing (2015). "VW Is Said to Cheat on Diesel Emissions; U.S. to Order Big Recall." *New York Times,* September 19, A1.

Dewey, John (1926). "The Historic Background of Corporate Legal Personality." *Yale Law Journal* 35: 655.

Donaldson, Thomas (1982). *Corporations and Morality.*

Donaldson, Thomas (1989). *The Ethics of International Business.*

Dubbink, Wim and Luc Van Liedekerke (2014). "Grounding Positive Duties in Commercial Life." *Journal of Business Ethics* 120: 527.

Dunfee, Thomas (2006). "Do Firms with Unique Competencies for Rescuing Victims of Human Catastrophes Have Special Obligations? Corporate Responsibility and the AIDS Catastrophe in Sub-Saharan Africa." *Business Ethics Quarterly* 16: 185.

Ewing, Jack (2015). "Volkswagen Cites 'Chain of Errors' in Emissions Cheating." *New York Times,* December 11, B1.

Ewing, Jack (2016). "VW Memos Suggest Company Misled U.S." *New York Times,* February 19, B1.

French, Peter A. (1979). "The Corporation as a Moral Person." *American Philosophical Quarterly* 16: 207.

French, Peter A. (1995). *Corporate Ethics.*

French, Peter A. (1996). "Integrity, Intentions, and Corporations." *American Business Law Journal* 34: 141.

Fried, Jesse and Nitzan Shilon (2011). "Excess-Pay Clawbacks." *Journal of Corporation Law* 36: 721.

Garrett, Brandon L. (2014). *Too Big to Jail: How Prosecutors Compromise with Corporations.*

Goodpaster, Kenneth (1983). "The Concept of Corporate Responsibility." *Journal of Business Ethics* 2: 1.

Hakim, Danny (2016a). "VW Admits Cheating in U.S, but Says its Practices Were Legal in Europe." *New York Times,* January 22, B1.

Hakim, Danny (2016b). "Cars Failed Fumes Test in Europe for Years." *New York Times,* February 8, B1.

Hansmann, Henry and Reinier Kraakman (1991). "Toward Unlimited Shareholder Liability for Corporate Torts." *Yale Law Journal* 100: 1879.

Hansmann, Henry and Reinier Kraakman (2000). "The Essential Role of Organizational Law." *Yale Law Journal* 110: 387.

Hansmann, Henry, Reinier Kraakman, and Richard Squire (2006). "Law and the Rise of the Firm." *Harvard Law Review* 119: 1333.

Hasnas, John (2010). "Where Is Felix Cohen When We Need Him? Transcendental Nonsense and the Moral Responsibility of Corporations." *Journal of Law & Policy* 19: 55.

Hsieh, Nien-hê (2004). "The Obligations of Transnational Corporations: Rawlsian Justice and the Duty of Assistance." *Business Ethics Quarterly* 14: 643.

Hsieh, Nien-hê (2006). "Voluntary Codes of Conduct for Multinational Corporations: Coordinating Duties of Rescue and Justice." *Business Ethics Quarterly* 16: 119.

Horn, Michael (2015). Letter to Volkswagen Owners (for specific model years), September 29 (on file with author).

Ivory, Danielle (2015). "VW Hires Feinberg to Create Compensation Plan." *New York Times*, December 18, B1.

Katz, Leo (1996). *Ill-Gotten Gains: Evasion, Blackmail, Fraud, and Kindred Puzzles of the Law.*

Khanna, V.S. (1996). "Corporate Criminal Liability: What Purpose Does It Serve?" *Harvard Law Review* 109: 1477.

Khoury, Andrew C. (2013). "Synchronic and Diachronic Responsibility." *Philosophical Studies* 165: 735.

Landes, David S. (2006). *Dynasties: Fortunes and Misfortunes of the World's Great Family Businesses.*

Lee, Ian B. (2002). "Fairness and Insider Trading." *Columbia Business Law Review* 2002: 119.

Lewis, H.D. (1948). "Collective Responsibility." *Philosophy* 23: 3.

List, Christian and Philip Pettit (2011). *Group Agency: The Possibility, Design, and Status of Group Agents.*

Loewenstein, Mark J. and William K.S. Wang (2005). "The Corporation as Inside Trader." *Delaware Journal of Corporate Law* 30: 45.

Maitland, Ian (1994). "The Morality of the Corporation: An Empirical or Normative Disagreement?" *Business Ethics Quarterly* 4: 445.

Miller, Seumas and Pekka Makela (2005). "The Collectivist Approach to Collective Moral Responsibility." *Metaphilosophy* 36: 634.

Morck, Randall K. and Lloyd Steier (2007). "Global History of Corporate Governance." In *A History of Corporate Governance Around the World: Family Business Groups to Professional Managers*, ed. Randall K. Morck.

National Public Radio (2015). "'Tie a Bow on It.' This American Life," episode 569, act three, http://m.thisamericanlife.org/radio-archives/episode/569/put-a-bow-on-it?act=3#act-3.

O'Neill, Onora (2001). "Agents of Justice." In *Global Justice*, ed. Thomas Pogge.

Orts, Eric W. (1995). "Reflexive Environmental Law." *Northwestern University Law Review* 89: 1227.

Orts, Eric W. (2015). *Business Persons: A Legal Theory of the Firm*, rev. paperback ed.

Orts, Eric W. (2016). "Theorizing the Firm: Social Ontology in the Supreme Court." *DePaul Law Review* 65: 559.

Pettit, Philip (2007). "Responsibility Incorporated." *Ethics* 117: 171.

Pettit, Philip (2008). *Made with Words: Hobbes on Language, Mind and Politics.*

Rakoff, Jed S. (2014). "The Financial Crisis: Why Have No High-Level Executives Been Prosecuted? *"New York Review of Books*, January 9, http://www.nybooks.com/.

Rakoff, Jed S. (2015). "Justice Deferred Is Justice Denied." *New York Review of Books*, February 19, http://www.nybooks.com/.

Rönnegard, David (2013). "How Autonomy Alone Debunks Corporate Moral Agency." *Business and Professional Ethics Journal* 32: 77.

Rönnegard, David (2015). *The Fallacy of Corporate Moral Agency.*

Scheppele, Kim Lane (1993). "'It's Just Not Right': The Ethics of Insider Trading." *Law and Contemporary Problems* 56: 123.

Scruton, Roger (1989). "Corporate Persons." 63 *Proceedings of the Aristotelian Society, Supplementary Volumes* 63: 239.

Sepinwall, Amy J. (2012). "Guilty by Proxy: Expanding the Boundaries of Responsibility in the Face of Corporate Crime." *Hastings Law Journal* 63: 101.

Sepinwall, Amy J. (2014). "Responsible Shares and Shared Responsibility: In Defense of Responsible Corporate Officer Liability." *Columbia Business Law Review* 2014: 371.

Sepinwall, Amy J. (2015a). "Crossing the Fault Line in Corporate Law." *Journal of Corporation Law* 40: 439.

Sepinwall, Amy J. (2015b). "Corporate Piety and Impropriety: *Hobby Lobby*'s Extension of RFRA Rights to the For-Profit Corporation." *Harvard Business Law Review* 5: 173.

Sepinwall, Amy J. (2015c). "Conscience and Complicity: Assessing Pleas for Religious Exemptions in *Hobby Lobby*'s Wake," *University of Chicago Law Review* 82: 1897.

Smith, Jeffery (2012). "Corporate Duties of Virtue: Making (Kantian) Sense of Corporate Social Responsibility." In *Kantian Business Ethics: Critical Perspectives*, ed. Denis Arnold and Jared Harris.

Strudler, Alan and Eric W. Orts (1999). "Moral Principle in the Law of Insider Trading." *Texas Law Review* 78: 375.

Thompson, Barton H., Jr. (2000). "The Continuing Innovation of Citizen Enforcement." *University of Illinois Law Review* 2000: 185.

Thompson, Robert B. (1994). "Unpacking Limited Liability: Direct and Vicarious Liability of Corporate Participants for Torts of the Enterprise." *Vanderbilt Law Review* 47: 1.

US Department of Justice (2015). Offices of the United States Attorneys, "Principles of Federal Prosecution of Business Organizations." November 2015, https://www.justice.gov/usam/usam-9-28000-principles-federal-prosecution-business-organizations.

Van der Heyden, Ludo (2015). "VW's Board Needed More Outsiders." *Harvard Business Review*, November 17, https://hbr.org/.

Velasquez, Manuel G. (1983). "Why Corporations Are Not Morally Responsible for Anything They Do." *Business and Professional Ethics Journal* 2: 1.

Velasquez, Manuel G. (2003). "Debunking Corporate Moral Responsibility." *Business Ethics Quarterly* 13: 531.

Weinrib, Ernest J. (1992). "Corrective Justice." *Iowa Law Review* 77: 403.

Index

accountability, corporate 56, 59
administrative responsibility 95–6, 97
affect
  and blame 144, 146–7, 148n12, 154n18,
    162–3
  and punishment 161
agency 124
  collective *see* collective agency
  conversable 20–2
  corporate *see* corporate agency
  corporate personality 116, 118
  group 90–5
  nature of 16–17
  rational point of view 183
American Law Institute 213–14
anger
  and blame 148–9, 151–2, 153, 162
  world without 149–51
Aronson v. Lewis (1984) 117
Arthur Andersen 100, 133n6, 217
"as if" attributions of mental states 129, 130, 132
atomism 181, 182
Austin v. Michigan Chamber of Commerce
  (1990) 113
autonomy 134–7, 139
  corporations' fitness to be held morally
    responsible 90–1, 92
  moral agency 144
Avi-Yonah, Reuven S. 116n7, 117

Bank of America 2, 109–10, 111, 112
banks
  corporate misconduct 2
  fraud 156n19
  Steinbeck on 1, 7
Barclays 2, 53n1
Beardsley, Elizabeth 153n17
belief, capacity for 200
beneficence 189, 190, 192–5, 199, 201, 213
Berle, Adolph 116
Blair, Margaret M. 115, 116
blame 8, 137, 143–4
  collective punishment 102, 103
  consensus 174n10
  conversability 29, 31, 32
  corporate personality 108
  corporations and 154–60
  diachronic moral responsibility 59
  emotional account of 149–54

emotions and moral responsibility 144–6
  implications 160–3
  moral agency and 146–7
  moral responsibility as prerequisite for 98
  nature and function of 147–54
  passionless 151–3
  Principle of Responsive Adjustment 54
  teleology 153–4
Bowie, Norman 193
BP
  Deepwater Horizon disaster 2, 140, 211
    collective agency 66, 80
    diachronic responsibility 57, 58, 59–60, 63
  punishment 103
  self-narrative 62–3
  Torrey Canyon disaster 57–8, 63
Bratman, Michael E. 4, 36–52, 53n1, 211
Brickey, Kathleen F. 217n9
British Petroleum *see* BP
Buckley v. Valeo (1976) 83n3
Buddhist psychology 150n14
Burwell v. Hobby Lobby, Inc. (2014) 80–1, 83,
  123, 143n4, 214
business ethics
  beneficence 193
  collectivism 140
  consensus 172, 212
  and corporate responsibility, distinction
    between 138–9
  importance 185
  positive duties 213
  renewed interest in moral
    responsibility 1–11

Caney, Simon 196
Carroll, Lewis, *Through the Looking-Glass* 56
Catholic Church 77
Charland, Louis 145
Christopher, Russell 161n25
Ciepley, David 196–7
Citigroup 2, 111
*Citizens United v. Federal Election
  Commission* (2010) 80–1, 82–4,
  112–15, 123, 143n3, 163n30
civil liability 107, 108
civil responsibility 95, 96, 97
Clinton, Hillary 113
Coates, D. Justin 153n17
Coffee, John 110, 111–12